Praise for Yang Erche Namu

Leaving Mother Lake

A GIRLHOOD AT THE EDGE OF THE WORLD

"Open the pages of *Leaving Mother Lake* and you'll learn what it's like to live in a Himalayan culture where women shun marriage and are encouraged by their society to have multiple men father their children. The book is a memoir of growing up in the Chinese mountain Moso culture where 'there is no word for father, marriage is a backward practice, and property is passed on from mother to daughter.'" —Jessie Milligan, *Fort Worth Star-Telegram*

"Your heart will race as Yang Erche Namu flees China's isolated Moso people for the modern world in this touching memoir."
—*Marie Claire*

"A gorgeously crafted story of a remarkable life.... Namu's discussion of the little-known Moso culture will come as a surprise even to hard-core fans of Chinese women's history.... Namu's musical career and her astute observations on Chinese political culture in the late twentieth century only make the story more compelling." —Linda Schlossberg, *San Francisco Chronicle*

"An absolutely wonderful history of a woman and a place. I was stunned by the lineage of women described in this 'country of daughters'—by their complete control over the customs of love, family, and property. Somewhere between Kingston's *Woman Warrior* and Robert Graves's *The White Goddess*, this book creates a world of magic and ritual, songmaking and passion that has the powerful ring of truth." —Victoria Cass, author of *Dangerous Women: Warriors, Grannies and Geishas of the Ming*

"*Leaving Mother Lake* is primarily a book about love, loyalty, duty, and desire. That Namu and Mathieu can convey these emotions across the vast cultural differences is a testament to their storytelling abilities; their use of exquisite imagery and rich description make the story all the more enjoyable."
— Melisa Gao, *Saginaw News* (MI)

"Namu vivdly details village life: women work the fields while men herd the yaks; a 'skirt ceremony' marks a girl's arrival into womanhood; and at her grandmother's burial a straw figure wearing a beautiful dress was put on a decorated horse and paraded around the village to represent the soul's last ride. . . . Rich in local color and lore, an evocative introduction to a unique way of life."
— *Kirkus Reviews*

"At last, a memoir that delivers a life worth remembering! This book enchanted me — the tale and the telling."
— Lynn Freed, author of *House of Women*

"Namu's journey, the likes of which would ordinarily only appear in an adventure novel, drew me from beginning to end into what appeared to be a life of ultimate freedom."
— Claire McClanahan, *Bust*

"Yang was born into what sounds like the ultimate feminist fantasy. . . . A beautifully drawn picture of a unique society — and of the familiar struggle between mother and daughter."
— Jan Richey Butsch, *Elle*

"A fascinating portrait of a young girl who grows up in a matriarchal society in a remote region of China and becomes a star. *Leaving Mother Lake* will take readers on an incredible journey to a part of the world most of us never knew existed."
— May-lee Chai, author of *The Girl From Purple Mountain*

Leaving Mother Lake

Leaving Mother Lake

A GIRLHOOD AT THE EDGE OF THE WORLD

Yang Erche Namu and Christine Mathieu

BACK BAY BOOKS
LITTLE, BROWN AND COMPANY
NEW YORK · BOSTON · LONDON

Back Bay Books / Little, Brown and Company
Hachette Book Group
237 Park Avenue, New York, NY 10017
littlebrown.com

Originally published in hardcover by
Little, Brown and Company, February 2003
First Back Bay paperback edition, February 2004

Back Bay Books is an imprint of Little, Brown and Company, a division of Hachette Book Group, Inc. The Back Bay Books name and logo are trademarks of Hachette Book Group, Inc.

The publisher is not responsible for websites (or their content) that are not owned by the publisher.

Library of Congress Cataloging-in-Publication Data
Yang Erche Namu.
    Leaving Mother Lake : a girlhood at the edge of the
world / by Yang Erche Namu and Christine Mathieu. —1st ed.
    p. cm.
    ISBN 978-0-316-12471-3 (hc) / 978-0-316-73549-0 (pb)
    1. Yang Erche Namu.   2. Women singers—China—
Biography.   I. Mathieu, Christine.   II. Title.
ML 420.Y38 A3 2002
782.42163'092—dc21   2002019109
[B]

10 9 8

RRD-C

Designed by Iris Weinstein
Map by George Ward
Printed in the United States of America

TO OUR MOTHERS

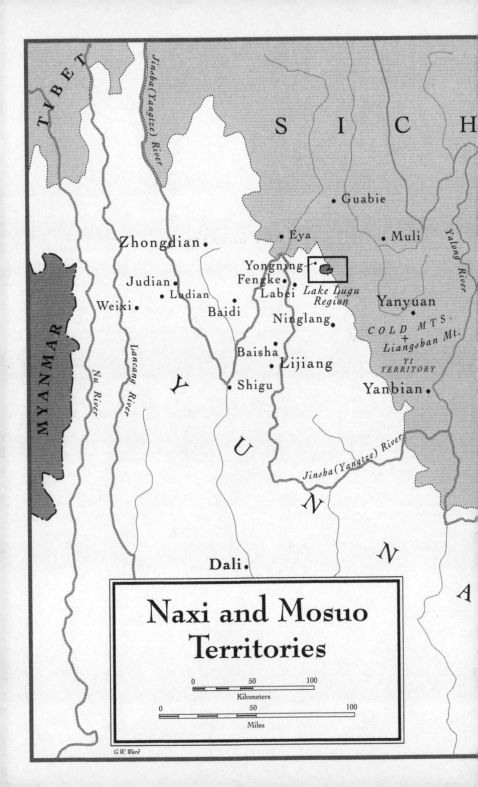

TIBET

Jinsha (Yangtze) River

SICH

MYANMAR

Nu River

Lancang River

• Guabie

• Eya

• Muli

Zhongdian•

Yalong River

Yongning•
Fengke•
Judian•   Labei•
•Ludian   Lake Lugu
Weixi•   Region
          Baidi•   Yanyuan
•
                Ninglang•
                                      COLD MTS.
                                      +
                                  Liangshan Mt.
        Baisha•
                                      YI
          •Lijiang   TERRITORY
    •Shigu
                              Yanbian•

Y

U

Jinsha (Yangtze) River

N

N

Dali•

A

Naxi and Mosuo
Territories

0   50   100
Kilometers

0   50   100
Miles

G.W. Ward

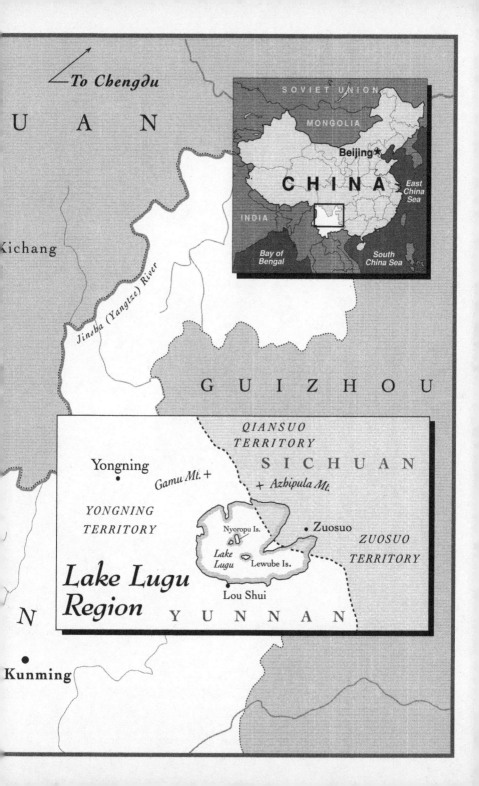

Leaving Mother Lake

A Lifetime of Tears

My mother doesn't remember when I was born. She does not remember the year or the month or the day. All she knows, she tells me, is that I cried too much. "From the moment you were born, you were trouble."

But I insist: "Ami, just try."

So my mother takes a sip of butter tea and says: "Ask Dujema, she was there."

Dujema is our neighbor. She is also my Ama's best friend and they spend a lot of time together, working and singing to keep their spirits up, and after coming back from the fields, sitting by the open fire, drinking butter tea and talking. Usually they talk about the weather and the crops but just as often they talk about men. Dujema is tall and strong and very beautiful, and she has many lovers. When my mother and Dujema talk about men, they laugh or they cry. Or both.

Right now Dujema is laughing, and in the glow of the fireplace, her beautiful brown face is shining like polished amber.

I slide on my hands and knees over to her side and sit close to her. "Tell me, Ami Dujema. What was it like when I was born? Do you remember?"

3

"Oh, yes, I remember," she says.

And I nestle under her arm, and she tells me.

It was the year of the horse, and early in the winter. The mountains were already white but my Ama did not feel the cold or hear the stillness settling over the snow-covered fields. Nor did she hear my sisters bickering and giggling on the other side of the fireplace. My Ama was aware only of one thing: the boy inside her stomach stubbornly refusing to come out.

Dujema knelt on the grass mat on the floor near the fire-place, where my mother was lying. She wiped the tears from my Ama's face and smoothed her brow. She ran her hands over the tight belly to make sure the baby was in the proper position. When the pain became unbearable, she put a dried-up corncob in my Ama's mouth and told her to bite on it. When at last my Ama was still, Dujema added wood to the fireplace and stared into the bright flames, and the same frightening thought again came to her. "This is her third child. It should be much easier." And when my Ama spat out the corncob and turned onto her side and clutched at her belly with trembling hands, Dujema said: "Latso, you know that boys always hurt more. This one must be a very big boy."

My mother closed her eyes and held back her tears. "Yes. A boy. It's worth the pain," she said. "It's worth the pain."

This went on for a whole day and a whole night.

The next morning, shortly after the rooster called for the sun to rise, Ama suddenly groaned louder and she gave a big push, and then another, and Dujema cried: "That's it, Latso! I see the head!" She laughed with relief. "It's a big head. A big boy's head!" Then she pulled me kicking and screaming into the narrow ray of dawn filtering through the opening in the roof, just above the hearth.

"Is he all right?" Ama asked anxiously. She tried lifting herself on her elbows to see me, but she was too weak. She fell back onto the mat and closed her eyes, leaving Dujema to examine me more closely by the warm light of the open fire.

"Yes, the baby is all right," Dujema said, covering me with a blanket and turning to silence my curious sisters. Awakened by my mother's groans, they had gotten out of bed, and they were now pushing against each other to get a better look at their baby brother.

Dujema gathered her long skirt from underneath her and stood up, her knees creaking from the long hours she had spent squatting near my Ama. She smacked her lips impatiently and shouted to my older sister to hurry and fetch the scissors from the sewing basket. Then she reached into the fireplace for a piece of kindling to light the holy sagebrush she had readied in the big iron pot almost two days before.

The sagebrush crackled. Thick, scented smoke drifted slowly throughout our log house and then upward through the opening in the roof and toward the gods in the heavens. And while the smoke cleansed every corner and crack of the house, Dujema ladled warm water into our blue enamel basin. After such a long labor, there was no time to waste in separating me from my mother. Dujema took the sewing scissors from my sister, passed them through the sagebrush smoke, and then cut the umbilical cord. After that she dipped me into the enamel basin.

"All is well, all is fortunate," Dujema chanted above my newborn screams. "The room is cleansed. The baby is well. The water is pure. All is in harmony."

When she had washed and dried me, Dujema anointed my forehead with a little pat of yak butter. She placed a cloth diaper between my legs, bundled me up in the traditional square cotton cloth, and tied a tiny red-and-green cotton belt across my belly.

And then she handed me over to my sleepy mother.

"It's a girl, Latso," Dujema said.

My Ama opened her eyes. "A girl?" she repeated, hoping she'd misunderstood.

Dujema looked at my crinkled little face and smiled above my tears. "Yes! It's a little girl!"

My sisters started giggling again. "Yes, it's a girl," they repeated. "It's a big girl, with a big head!"

And now I too giggle as I press my face into Dujema's skirt. "So why did it hurt my Ama so much to give birth to a girl?" I ask.

"Maybe you didn't want to come out and disappoint her!" she jokes.

My mother laughs. With her sleeve, she wipes little Howei's face, who is happily burping up his milk, and she takes another sip of butter tea.

MY MOTHER'S DISAPPOINTMENT at my birth was unusual. For we Moso tend to favor daughters over sons—which is why the Chinese call our country the Country of Daughters. Among us it is women, not men, who inherit the family house and rule the household. But a family needs sons as well as daughters. We need men to herd the yaks in the mountains, to travel with the horse caravans to trade in the outside world, and to make the long journey to Lhasa to study the holy Buddhist scriptures and become lamas. Without our lamas we could not name our children or send the souls of the departed on to the next cycle of life.

There were no men in our family. We had no uncles, no brothers, and no sons living with us. But also we had no grandmothers and no aunts. We did not even have relatives nearby. Our family was unlike any other in the village, and all this because, years ago, my mother had broken with Moso custom.

According to our tradition, a family should never divide.

Daughters and sons should remain with their mother and other maternal relatives for their entire life. Ideally, all family members should die in the house where they were born, the house of their mother and grandmother. But when my Ama was a very young and very beautiful girl, she ran away from the house of her grandmother. She was curious and restless and she wanted to see the world, the marvelous world where her uncles traveled with the horse caravans. But she did not go very far. She stopped only two days' walk away on the other side of the mountains, in the valley of Zuosuo, where she lost her heart to a handsome young man and soon abandoned the dreams that had beckoned from beyond the mountains. When her belly was round as the full moon, she decided to build a house and raise her own family near his village.

A few months after our house was built, my oldest sister, Zhema, was born. Then, not long after Zhema began to walk, my mother sang the courtship songs again, with another handsome young man, and some months later she gave birth to another daughter, Dujelema. Then she fell in love with another man. His name was Zhemi and he was from Qiansuo, where my grandmother lived. He often passed through Zuosuo when he traveled in Tibet with the horse caravan. Zhemi was tall and he had the finest and most beautiful hands. Many times my Ama told Dujema that she fell in love with Zhemi when she looked at his hands.

Zhemi was my father.

Among my people this is how families usually live together. Women and men should not marry, for love is like the seasons—it comes and goes. A Moso woman may have many lovers during her lifetime and she may have many children. Yet each of them will perhaps have a different father, and none of the fathers will live with his children. Moso children should be raised in their mother's house and take the family name of their maternal ancestors. They should grow up side by side with their cousins—the children of their mother's sisters. The only men who live in the house are the brothers and uncles of the women. So in place of one father, Moso children have many uncles who take care of them. In a way, we also have many mothers, because we call our aunts by the name *azhe Ami,* which means "little mother."

When I was born, my father was away at his own mother's house in Qiansuo, and since we had no relatives living with us, there was no one to help my Ama. There were no sisters to help chop the firewood or cook dinner and no uncles to hold her newborn baby. So when Dujema had fed her enough eggs and chicken soup and corn gruel and my Ama was strong enough to stand up, she bound me to her back, and with my two sisters trailing behind her long skirt, carried me with her everywhere she went as she cooked and cleaned and tended the chickens and the pigs.

I soon proved quite a burden.

From the moment I was born, I cried. I cried all day, and often through the night as well, week after week, month and month. No one could understand why I never stopped crying. My mother tried everything. She sang me lullabies. She cradled me in her arms and bounced me softly on her shoulder. She nursed me until her breasts emptied.

When she could not stand my crying any longer, she sometimes bundled me tightly into a goatskin and placed me under the kang, the wooden platform where the family sits at night around the hearth. Then she covered her ears with her hands and rushed into the courtyard, where she shouted at the pigs and the chickens. And when she was done with shouting, she paced back and forth until she felt calm enough to retrieve me from underneath the platform—still crying and kicking.

One night when she left me crying alone under the kang, I wriggled my arms free of the goatskin and reached out to the bright embers that had fallen between the cracks from under the stove. My tiny fingers closed around the glowing coal, and I screamed with all the force of my baby lungs. My Ama rushed back into the house, but already my hand was horribly burned. To this day, when she sees the scar on my right hand, my mother's eyes fill with tears.

After I burned my hand, Ama decided to seek some help. She snipped a corner of my clothing and set off with a large bunch of wild sagebrush to consult with old Lama Ruhi.

The holy man shooed away his chickens and piglets, and my Ama stepped through the wooden porch and into his courtyard, where, as custom requires, she respectfully undid her headdress and kowtowed three times, each time touching her forehead to the cold earth. When she stood up, she straightened her long skirt, picked up her things, and followed Lama Ruhi across the yard into another interior court, enclosed on two sides by the women's bedrooms and, at the far end, by a little chapel. There Lama Ruhi directed my mother toward a large clay burner next to the chapel wall, where she piled her sagebrush and the old man struck a match.

The twigs crackled and the smoke rose up the chimney and into the sky.

Lama Ruhi stared at the smoke for a while before he led Ama upstairs and into his little chapel cheered by the perfume of sagebrush smoke and burning incense and the glow of tiny flames dancing in the butter lamps on the altar. Again Ama lowered her forehead to the floor, this time to honor the portraits of the yellow Buddhas gazing in serene benevolence from above the altar. When all these formalities were finally over, Lama Ruhi sat himself on a large red cushion while my mother knelt in front of him, on the bare floor, and politely joined her hands together with her fingers pointing up toward heaven and her thumbs touching her heart.

"Uncle Lama, how is your health?" she asked. "How are your fields?"

"And how is your family in Qiansuo?" he replied, smiling. "Do you have news from your mother? And your sisters and brothers?"

"Thank you for asking, Ape," she said, "but the horse caravan has not arrived and we have no news."

"There was hail in Qiansuo this summer," he told her. "Did your family manage to reap a good harvest?"

"Thank you for your concern, Ape. Everyone is well. But I have not come because of my mother or sisters or brothers, or because of the crops. I have come because my third daughter won't stop crying. I have enough with the noise of the pigs and chickens and cows. I can't sleep at night. I am so tired. I am afraid I'm going to lose all my hair. She cries and cries. No matter what I do she will not stop."

My mother undid her hands and reached under her belt for the little piece of my clothing. "Please, Uncle, help me," she pleaded.

Lama Ruhi leaned over, took the cloth from her, and brought it to his nose. He sniffed it, closed his eyes, and sniffed again carefully, and then he looked at my Ama and asked, "When was the baby born?"

Ama hesitated. "When the rooster crowed."

"Yes, and what is her zodiacal sign?"

Ama frowned. "Well, it is a horse year, so she must be a horse. . . ."

Lama Ruhi laughed. "What do you mean, she must be a horse? Don't you know when your daughter was born?"

Ama lowered her eyes. "I know that it's time she had a name. Maybe she's more than two months old already. With four mouths to feed and the pigs and chickens and horses to tend and without brothers or sisters to help me, I don't even remember my own birthday!"

The old monk repressed a smile. He half closed his eyes and began chanting a sutra in a deep, low voice. When he finished, he gazed calmly into my mother's face and said, "Latso, your third daughter has a very special destiny awaiting her. But to solve your problem, you must first of all find a suitable name for her."

"But how will I find this name?" my mother asked eagerly, at once relieved to hear that there was a solution and anxious to find it as quickly as possible. "Why don't you give her a name, Uncle?"

"On the fifteenth day of the month," Lama Ruhi answered gravely, "you must leave your house before the cock crows and take this baby to the crossroads at the center of the village and you must wait there. You will ask the first person you meet to give her a name. Then she'll stop crying."

On the fifteenth day of that month, Ama got up well before sunrise. She wrapped me up tightly and tied me over her back, slung a canvas bag filled with food over her shoulder, and set off down the road. At the crosswalk she spread a goatskin on the ground and placed me on it. She took her food offerings out of her bag and carefully laid them on the ground for the local spirits—a bowl of red rice, a slice of ham, and a whole boiled chicken—all the while thinking that it was so dreadfully cold that no one in his right mind would dare venture out of his house before the sun came up. And what if no one came? Would the baby cry forever? And what would the other girls do if they woke up and found she was gone? And what if the baby caught a cold?

She reached for her prayer beads and worked a swift miracle. For she had chanted only a few mantras when the tinkle of a lama's bell rang in the nearby darkness. Ama squinted toward the dark shape moving toward her along the road and smiled. It was the old Bonpo monk Lama Gatusa. He was walking very slowly, bent over his wooden cane, his eyes fixed on the ground. He was on his way to the lake to collect water for the morning prayers.

"Uncle Lama! You are so early!" she called out as she kowtowed.

The dear old man looked at my mother prostrate on the hard, cold road and at her offerings and at the whimpering child on the goatskin.

"What's the matter with this child?" he asked.

"Uncle Lama," Ama replied, raising her forehead from the ground, "this is my third daughter. She cries too much. I went to see Lama Ruhi and he told me that today was a good day to name her, to come to the crossroads and wait. I never imagined that the first person we would meet would be a lama. My daughter is so fortunate. Please, Uncle, could you give her a name?"

Lama Gatusa bent a little farther toward the ground and reached out to my mother, somewhat shakily, to invite her to stand. He then tried to reach for me but thought better of it and asked my Ama to pick me up from the goatskin so that he could take a better look. "She is pretty as the moonlight," he said, his ancient face creasing into a kindly smile. He placed his hand on my belly and gave me a long look and began chanting in a low, trembling voice. When he stopped he said, "Her name is Erche Namu."

Ama nodded. In our language *erche* means "treasure" and *namu* means "princess." And since, at that moment, I happened to be both awake and quiet, my mother was immediately impressed by the apparent magic of my name. "My Treasured Princess," she repeated softly to herself. And when the old lama resumed his slow walk to the lake, Ama followed after him, squeezing me in her arms and gratefully checking her own impatient steps in his unsteady wake.

We Moso say that very early in the morning, before the birds drink from it, the water of Lake Lugu is the purest. This is why lamas come to the lake so early to fetch the water for their morning prayers. When Ama and old Lama Gatusa reached the shore of Lake Lugu, the night was still perfectly quiet, but the moon was fading and the approaching dawn already glowed faintly in the darkness above the tall, jagged mountains. We had arrived at the lake just in time, because the birds wake with the sun.

Following the lama's instructions, my mother dipped her right hand into the lake and scooped up just enough water to wash my face. Then she held me up to the sky under the approving gaze of our great mother goddess, the mountain Gamu.

As for me, I was now thoroughly wakened by the icy water on my face, and I was screaming with all my might.

INDEED, FINDING A NAME FOR ME, even such a beautiful name, did not stop my crying. In fact, and quite in spite of Lama Ruhi's prediction, it seemed that my screams grew louder as the days passed by and my body grew stronger from my mother's milk. So much so that word now went around all the neighboring villages and far beyond that my mother had given birth to a daughter who was supposed to be a son and who would not stop crying. My tears had become legendary.

One day during the summer, Dujema came to our house to visit. She had brought barley cookies and wanted my mother to sit with her near the fireplace and have some tea. As usual, I was crying. So while Ama placed Dujema's cookies on the ancestral altar and went to fetch the butter and the salt to churn the tea, Dujema took me in her arms and began to pace back and forth, singing to me softly and bouncing me over her shoulder.

When tea was ready, Dujema sat down at the fireplace at the spot reserved for honored guests. Ama sat across from her, on the left-hand side, where the mistress of the house always sits.

"Look at this loud little piggie," Dujema said, holding me up in the glow of the fire. "Little piggie," she commanded me, "little potato! Stop crying!" And she gave me her breast. I took it greedily and Dujema concluded: "Look, Latso! She's not such a bad one after all." And after a pause, she added, "You really are fortunate. You have three girls now. I have only two boys!"

My Ama did not answer. She chanted the usual incantations and calmly poured several drops of tea over the hearth to honor the fire god Zabbala. Then she poured two bowls of tea and, according to our custom, politely extended a bowl to Dujema using both her hands. After this she placed the plate of cookies on the wooden floor in front of Dujema.

Dujema took a sip of tea and bit thoughtfully into her cookie. "Without girls," she said, "who will give me grandchildren? Everyone knows that the wealth of a house is its women."

My Ama watched me gurgling at Dujema's breast and wondered if perhaps Dujema's milk was sweeter than her own, but she kept silent and stared at the fire.

"She likes you," she said at last.

Dujema nodded.

"You can have her," my mother said.

Dujema smiled. She had expected no less. She looked up at my Ama's tired face and said, "I will give you Tsili in exchange for this one. He's already two years old and he's not much trouble anymore. And you know what people say, Latso. If we exchange our children, the next time you become pregnant, you will have a son for sure."

Thus, my Ama and Dujema agreed to exchange their children—a daughter for a son.

I, unfortunately, appeared not to like this new arrangement, for I resumed crying as soon as I arrived at Dujema's house. And now I cried so hard and so long that all the members of the household spent the night holding their hands over their ears. I cried so loud that my Ama said she could hear me through the log walls of our house all night long.

After fourteen sleepless nights, Dujema's mother ordered: "Give her back! If she continues like this, the whole house will break apart and fall down."

So Dujema returned me to my Ama, and she took back her Tsili.

A year later, a woman from a neighboring village who had heard that my mother had grown weak from caring for a girl who wanted to be a boy came to our house with offerings of tea, ham, chicken, eggs, and barley cookies. She left with me.

The poor woman had tried for years to have children, but she kept me only two nights. On the third day she brought me home, her eyes red and swollen from lack of sleep. "This little girl has a terrible temper. We tried everything. To have no child at all is better than to have a girl who will not stop crying."

And so I was back with my Ama.

Weeks passed, and then months. The trees around the lake turned red and orange, and the cranes flew in from above the mountain peaks. Then snow fell on the hills. And then, one day, the cuckoo sang in the forest and spring came again.

One sunny afternoon, a woman who looked just like my

Ama appeared in our courtyard. She was holding a little boy by the hand.

"This is your Aunt Yufang," my Ama said. "And this is your cousin Ache. They have walked all the way from Grandmother's house to meet you."

A few days later, Aunt Yufang loaded her little mountain horse, and my mother bundled me up in some warm clothes. We waved good-bye to my Ama and my little cousin Ache and started on the trail back to Grandmother's house in Qiansuo. But as soon as we reached the last mud wall at the edge of the village, I began pulling on Aunt Yufang's hand and refused to walk. And when Aunt Yufang picked me up in her arms to sit me on the little horse, I screamed and I kicked and I scratched. We had not gone more than a few miles before she gave up and we turned around. My Ama then swapped me for my older sister Dujelema and she kept Ache. And I became known as the girl who was given back three times.

But certainly there was something fortuitous in this last exchange. For only a few months after she had sent Dujelema to live with Aunt Yufang, my mother gave birth to my little brother Howei—thus proving the truth of our tradition regarding the exchange of children. And that was not all. From the moment my adopted brother, Ache, came to live with us, I became entirely fascinated by him and stopped crying. It was as though, in a matter of a single day, I had become a normal child. Or at least it seemed that way at first. For the strange thing is, after I stopped crying, I never cried again.

According to Dujema, this was because I had shed a whole lifetime of tears in my first three years.

Latso

My mother, Latso, grew up in the region of Qiansuo, in the house of her maternal ancestors, a traditional log house with three courtyards, a vegetable garden, and flower gardens. My grandmother loved flowers. She especially loved yellow chrysanthemums because they made the best offerings at the Buddhist temple. But my grandmother grew all sorts of flowers, and because of all the bright colors, you could see her house from a long way off on the mountain road.

In her house, my grandmother was Dabu, the head of her household. As a mark of her status, she wore the key of the granary on her belt and a proud expression on her face. She was the one in charge of planning and organizing work and distributing food and other goods, and everyone in the family owed her their special respect and attention. Still, one should not think of my grandmother as a strict matriarch. In Moso families, decisions are always made in consultation with the other adults, and Dabu do not really rule over anyone. Rather, they are entrusted with responsibility because they are wise. My grandmother was Dabu, not because she was the oldest, and not only because she was a woman, but because among all her siblings, she was the smartest and the most capable. Her sisters also helped run the house and worked in the fields, and they were like all Moso women, hardworking and skillful. They could do anything, from plowing the earth and chopping wood to sewing clothes and butchering animals. As for my grandmother's brothers, they did what Moso men have always done: they helped in the fields, built houses, and made furniture, and they took care of outside business.

My first great-uncle traveled with the horsemen to trade local products, musk, and medicinal herbs from the forests, and also opium, in exchange for tea, salt, and metal tools. Sometimes the caravans went north to the market towns in Sichuan; other times they went south into Yunnan province, to Lijiang or even as far as Dali, and they also traveled west, into the Tibetan interior. In those days it took almost a week just to reach the Tibetan town of Zhongdian, the first major town in eastern Tibet, and at least four months to reach Lhasa, and the horsemen were often gone for a year at a time.

My grandmother's second brother was a herdsman. He spent all his time in the mountains, where he took care of our family's and the other villagers' yaks and came home once a month to deliver butter wrapped in dark green leaves.

After the older generation had passed away, with her first brother trading in distant places and her second brother herding yaks in the mountains, my grandmother's household consisted most of the time of her two sisters and the children — all of them her own because, although my great-aunts were beautiful and had many lovers, they never had children. Strange as this may seem, it is not uncommon in Moso families. Many Moso women cannot conceive, though we do not know why. Some people say that it is because we live in high mountains. And according to others, it is often the prettiest women who remain childless. As for my grandmother, she was at least as pretty as her sisters but she had five children: three daughters and two sons.

Following our custom, my grandmother educated her daughters to take care of the fields and the house, and she entrusted to her brothers the rearing of her sons. When Grandmother's eldest son came of age, he joined the caravans on the long journey to Tibet and left his uncle and younger brother to trade in nearby Sichuan and Yunnan. Whenever her oldest son was away, my grandmother counted the months, and then the weeks and the days, to the time the caravan would return. On one of these trips, she counted and then she waited, but neither the men nor the horses appeared on the mountain road. After a few weeks, she got word that the whole caravan had disappeared on the way to Lhasa. After that there was another rumor, that the horsemen had gone to India. But whatever happened, they never came back.

For years, when she was finished with her chores at the end of the day, my grandmother quietly walked away from her house down the same mountain trail where her son had left. She went some distance to the turnoff, where, if you stop to look back, the houses clinging on the hillside abruptly vanish from view. There, she sat on a rock and listened for the horse bells, and she stared toward Lhasa, into the strip of heaven hovering just above the mountain peaks. She stared and stared but no one ever came. When Grandmother got old, she went blind. The people said that it was from staring into the empty sky looking for her son.

Some months after her eldest son disappeared, Grandmother told her two brothers: "The caravan took one son from me. That's enough." So her second son stopped traveling with the horsemen and went to herd the yaks in the mountains with his second uncle.

My mother, Latso, was my grandmother's third daughter, and she was also her favorite child. Grandmother believed that my Ama had all the qualities needed to become Dabu and to succeed her as head of the family. And because Grandmother had such hopes for her, my Ama says that third daughters are always smarter than the other children. Perhaps she means it. But perhaps third daughters are not only the smartest but also the most troublesome, because my Ama became a great disappointment to her mother—in truth, as I was to be to her.

My mother grew up without toys. Her only prized possession was a small mirror in a pink wooden frame that her uncle had brought back from one of his trips to Lhasa. When she became a young woman, she spent a lot of time looking at herself in this little mirror, practicing pretty faces, dreaming of summertime, when all the villagers would gather at the hot springs for the festival of the mountain goddess. She imagined the young men watching her bathe, standing helpless with love at the sight of her full figure, her smooth brown skin, and her long black hair that graced her perfectly rounded buttocks like a yak's tail. She imagined the young men falling over each other to offer her the traditional multicolored belts in token of their admiration. And then she saw herself, at night, coming out to dance in the light of the fires, wearing all her trophies attached to her waist, whirling in the glow of the flames, with the bright-colored belts flying wildly about her waist as though she were stepping through a blazing rainbow.

But my Ama could do a lot more than daydream in front of her mirror. She spoke the language of the Yi tribes and some Tibetan, and she was a hard worker, a good cook, and a skillful horsewoman who could use the bow and arrow as well as any man.

Aunt Yufang says that my Ama was both woman and

man. She also says that my Ama was too smart and too beautiful for her own good. Everyone gave her too much attention, and not only the men but also my great-aunts, who could not have children of their own and who spoiled her rotten. "Who in their right mind would ever want to leave their own mother's house?" Aunt Yufang asks herself as she draws on her clay pipe and blows out a little puff of gray smoke. She stares at the smoke for a while and then she smiles at me knowingly. "Your Ama was a bit like you, really. She was spoiled by all her talents. She was spoiled and she became bored with the life that she knew."

So, it was boredom that turned my mother into a revolutionary.

TOWARD THE END OF WINTER IN 1956, the People's Liberation Army (PLA) left Lijiang town and marched across the mountain to the banks of the Yangtze River. There the soldiers exchanged some shots with a few resisting Moso who were firing their old guns from the other side, then they crossed the river and pushed on over the hills. In less than three days, the Communists had reached Yongning, the Moso capital, where our feudal lords had resided since the Mongol conquest of 1253, when the great Kublai Khan left an officer to rule over our ancestors. In actual fact, we know nothing about this officer, not even his name, but legend has it that he married a Moso woman and that it was not until much later, under pressure from the Qing emperors, that our Country of Daughters came to be ruled by chiefs, who passed their charge from father to son. In any case, when the Communists arrived in Moso country, the Moso feudal lord had already been deposed.

About a month before the People's Liberation Army marched on Yongning, the Communist authorities had summoned the Moso feudal lord and his younger brother Losan, our greatest saint and Living Buddha, to Kunming, the capital of Yunnan province. From Kunming, the Living Buddha had been sent to Ninglang, the county administrative capital some days' walk east of Moso country. The Living Buddha needed to learn to work for his keep like everybody else, the Communists had said. As to our feudal lord, he had died on the way to Kunming. Of natural causes, they said.

On that fateful day when the people heard the approaching Communist army, they ran away to hide in the mountains. There had been reports of bloody fighting in nearby Tibet, and without their chief to organize resistance or to speak on their behalf, the Moso were terrified of the Chinese army. But the Communists had not come to fight. They had come to liberate the Moso and bring about democratic reform — to free the serfs and redistribute the land among the common people and to organize mass meetings, where they encouraged peasants to speak against Buddhist monks and former overlords and aristocrats, whom the Moso had long regarded as a divine class of persons. China had "turned over," the Communists explained; the old feudal order was dead, and a new era had dawned. The people needed to learn new attitudes and new ideas. This was a period of great confusion and strange new hopes for the Moso.

While they were helping the people of Yongning "turn over," the Communists dispatched soldiers to carry out the revolution in the rest of Moso country. That was how eight members of the PLA set off on the long trek to my grandmother's village in Qiansuo, where they changed our family history forever.

FEW OUTSIDERS EVER CAME to Grandmother's village, and those who ventured in on occasion were almost always of nearby tribes: Lisu hoping to trade their fertility medicines for Moso butter, or Yi slaves running away from their masters. When the Communist soldiers arrived very late in the afternoon, exhausted and filthy from a seven-day walk across the mountains, the villagers came out of their houses to take a closer look. At first the children hid behind their mothers' skirts, but the mothers, although they said nothing, were more curious than anyone. Moso women do not travel very far, especially when they are young, because they are responsible for the crops and the house. So most of the women had never gone beyond the mountains of Qiansuo. Very few had ever seen Chinese people before. And no one had ever seen Chinese in the dusty green uniforms of the People's Liberation Army.

The soldiers smiled and greeted the curious villagers crowding around them. Then one of them crouched before a little girl hiding her face in her mother's skirt and extended his hand. And the little girl, perhaps sensing her mother's own interest, took a few steps sideways and crept up toward him, in crablike fashion, until she was close enough to touch the strange cotton clothes, the boots, the cold gun. The soldier stood up and patted the little girl on the head and asked if anyone could speak Chinese. A horseman stepped forward.

"Our point of departure is to serve the people," the soldier explained. "We are wholly dedicated to the liberation of the people and work entirely in the people's interest. Do you understand?"

The horseman shook his head. He turned toward the villagers and said that the Chinese were tired and hungry. Soon after, a woman made her way through the small crowd, carrying a tray with bowls of butter tea. After her, another appeared with a plate of barley cookies, and then another with walnuts and pears. The soldiers squatted on their heels and ate and drank gratefully. Meanwhile the villagers looked on and commented on the way they ate, on their soft, pale yellow skin, the short hair that stuck out from under their caps, the shiny guns, the dusty uniforms. Eight soldiers, they agreed, was not a big army. You couldn't kill a lot of people with only eight soldiers.

And since it was dark already, some volunteered to invite the Chinese into their homes, where they fed them chicken soup and told them to sleep near the fireplace.

The next morning the soldiers were ready to get on with their revolutionary work. With the help of the horseman, they gathered the villagers and began speaking with great enthusiasm about the modern world beyond our mountains — the airplanes, the cinemas, the cars and trucks, and the Communist Party.

"China has turned over," the horseman said. "Chairman Mao will give you everything you need."

"Really, he will give me *everything* I need?" a young woman called out with a mischievous smile.

The villagers laughed.

In Grandmother's village, there were no aristocrats or feudal lords to overthrow, and the people already had their fair share of the land, so the revolution was over quickly. But the Communists did not leave immediately. Instead they hung red banners with large Chinese characters that no one could read all over the village. Then they selected the largest courtyard, where they began to hold daily political meetings in order to reeducate the local masses.

The villagers learned about many new things. For example, they learned that Tibet and Moso country had always belonged to China and that the Moso were no longer Moso but members of the newly established Naxi Minority Nationality, one of forty or so official Chinese nationalities that made up the People's Republic of China.° "Oh!" the people said. The Naxi are our neighbors in Lijiang, on the western bank of the Yangtze River, and although we do not speak the same language or eat the same food or dress in the same way, the Chinese had always insisted that we were the same people. Except that, up to the revolution, they had also insisted on calling the Naxi by the name Moso.

"The Chinese have always had strange ideas," the horseman explained.

The villagers nodded their heads slowly.

Overall, the meetings had a mixed success. The old people got bored, and the horseman soon grew tired of trying to find Moso words that did not exist, but the young people were captivated. The Communists said: "The young people are the most active and vital force in society. They are the most eager to learn and the least conservative in their thinking. This is especially so in the era of socialism."

My mother never missed a session. When she got up in the morning, she could hardly sit still long enough to eat her breakfast before she gathered her long skirt and, barely taking the time to take one last glance at herself in the pink mirror, flew out of the door. She made rapid progress in Chinese, learning to shout slogans against class oppressors and to sing revolutionary songs. She truly loved the songs. She can still sing all of them today. Their rhythms were so different, so inspiring: they made you feel like marching to the top of the mountains and going to see what was on the other side.

°By the 1970s, the People's Republic of China counted fifty-five official nationalities, among which the Han made up 93 percent of the total population. In 1978, however, the Jino were added to the list of Chinese national groups. Thus, today, China has fifty-six nationalities, of which fifty-five are also known as minority nationalities.

Every night when my Ama came home from the evening meeting, her cheeks were flushed and her eyes shining.

But Grandmother knew that this had nothing to do with love.

Indeed, it did not take long for Grandmother to realize that the class struggle was threatening to undo all the education she had given my mother. Since the Communists had come to the village, my Ama had neglected the crops and the animals. She even refused to do some of the house chores. "China's women are a vast reserve of labor power. This reserve should be tapped to build a great socialist country," Comrade Latso lectured Grandmother.

Because custom forbids us to shout at our relatives, Grandmother shouted at the pigs: "What do you think you are saying? You're just spoiled rotten! Don't you have any shame? Don't you have any responsibilities?"

But the pigs grunted and ran away.

Late at night, when my mother had done enough struggling against feudal oppressors and she had gone to bed, Grandmother pounded her soybeans and sang the words we sing when we conduct rituals for people who have lost their souls.

"Latso, ah! Come back to me. Don't go into the far mountains, don't go walking near the rivers far away. You don't have any friends or family there. Tall trees cannot protect you. When the wind blows, the trees will topple over you. Don't try to hide at the bottom of the cliff; if the earth shakes, the rocks will crush you. You must not go to the wild side of the mountain, no one there can rescue you. All the gold and silver is at home. Outside, there is only wind and rain. Your sisters and your mother are at home. Listen to your mother's song. Let your soul come back to me, quickly."

Everybody in the family knew that a great change had come over my mother. Even the neighbors knew. But no one said anything. My mother's uncles and her brother kept quiet. Being men, they could not interfere in women's affairs, and least of all, in a fight between mother and daughter. As for my great-aunts and my aunts, they did not dare talk because my mother was too headstrong for them. So the whole family listened to my grandmother's song and hoped that my Ama would heed her mother's words.

But she did not.

One day the Communists announced that they were leaving. They were off to liberate the Moso people of Zuosuo, and everyone in the village was welcome to join them. When Grandmother heard that my mother and her girlfriends had volunteered for the revolution, she pushed my Ama out the front gate, locked the door behind her, and said angrily: "If you want to go with the Chinese, then go!"

That night my Ama went to sleep at some relative's house.

The next morning she woke early and jumped straight out of bed to find that the sun had risen with a golden glow, that the air was crisp and pure as only mountain air can be, and the sky was cloudless. This, she thought, was going to be a beautiful day. It was going to be a perfect day for singing marching tunes and walking along the mountain path. It was going to be a perfect day to discover the world.

When she arrived at the revolutionary headquarters, however, my mother discovered that of all the volunteers, only two young villagers had come to join the Communists, and that her girlfriends were missing.

"Isn't anyone else coming?" she asked, as the eleven-strong battalion set off down the narrow mountain road, marching in step and singing in one voice. And when the revolutionaries reached that part of the trail where, if you turn around, the village disappears from view, my Ama fell back and turned to look for her friends, and also to take one last look at Grandmother's house—the house where she was born and where, one day, she ought to return and die.

And she saw her mother standing outside the gates, looking toward her, silently pleading for her to return.

After the rough way in which Grandmother had pushed her out the gate, my Ama had not expected this. So she stood there, on the mountain path, her eyes fixed upon the miniature stature of her mother, not knowing what to do or feel. She had never thought that her mother could look so small. And then she squatted on the side of the road and hid her face in her hands and cried bitterly, while the Communists kept going, their marching songs growing fainter, slowly fading into the silence of the mountains.

When she could no longer hear the songs, my Ama turned her back on Grandmother and stared through her tears at the diminutive soldiers marching ahead on the distant narrow trail, walking toward the world, carrying away her dreams. And when she turned toward the village again, her mother was no longer standing outside the gates. Then she remembered the harsh words spoken the night before, and once more she hid her face in her hands and cried as she told herself that she could not bear to leave her village, and yet, she could not humiliate herself and return to her mother's house.

Who knows? Perhaps my Ama would have swallowed her pride and eventually run back to Grandmother—if it had not been for her girlfriends, who, some time later, arrived by her side, hot and out of breath and filled with revolutionary spirit. They had woken late, they explained, and missed the meeting. Then they had lost more time because of Grandmother, who had called out to them as they passed by her gates and asked them to take some food for the road. "Please take this for Latso," Grandmother had said.

My mother looked at the basket her friend was holding out to her, and the tears came flooding back.

But the girlfriends were in a hurry. "Latso," they said, "if you're so unhappy, you should go home."

And because she hated being told what to do, my mother made up her mind. She repressed her tears, picked up the food hamper, and headed down the path in the direction of Zuosuo with her two girlfriends following after her.

When the sun was high up in the sky, they sat down to take a rest and picnic on the ham and boiled eggs Grandmother had given them. They opened a bottle of Sulima wine and drank a cup to the Communist Party and a cup to the health of Chairman Mao and another cup to the revolution. And when they had finished the whole bottle, they thought of all their relatives and friends who lived in the villages on the road to Zuosuo and who too should hear about the revolution.

They never caught up with the soldiers.

Zuosuo is not very far from Qiansuo: only two days' walk away, and there are not many villages on the way. But my Ama and her friends managed to stop with so many people and to have such a good time that when they arrived in Zuosuo, the Communists had already left.

"The Chinese can't stand butter tea, and they can't take the fleas," someone said by way of explanation.

"But where did they go?" my mother asked.

"They've gone to meet up with the rest of the People's Liberation Army. They're on their way to the Cold Mountains to liberate the Yi tribes."

The three girls looked at each other. The Yi were terrible people who raided Moso villages and stole little children to make slaves of them. If the Communists had gone to fight with the Yi, they would never come back. For no army,

Chinese or Tibetan, had ever managed to subdue those ferocious tribesmen. Not even the great Kublai Khan had dared enter the Cold Mountains.

As things happened, the PLA waged a bloody battle in the Cold Mountains and brought democratic reform to the Yi tribes—but it did so without the help of my mother or her girlfriends.

The night they lost the Communists, my mother and her friends went to stay with some relatives who lived in the village of Wuzhiluo, near Lake Lugu. After a restless night spent discussing impossible dreams, they breakfasted on roast potatoes and butter tea, and the girlfriends resolved that, after all, they had been away long enough and it was time to go back to their mothers' houses in Qiansuo. But my Ama was too embarrassed to go home. Too proud to admit her foolishness to her mother. Too stubborn to change her mind.

My mother stayed with the people of Wuzhiluo, helping with the house chores and the work in the fields. Before long the summer rains began pouring and the narrow mountain path back to Qiansuo turned into a sloshy, slippery, and dangerous prospect, and my Ama decided that it would be best to stay and wait until the people gathered for the yearly festival of the mountain goddess to catch up with her family. She would return to Qiansuo after the festivities.

In truth, quite aside from the problem of the weather and that of her pride, my Ama had begun to enjoy herself too much to want to go home just yet. The young men found her exotic ways from Qiansuo hard to resist, and although she proved equally hard to please and no one had won her heart, she had already amassed an impressive collection of new belts and could not wait to show them off at the festival.

That year, when the people came out to dance under the

stars in honor of the mountain goddess, all the men's eyes were on my mother.

Around the bonfires, the men danced in a group and faced the women, who likewise danced arm in arm, their multicolored belts tied around their waists. My mother's waist was thick with all her trophies. Stomping the ground with their leather boots, the men moved toward the women, and soon both groups were dancing in one circle, stepping and swaying their hips in a single rhythm. Then the women pushed my Ama to show off in the center, and while she danced, a young man broke out of the circle and snatched a belt from her waist.

But my mother kept dancing by herself and the young man withdrew from the middle back into the men's group, and he threw the belt to one of his friends, who caught it and then threw it to another. My mother laughed and skipped from man to man, but she did not catch her belt. She would take it back only when a man worthy of her songs caught it. And so the belt flew from hand to hand in one direction and then the other, and still my mother could not make up her mind — until Numbu caught it, and he did not throw it to the next man but stepped into the circle and handed her belt to my mother.

My Ama did not move, but Numbu smiled and stood his ground. My mother hesitated, and then she snatched her belt from his hand and ran back to the women's group. But the women, who had seen the way she had looked at Numbu, pushed her back into the center.

His hands on his hips, Numbu began the courtship song:

Little sister, you are like moonlight in the middle of the
*   night sky,*
But the moon needs a star above it.

And my Ama answered:

Night has not fallen and the moon has not risen,
But the butterfly is already looking for honey.

Then Numbu sang:

The butterfly has found a beautiful flower, and
The moon is already high up above the lake.

She answered:

If the moon is high above Mother Lake, the water
is untainted.
Mother Lake is where I wash and comb my hair.

And Numbu sang:

But why do you comb your hair, little sister?
Oh, little sister, for whom do you comb your beautiful hair?

My mother and Numbu danced together in the middle of
the circle, arm in arm, until a new song began and another
couple took their place. Late in the night, as the fires began to
die and couples melted into the darkness, my mother followed Numbu to the shore of Lake Lugu.

AFTER SHE FELL IN LOVE WITH NUMBU, my Ama told
herself that she was not ready to go back to Grandmother's
house. Qiansuo was such a long way, two days' walk away:
Numbu might get tired of visiting her there. And when she
felt her daughter kicking inside her stomach, my Ama sent
news with the horse caravan to let Grandmother know that

she was going to set up her own house in Zuosuo, within walking distance of Numbu's village.

Grandmother sent some small presents in return, and a message: "Tell Latso," she told the horsemen, "tell her: I can't hold your heart back."

At these words my mother again cried bitterly, but she did not return to Qiansuo.

My mother's decision to start her own family was a shocking one. Dividing the maternal house goes very much against Moso tradition. Nonetheless, all the villagers helped her. Someone gave her a patch of land, and Numbu and his friends went into the mountains to cut the timber to build the house. In those days people did not use money and it seemed natural to get together to help each other. Besides, working together was always an excuse to dance and sing and have picnics.

"Can you sing for us, Latso?" one of the young men asked.

Another joked: "Latso, I hope you won't mind if my nephew comes to visit your daughter in the evening!"

And another, "Yes, and I hope you won't close the gates to mine!"

My Ama laughed. "In that case, you better not hinge the gates too tightly!"

So, in less than a year, my mother's house and all the gods and spirits who inhabited every nook and cranny had been blessed by the lamas, and she was moved in.

Hers was like all the other houses in the village. A log house built around a single courtyard, with a mud wall six feet high forming one side and the outer walls of the house proper forming the other sides. Behind the house, also enclosed by mud walls, was the vegetable garden.

Through the wooden gates and courtyard was the main room, which we call the Mother Room. This was where my

Ama cooked and ate and received guests, and where she slept. It was large and rectangular in shape, with a *ðurami* and a *ðuraðo*, the sacred female and male columns that support the roof of all Moso houses — and by extension, the sky — and two open circular hearths: the high hearth of the god Zabbala on the kang, and the cooking stove on the lower level. Aside from the small ancestral altar that was behind the high fireplace, all the furniture was arranged against the walls on the lower level and consisted of a tall pantry, where we kept dishes and cooking utensils and foodstuff; a large alcove bed built over a grain storage trunk, where my mother slept; and finally, against the far wall, a long bench where various things were stored off the earth floor, including, with his snout pointing eastward, the salted, boneless whole pig we call *bocher.* There were no windows, and the only light came from the openings in the roof above the fireplaces, and the front door.

On either side of the main room was a wing two stories high, with a balcony on the second level. The wing on the right, at ground level, was a chicken coop and a storeroom for tools and animal feed; upstairs there were four bedrooms divided from each other by plank walls, each with a door and a small window that opened straight onto the narrow balcony. Those bedrooms were for the daughters my mother planned to have. As for the other wing, it housed the stables for the horses and the pigs, and above those were three rooms for guests and for my mother's sons until they became men and could walk to their own girlfriends' houses in the evening.

My mother did not have any close relatives in Zuosuo but she had many friends — mostly because of her accent from Qiansuo. All Moso speak the same language, but every village seems to have its own dialect and special intonation. People loved my mother's accent, and they came to visit her just to hear her speak, so that before long she had become the villagers' favorite confidante. Our beautiful neighbor Dujema came to our house more often than anyone else. She came for a chat and a bowl of tea, and until my Ama's own garden began producing, she also brought her vegetables.

In the spring Dujema took care of my Ama when she gave birth to my older sister Zhema. Meanwhile, Numbu lived in his own mother's house, with his grandmother and great-aunts and great-uncles, and aunts and uncles, and nephews and nieces — three generations all related through the female line. Following Moso custom, he visited my mother every night and sometimes even stayed for a few days to help out with some chores, but eventually he always went home to work for his own relatives.

Toward the end of summer in the following year, my mother did not see Numbu for a few weeks. He had left with the horsemen to accompany the caravan to the Tibetan town of Zhongdian. And there he had met a beautiful Tibetan woman, who had come home with him.

My mother had waited and waited for Numbu to come and visit her in the evening, but instead it was the Tibetan woman who came calling for her at the gates. Numbu had a new lover, the woman explained as well as she could in her broken Moso. As for herself, she had no family or friends in the village and she was lonely. Answering her in Tibetan, my mother invited the woman to sit around the fireplace and drink a cup of Sulima wine. That evening my Ama made a new friend and decided to forget about Numbu.

Some months after the Tibetan woman and my mother had become friends, Dujema introduced my mother to a handsome young man.

The man was really very beautiful. My Ama did not love him but she had only one thing on her mind: to raise her own family and have her own big house, with her own daughters and sons and grandchildren. When the man came knocking on her bedroom window in the evening, my Ama opened the door for him, but when, a few months later, she was certain that she was pregnant, she hung his bag on a nail outside her door—which, according to our custom, is the proper way for a woman to break off with a lover. When he visited that night, he understood that she did not want him to come and see her anymore, and he left.

My mother's time came and the Tibetan woman helped her deliver my second sister, Dujelema. Then one day, when the Tibetan woman was holding the baby asleep in her arms, she suddenly burst into tears. She was missing her own family. The next morning she said good-bye to Numbu and went back to Zhongdian. I am not sure how Numbu felt, but my mother says that she missed her terribly.

Sometime toward the end of autumn, my Ama was putting out some corn to dry up on the roof of the house when she heard the bells of the horse caravan. As the riders got closer, she recognized one of her cousins from Qiansuo, and her heart leaped in her chest. She was always so happy to receive visitors from Qiansuo because they brought news and small gifts from her mother's house. She waved and shouted to them:

"Hey! The sun is almost gone. You better come in." And she climbed down the ladder and rushed to open the gates of her courtyard.

While the men unloaded the horses and took out the gifts that came from my grandmother, my Ama brought hay and water for the horses. And when the horses were watered and fed, the men sat on the ground and rested their weary backs against their knapsacks, leaving the youngest to do all the work: to light the campfire, take out the cooking utensils, cook their dinner, wash up, and tidy up. He was a tall and good-looking young man, and when my Ama came out again to offer the horsemen her best homemade wine, she made a point of pouring the young driver a full bowl. He smiled at her and took the bowl with both hands, with all the respect our custom requires. And that was when she saw that his were the most beautiful hands.

When the older men had stretched out their blankets and prepared to sleep near the campfire, Zhemi came inside the house. He played with my sisters and told my mother stories. And when later in the night the little girls fell asleep, he stayed up with my mother and they talked for a long time.

"Latso, why did you leave your mother's house?" Zhemi asked. "It must be so hard to manage everything on your own. Why don't you go home? You could come with us. If you wanted to, you could leave tomorrow."

My Ama's eyes filled with tears. Zhemi was right, life on her own was so hard.

"Come home with us, Latso. Don't be so proud."

But my Ama was proud. She dried her tears with the back of her hand and said, "I am going to show my mother that I can raise my own family."

The next morning the caravan left without Zhemi.

He stayed for a few weeks. He helped my Ama repair the pigsty and gather a year's worth of firewood and kindling for the winter nights. He was very quiet and very kind. When he was sure that everything was set up for winter, he went back to Qiansuo, and my mother sang softly in her empty house.

To the west of the mountains, the moon is full,
Why do you have to leave in such a rush?
The fireplace is still warm, my love,
My body is still warm for you.
One day without you seems so long.
Long too is the road where you ride your horse,
But my heart is following you.

Zhemi came back in the spring, and again he stayed with my mother for some time. One morning my Ama woke earlier than usual, and when she sat near the hearth to drink her bowl of butter tea, she felt a familiar sickness in her stomach. She smiled. She loved Zhemi and she was going to have a son. She was going to raise her own big family.

Latso Comes Home

Instead of a son, my mother had me, the crying one, and when I was about three years old, sometime after my cousin Ache came to live with us, she gave birth to my little brother, Howei. With two daughters and two sons, my mother's family was beginning to look impressive.

Nevertheless, after Howei was born, Ama did not hang Zhemi's things on the nail outside her door. She loved him dearly, and he continued to visit her, spending a few days with her every month. Whenever he visited, my mother washed and combed her long black hair, and she took out her cotton bedding to air and fluff up in the sunlight. In the evening she brought out the Sulima wine, and the house was filled with quiet joy. Sometimes Zhemi came alone. Other times he came with the caravan traders or with people from his own family. I especially remember his older sister. She was a tall woman with a kind and wide face. She loved to weave and she always carried a wooden spindle with her.

When my father stayed with us, our little brother, Howei, sometimes slept with Zhema and me in a bed in the store-room, and sometimes he slept with Ache in the room above the stables. My father always slept in the alcove bed with my mother. Once, when Zhema was fast asleep, I sneaked out of bed and peeped through the crack between the planks in the wooden partition. In the glow of the fireplace, my mother's skin shone like red gold and my father's back glistened with sweat and he whispered sweet names to her and she called him by his horse's name.

One day when my sister and I came home from cutting grass for pig feed, we found a tall black horse tied up in the courtyard. I could not wait to find out who the visitor was and rushed inside. No one we knew owned a black horse, and I immediately thought that Zhemi must have bought a new horse.

Inside the house, the fires were burning low and it was very dark. My mother was up on the kang, stirring the embers, her crouching figure outlined by the gray misty light that fell from the roof opening above the hearth. Near the kang, standing on the lower level, a man melted into the general darkness, barely visible against the sooty log walls, blackened by the smoke of the open fires we must never allow to die.

Zhema's voice startled me: "Namu! Do you think people want to eat your pig food?"

As usual my big sister was right. I had been so curious about the black horse that I'd walked into the house with my little basket on my back. Just the same, I did not like to be told off and I pulled a nasty face.

Ignoring our bickering, Ama blew on the kindling. A bright orange flame lit up a deep scowl on her forehead, and my uncle's tearful face emerged from the darkness. My mother then turned her worried forehead toward Zhema and said: "Grandmother is very sick. We have to go to Qiansuo tomorrow morning."

The black stallion tied up in our yard had brought us very bad news.

My Ama had not been back to Qiansuo in many years, and she had a lot of things to prepare. Following our custom, she had to bring a gift for every member of her family as well as for every family in Grandmother's village: brick tea, sugar, wine. While my sister helped her with the gifts, Ama sent me next door to Dujema to borrow a horse. I was hungry and tired from gathering pig feed and wished Ache had gone instead of me, but he was not home yet, and my mother's voice was harsh and flat. So I did not argue, and after I had closed Dujema's horse in our stable, I kept out of the way.

Very early next morning, while we were still sleeping, Uncle loaded the horses with the gifts and saddled Dujema's pony for us to take turns at riding. My brother, Howei, was still a toddler and he needed to be carried. As for me, although I could walk, I was much too young to hike all the way to Grandmother's village.

As soon as we'd had our breakfast, we set off on the road with our little mountain horses trotting like obedient dogs behind the big black horse. My Ama set the pace and we followed — across the village fields in the valley and then up the hill and into the oak forest, and yet higher up the mountain and into the pine forest, leaving the blue immensity of Lake Lugu shimmering behind us. We pressed on behind Ama, in the wake of her long skirt swishing about her ankles and trailing the red dirt. When the path was wide enough, we walked alongside the horses; when it narrowed, we walked behind them. At times the trail turned to sludge but this hardly slowed us down. When we slipped, we just picked ourselves up, shook the mud from our backsides, and walked on, without talking, without even thinking that we needed to pee or that we were hungry. Ache and I took turns riding Dujema's pony and running beside it. Uncle, Ama, and Zhema took turns carrying little Howei.

Our collective breathing and the dull thudding of the

horses' hooves on the ancient forest floor barely ruffled the anxious silence that enveloped us. We slowed down only where the trail narrowed dangerously on the edge of precipices. We stopped only at the crossroads marked by the piles of rocks we call *mani* piles because of the rocks engraved with the mantra *Om mani padme hum*, where Ama and Uncle lit sagebrush in offering to the mountain spirits. Only then did we take the time to listen to the rustling of the pines, to look up at the eagle spanning its wings in the cloudless sky, or to look down at the river churning yellow water, a long way below us, between white sandy banks and the sheer gray walls of deep gorges.

At night we stayed with relatives, and Ache and I ate our dinner listening to the adults talking in grave tones. And when the adults were done with talking and eating and smoking and drinking wine, we huddled together near the fireplace for what seemed a very short night. We woke up for breakfast and then we resumed our walk in the pink glow of dawn.

On the third day the sun was already high in the sky when we reached the turnoff where Grandmother's house comes into view, and my Ama suddenly gave a loud cry and I looked on in terror as she ran down the path, ripping her headdress and tearing at her long black hair.

"Ama!" I screamed.

"It's too late," my sister said. "It's too late. She's dead."

"Who's dead? Who's dead?" I cried.

Zhema pointed to the white flag floating over the roof of Grandmother's house.

Then we ran too. We ran after Ama, with Uncle carrying Howei on his back and the horses following after us. We ran until we reached the entrance of the village, when we had to slow our pace and compose ourselves and walk with the rest of the people who were going to Grandmother's house. At the gates the villagers moved to one side and let us pass ahead of them. "Latso has come back," I heard someone say as I stepped through the gates and into the courtyard.

People were milling about between long banquet tables, coming in and out of the house, talking and sobbing. Two women I had never seen before were tidying up the leftovers from lunch, their long skirts brushing the dirt between the tables. At the front door, my mother was standing with Aunt Yufang. She seemed calm now, but she looked strange with her hair loose about her face. Aunt Yufang looked even stranger. She had plaited her long hair into a single braid and her head was covered with clay. Her face was gray and sooty. Aunt Yufang looked so strange that in spite of the still half-filled dishes on the tables, I forgot I had not eaten since very early that morning.

I grabbed my sister's hand. "I'm scared!"

"Why?"

"Did Aunt Yufang die too?" I asked.

"Of course not! What's wrong with you?"

"She looks like a ghost," I continued in a low voice.

"People always look like that when someone dies," Zhema said and she squeezed my hand to reassure me. "Anyhow, how do you know what a ghost looks like? Come, let's go into the house."

We followed Ama and Aunt Yufang inside. In spite of the pine torches and the fires burning in the hearths, the room was obscured by the thick smoke of smoldering sagebrush and cypress leaves and by the sheer number of people. The smoke stung my nose and made my eyes water. The people made me dizzy. I had never seen so many people gathered together in one house. They were everywhere, men and women, standing near the kang and blocking the light of the fire god, others squatting near the cooking stove, chatting and drinking tea and wine — and in the half-light of the fires and the haze, they were but shadows of men and women. Shadows with sad, unknown faces.

Zhema pointed to three men squatting on the floor next to a cane basket who were cutting up strips of white cloth with scissors.

"They're Great-Uncle's helpers," my sister said.

"Why does Great-Uncle need help?"

"They're going to bathe Grandmother."

"Isn't it wrong for a man to wash a woman?" I whispered.

"It's not wrong when the woman is dead," Zhema said.

As I took in this bewildering piece of information, the shadows parted and my mother kowtowed to the old Daba sitting on the kang, near the hearth. He was wearing a white cape and a brightly colored crown and chanting to himself, his lips barely moving in his wrinkled old face. And since all I knew of Dabas was that they cured sick people, the old man was a comforting sight.

In actual fact, although Buddhism now dominates all Moso religious life, the Daba is the true Moso priest — the keeper of a much older tradition, who does battle with malevolent ghosts and sacrifices animals and drinks great quantities of wine. Unlike the lamas, Dabas have no temples or chapels or even written books, and they do not go to Lhasa to study in the monasteries. They learn all they know from their uncles and keep all the songs of their ceremonies in their memory. Of course, I was much too young to know any of these details, but at the time of Grandmother's funeral, the Chinese authorities had long labeled the Daba a backward superstition and had forbidden its practice. This did not mean very much, since there were no police or officials to enforce the rule, but the Dabas had stopped teaching their nephews, and they were already so few and most of them so old, people feared that when time came for the last of the old men to join our ancestors, so would our most ancient knowledge and ceremonies go with him.

Now, when a person dies, we need to ask a Daba as well as several lamas (and the more lamas that come the better) to perform the funeral rites because we believe that a person does not have one soul but five, and that different fates await them in the afterlife. Thus, the lamas must oversee the cremation of the body and guide the departed on the path of reincarnation, while the Daba sends them to the land of Seba'anawa, the paradise where our ancestors came from and where they still dwell, which is somewhere north of Moso country in eastern Tibet.

The old Daba looked at my mother prostrate on the floor and took a sip of wine before he resumed chanting, his eyes half closed, his head slightly shaky. My Ama lifted herself off the floor, and with Ache, Zhema, and me in tow, she followed Aunt Yufang across the main room to the storeroom. As they were about to enter, Aunt Yufang told Ama that the lamas were praying in the family chapel and that an auspicious day had already been decided for the cremation. My mother suddenly looked very sad, but she said nothing, and then she disappeared into the storeroom.

"What's cremation?" I asked Zhema.

"Hush. I'll explain to you later," she answered. "Let's go in."

But I did not want to go in. I wanted to go home. "Why are we going into the storeroom?" I asked.

"Because Grandmother is there."

In our house the storeroom was where we slept when our mother needed privacy, but in all Moso houses, it is also where grain and other things are kept and where women give birth, secluded from their male relatives. And then, it is the place where we lay out the dead — so that at death people return to the place of their birth and the cycle of life is complete. Because there were no men in our family, my mother had given birth to her children near the cooking stove, on the floor in the main room of the house. But this, as many other things about our family, was not the usual custom.

I had never yet entered a place where the dead lay in wait. I had never been near a dead person before. And so I stepped in cautiously, reluctantly.

The little room was cramped — my aunts and great-aunts and uncles and Dujelema, my second sister, who had been given to Aunt Yufang, and my mother were all standing around Grandmother and sobbing quietly, almost silently. Poor Dujelema! She had been crying so much, her eyes looked like walnuts, and I could not help wondering if that was what I'd looked like when I had cried so much, when my Ama had given me away to Aunt Yufang. And here, too, the air was thick with smoke. Perhaps it was even thicker, more concentrated, because I could barely make out Grandmother's face in the soft glow of the butter lamps.

Because we lived in Zuosuo, I had seen very little of Grandmother during my short life — a few times during the summer festival — and I could not feel true grief. I was also too young to understand what the death of a person meant. The only dying I knew was that of the animals Ama killed for us to eat. Yet, as I stood close to my grandmother sleeping so still in the hazy light, I felt moved by a strange and unknown emotion, and I looked about the room for a place to go to, perhaps to escape. And that was when I saw the pit in the earth floor. I looked at the pit, and I felt chilled, and I felt sick inside my stomach, and then I felt very, very hungry.

Without saying anything, I walked back into the main room and straight to the pantry, where I helped myself to a plate of rice cookies. Eating made me feel a lot better — at least, until my sister Zhema peeked through the doorway and saw me sitting by the cooking stove. She frowned and rushed over to me.

"People are dead and all you can do is eat! Namu, you have to show some respect!"

This scolding, coming after the pit in the storeroom and my mother's silent tears and the fatigue of the long journey, broke me down. I began to howl in that peculiar tearless way I knew how to cry. And now it was Aunt Yufang's turn to rush out of the storeroom.

"Hush," she said gently. "It's too early to cry. If we cry now, it will make Grandmother very sad, and she won't want to leave us."

Of course, I did not want Grandmother not to leave us. I did not want Grandmother to become a hungry ghost who would roam forever among the living. I wanted Grandmother to join our ancestors in the land of Seba'anawa and to take care of our family from there.

Aunt Yufang took my hand, and I walked back into the smoke-filled room, where I knelt in front of Grandmother and then, as instructed, kissed her forehead. Grandmother looked peaceful. She seemed simply to be asleep.

For the first time since we had set off on the road that morning, Ama turned her attention toward me. "We must go now," she said in a flat voice. "Uncle and the helpers are going to bathe her."

I reached out for my Ama. But she was so distant, and her face was streaming with tears. I was not sure that she knew I was holding her hand. Even as I think of this today, I do not believe that she had noticed my sister Dujelema standing next to her. I squeezed her fingers a little harder. Ama did not look at me, but she took my little hand in both of hers. My mother's hands were very warm and very strong and very rough from all the hard work.

In the main room, a young man was waiting with a blue

ceramic bowl filled with water and yellow chrysanthemums. And now that we had all left the storeroom, Great-Uncle motioned him in, while his helpers, one of whom was carrying the basket with the white strips of cloth, followed him in and closed the door. Zhema gave me a small push between the shoulders. "You should go in the yard with Ache," she said.

I didn't need to be told twice. I squeezed between the people and went out into the courtyard, but Ache and the other children had left to go and play somewhere, and I did not feel like going to look for them. I felt tired and disturbed. So I sat down on a little wooden bench on the porch and closed my eyes, taking in the warmth of the sun. I stayed there until I got bored and remembered that I was still hungry, and again I went into the house.

Ama wasn't there. She wasn't sitting by the cooking stove, and she wasn't standing near the kang with the other mourners. She wasn't in the storeroom either. Only the helpers and Great-Uncle and Grandmother were in the storeroom.

Great-Uncle was holding Grandmother, supporting her while the other men were binding her body with strips of white cloth — the strips they were cutting up when we arrived. They had folded her knees under her chin and were binding her arms around her legs. Her head was leaning to one side. Her nostrils were filled with butter.

I didn't ask why. I knew I should not be there, but no one had noticed me. I squatted on my heels and made myself smaller, and I watched — at once dazed and fascinated — as the three men put my bundled-up grandmother into a big white sack and carried the sack from the table to the pit in the ground.

But that was as much as I was to see. For just as he was lowering Grandmother into the pit, Great-Uncle lifted his head and looked straight at me. His mouth dropped in surprise, but before he could say anything, I ran out of the room, wiggled through the crowd of mourners, and stepped over the doorstep and into the sun-drenched courtyard.

When I had caught my breath and my heart had grown quieter, I wondered how Grandmother felt in the hole in the ground, and how she could breathe with butter in her nose, and if she was afraid. Then I thought of how Great-Uncle had bundled Grandmother's legs against her chest and wrapped her arms around her knees and I understood why Ama always scolded me when I sat at the fireplace holding my knees against my chest.

AFTER GRANDMOTHER WAS BURIED in the storeroom, everyone was allowed back in again. But now the pit had been covered up and there was in its place a little white clay mound, like a strange termite mound, with two small flags sticking out of the top. In front of it was a small table with some food offerings and butter lamps. When everyone had taken a place around the mound, the Daba came in to sing the song for the dead.

> *O Grandmother,*
> *When you reach the land called Seba'anawa,*
> *All the ancestors will come to greet you.*
> *Please tell my ancestors*
> *That I wanted to bring them gifts*
> *But the Pumi came down from the mountains*
> *And blocked my path,*
> *And I cannot speak their language.*
> *Please tell my ancestors*
> *That I wanted to bring them gifts*
> *But the Han Chinese came down from the mountains,*
> *And I cannot speak Chinese.*

On the road, the horsemen lead the caravans,
But they have poor memories,
And I don't dare trust them with these precious gifts.
Please, Grandmother, tell my ancestors
That I cannot bring them my gifts.
But you, since you must leave our village,
Since you must return to the ancestral land,
You must take my gifts with you.
These gifts are not heavy.
And the mountain wind will carry you
All the way to the ancestral land.

And when the Daba had finished, Aunt Yufang's voice rose above the quiet sobbing:

O my Ama,
My heart will ache for the rest of my life,
You brought me up from when I was so little,
You chewed my food when I had no teeth, and you wiped
*   my bottom.*
Now your house is filled with grown children and
*   grandchildren.*
Today even Latso returned with her children.
Why don't you open your eyes? How could you just go
*   like this?*
O my mother, how will I bring your tea tomorrow morning?
O my mother, how could you leave like this?
You promised you would help me finish the blanket,
Now the blanket is half woven and you have gone!
How could you leave me like this?

On hearing Aunt Yufang mention her name, my Ama had let out a cry and begun sobbing uncontrollably. But when her turn came to sing, she held back her tears.

O my mother,
I love you from the deepest of my heart.
I know I did a lot of things that made you sad.
I know you had a lot of hope for me.
But I never had a chance to prove myself to you.
You left me too soon.

I had never heard anything so beautiful as these songs. I had heard people sing for our mountain goddess, and I had heard them sing for Mother Lake. I had also heard my Ama and Dujema sing the working songs, and I'd heard my mother whisper love songs to Zhemi in secret. But I had never heard people sing from so deep in their hearts. And I had never heard such a beautiful song as my Ama sang for her mother, when she knew that she had come home too late. Forever.

WITHIN A FEW DAYS, we all looked like Aunt Yufang. No one was allowed to wash until forty-nine days after Grandmother's death, and our hair was covered in mud from all the kowtowing to the lamas and to the Daba and to every arriving guest. My mother's face was drawn from lack of sleep and black from soot. Her eyes were red and swollen. But she was exhausted not only from sadness but also from cooking, and feeding the guests. Since my grandmother had three daughters, each was responsible for preparing one of three daily meals, which was then served on the banquet tables in the courtyard. Aunt Yufang, who was the oldest, was responsible for the evening meal, the most important. My Ama, being the youngest, had to cook breakfast. But since she was also the proudest and she did not want to be outdone by her sisters, every meal she prepared was a feast, and to do this, she had to get up very early in the morning.

People were still arriving from neighboring villages. The relatives with whom we had stayed on our way to Qiansuo had also arrived. Perhaps eight entire villages came to my grandmother's house in those few days. Every guest brought a bamboo box with a gift of tea and salted pork for Grandmother's family, and my mother and her sisters had not only to cook the meals, but also to make sure that no one went home with empty boxes.

There was so much food, and so many gifts of grain and pork meat and flowers. I had never smelled so many pungent things or seen so much wealth displayed at once. Inside the main room, my aunts had set up another table with more rice and cooked meats, and chrysanthemums and butter lamps. Above the table they had hung a set of brand-new clothes and two yellow-and-red umbrellas. This was Grandmother's table. Grandmother should have no regrets. She was about to depart from this world, and she should enjoy eating her last meals with her family, she should wear beautiful clothes, and when she finally departed, she could use the umbrellas if it rained on the way to the ancestral land.

One afternoon, straight after lunch, my great-uncle and my uncle brought a large square wooden box into the yard. It was very pretty, made of a light pinewood and decorated with flowers and fishes. My uncles took the box into the house and into the storeroom, where the Daba hung yellow chrysanthemums from the rafters. Then they took my grandmother out of the earth and brought the coffin back into the main room.

Now everyone was crying. Grandmother was about to leave us and it was all right to let her know how much we loved her. All the adults kowtowed, and my great-aunts, my aunts, and my mother wailed and cried very loudly, leading the rest of the mourners. Meanwhile, above all the sobbing and the crying, the Daba proceeded with the last rites. First he chanted the Road Leading Ceremony, when he told the story of the Moso people and explained to Grandmother how to find the road to our ancestral land. Then he led the ceremony we call Washing the Horse, and Ache and I ran after the crowd of mourners who followed Grandmother's soul as she took her last ride around the village. Grandmother's soul was made of straw and wearing a beautiful blue dress, and it was sitting on a magnificent horse with feathers and flowers in its mane.

The next day the mourners set off in a long line behind the lamas, Grandmother's coffin, the Daba, my great-aunts, Great-Uncle, Aunt Yufang, Second Aunt, my Ama, and Uncle. Behind them, just ahead of the rest, was a small group of men. They were Grandmother's special friends, and perhaps my mother's father was among them. But perhaps my mother's father was already waiting for Grandmother in the land of Seba'anawa. And perhaps, as my Ama followed her mother's coffin to the cremation grounds, she held such thoughts about Grandmother's lovers, but perhaps not. People of my mother's generation did not inquire about their fathers: whatever happened in a woman's room, in the warm light of her own private fire, was a woman's private affair. If she wished to invite her friends into the house, to drink Sulima wine or dine with her relatives, that was fine, but if she wished to meet her lovers only in secret under the cover of night, that was also fine. And while it was quite all right to talk and joke between neighbors and friends, it would have been worse than unseemly for people of the same blood to discuss these things.

While the mourners walked down the mountain path, crying and wailing and falling backward into each other's arms and pulling at their hair, I stayed behind with Zhema and Ache and Howei and all the other children because, according to our custom, people under the age of thirteen should not mingle with death or any other business dealing with the ancestors. So we stayed with the pregnant women, who, on account of their unborn children, cannot witness the burning of the dead.

Just a few days after Grandmother departed for the land of Seba'anawa, my Ama returned to Zuosuo. She took my sister Zhema and the horses with her, and she left me, Ache, and Howei at Aunt Yufang's house. We stayed in Qiansuo for a long time. We ran in the fields with our sister Dujelema and the rest of the children, and we laughed, and we played with the water buffalo. Then one day we washed our hair and took a bath and changed our clothes, and Uncle brought us home, where my mother cooked for us in silence.

The Cultural Revolution

After Grandmother's funeral, we did not see my father very much. For many months Ama was too sad to receive visitors. Then winter came again. Snow covered the mountain roads, and Zhemi stopped traveling west to the Tibetan towns, going east instead, where he traded goatskins and yak tails in exchange for tea and salt. "Because yak tails make the best brooms," Ama explained. But when the worst of winter had passed, before Zhemi came back to visit my mother, the Red Guards came to Zuosuo.

It began with the banging of gongs coming from over the mountains.

My Ama hitched up her long skirt and climbed up the ladder onto the roof to have a better view, while Ache and I ran out of the house and followed the village children toward the commotion. We ran down the path, under the blossoming apple trees, between the vegetable gardens and the newly planted cornfields, and then we stopped dead in our tracks. Coming toward us was a large group of people with pale skin, all dressed alike in blue uniforms, with blue caps on their heads and red bands around their arms. They were singing at the top of their lungs, a strange alien song that to our children's ears was not just strange—it was terrifying.

These were not mountain people.

These were not Moso or Yi or Pumi or Lisu.

"Han people," one of the children said. "They're Han people."

We did not need to hear anything more. We ran in the opposite direction back toward the village, screaming for our mothers.

None of us children had ever seen so many Chinese people all at once. We had seen small groups of officials who occasionally visited our villages, and of course, there were the few Chinese who lived among us. But those Chinese were just like us; they spoke our language and sang our songs and their faces were brown from the sun and all the hard work. The Chinese of Zuosuo were no longer Chinese; they had become Moso. But if we never had much to do with the Han Chinese, we heard of them often enough: "If you are naughty, the Han will come and get you," Moso mothers tell their children.

And now the Han had come to get us.

When the Han reached the village and the adults came out to take a look at their ugly clothes and their sickly skin, we children hid behind our mothers, straining to make sense of the strange words passing above our burning ears. The Han, it appeared, had traveled a long way to get us. All the way from Chengdu, the capital of Sichuan province.

The Red Guards pasted the mud walls of our village with bright red propaganda banners, and as the Communists had done in the 1950s, they summoned the villagers to one of the larger houses. There they asked our village leader to translate for them as they denounced capitalist roaders, stinking bourgeois intellectuals, venerable masters, and all the other revisionists and running dogs of America. When our village leader was stuck for words, everyone had to sing. There was a lot of singing, although the people did not enjoy the songs this time around as they had done two decades or so earlier. Also like the other Communists, these Chinese did not like butter tea, but they had not come to drink and have dinner, they had come to make revolution—and they did like the apples. They had a strange way of eating apples. No one we knew ate apples in this way. They peeled the apples with their knives, starting from the top and going around and down, so that the whole skin came off in one piece like a ribbon, and we children, who knew by then that the Han hadn't come to get us, applauded with delight.

It took but a few days for the fleas, the butter tea, and too many apples to get the better of the Red Guards, and they soon left to visit other villages in the valley, where they did more singing and pasting of red banners. There really wasn't a great deal to destroy in our villages—we were all poor, illiterate peasants living in log houses surrounded by mud walls. In Zuosuo the Red Guards had to content themselves with scratching the eyes and digging out the faces of the gods on the temple murals—until they found Xiao Shumi's house, where they tore down and burned the gates and at last struggled with the enemy of the people.

Xiao Shumi was our old leader's wife but she was Chinese, from Sichuan province, and the daughter of an important military family. Our feudal lord had married her in 1942 with a view to securing the protection of the Sichuan warlord. As for our feudal lord, his family name was La, which means Tiger—but by the 1940s these tigers had long lost their teeth and their claws. Almost all the men in the La family were opium addicts, and our feudal lord himself was helpless to protect his people from the Tibetan bandits and Yi tribes who raided the villages whenever the need or the fancy took them—stealing grain and livestock and burning houses, and kidnapping little children to sell into slavery. The situation had got so out of control that in one infamous raid, the Tibetans had almost succeeded in kidnapping our leader himself, and in another, the Yi had set his house on fire.

In 1942 it took a whole month for Xiao Shumi and her retinue to make their way across the bandit-infested mountains to the narrow valley of Zuosuo, where her husband awaited her in his burned-out house. She was only sixteen years old and had been forced into the marriage, and the trip must have seemed awfully long to her, but she accepted her duties with dignity and soon proved very useful to her husband. Although her marriage turned out to be a political disappointment (the Sichuan warlord showed no interest in protecting Zuosuo), she was very smart and well educated, and she became famous on account of her skills with the abacus. After the People's Liberation Army brought democratic reform to Moso country in 1956, our feudal lord and his wife, along with all the other members of the La clan, became common people. Xiao Shumi took to her new lot without complaint. She soon became friends with many of the people, including my mother, and by the time the Red Guards came to Zuosuo, everyone had grown to respect her.

To the Red Guards, however, our leader's wife was still a feudal oppressor who deserved to be humiliated and punished for the evils of history. After they burned the gates of her house, they put a big tall hat on her head and paraded her through the villages. Every so often they stopped and shouted at her and rough-handled her. They forced her to kneel and to bow her head to the ground. They yelled in her ears: "Long live Mao Zedong! Long live the Communist Party! Down with the exploiters! Struggle against the bitch!"

At first the villagers followed Xiao Shumi through the narrow village streets and looked on, horrified, not knowing what to do. But when they understood that she was to be put through this humiliation every day, they stopped following.

When the people stopped following Xiao Shumi, the Red Guards took her from door to door and called for everyone to come out of their houses and look.

The villagers came and looked. Then they went back in, and they did not dare come out again. Now only the children went outside—to cut grass to feed the pigs. And this was how my sister and I got to see Xiao Shumi for the last time.

We were by the lakeshore, gathering pig feed, when Zhema said:

"Look! It's her!" She pointed to a tall white cone covered with Chinese characters that was hovering above the tall grass.

It was. It was Xiao Shumi under the cone. I followed my sister and walked over toward our old leader's wife. She was bent over, working very hard. Her forehead was shining with sweat. A little way from her, two Red Guards were lying back in the grass, smoking cigarettes.

"Why don't you run away and hide, Ami Xiao Shumi?" I asked in a low voice.

Xiao Shumi straightened her back and looked at us for a moment without saying anything. Then she touched her hat: "Where should I hide?" And she smiled. "But don't you worry for my old bones. How is your mother?"

She ruffled my hair and said that she had more work to do, and went on cutting the grass. When she was done, she lifted her basket onto her back. I watched her leave between the revolutionaries, looking very short and wobbly under that tall white thing. We would not see her again for many years.

Some days after we saw Xiao Shumi that last time, we had news that the Red Guards had paddled across Lake Lugu to Yongning plain, where they had joined another contingent of critics of the feudal order—and where they insulted and beat the lamas and took some people away from their homes—perhaps to prison, perhaps worse—and they pounded and they burned the great lamasery and the houses of the old native chiefs, the descendants of the fearless Kublai Khan. In the rubble and the ashes, seven hundred years of our history disappeared.

But even catastrophes cannot last forever. Once the crops are devastated, the locusts move on. Their belly filled with destruction, the Red Guards returned to where they had come from, and after they left, the old oaks turned yellow on the mountainside, and after them the pear and walnut trees in our valley, and then the propaganda banners turned pink on the mud walls, and life slowly returned to normal. The old people dried their tears and comforted themselves with thin butter tea and the thought that they had lived through worse times.

But in our house, my mother went on serving our dinner without speaking. Her heart was cold. Her thoughts were in Qiansuo, where Grandmother was no more and where Zhemi, whom we had not seen in such a long time, was sleeping without her. I searched my mother's face for an end to her sadness, and then I looked at my big sister, but Zhema had no answer for me. So I looked at the bowl of food in my lap.

I wished we had some meat. It had been a long time since we'd eaten meat.

A Pair of Red Shoes

When we ran into the courtyard, blowing on our cold fingers and wiping our noses on our sleeves, the first thing we saw was that Ama had changed her jacket.

She had swapped her everyday black vest for the red one she wore on festival days, but she was chopping wood, and when she lifted her head up from the stack of wood, her eyes were shining. She put down the ax and walked over to help me take the basket off my back. Then she took Ache by the hand and we went into the house, the three of us together. Ama had not paid us so much attention in a long time.

Inside the house, the fires were burning bright, and our new baby brother, Homi, was sleeping happily in Zhema's arms. The aroma of pork soup filled the air. It was not fresh pork, of course. Ama had only cut up slices of *bocher*, the salted boneless pig that all Moso keep, like a mattress, on the bench in the main room, and sometimes for so many years that the fat goes dark yellow. No, it was not fresh meat, but it was meat, and it smelled good.

And my father was sitting next to the fire.

"Uncle, you're back!" I called out.

"And where have you been?" Zhemi asked, smiling.

"Cutting grass for the pigs."

"That's good," he said.

My father got up and poured me and Ache some butter tea. "Make sure you spit out the seeds," he said, "otherwise you will have a big tea bush growing at the top of your head."

My Ama laughed.

My father went back to the kang to sit near the fire, with his legs crossed in front of him. His handsome face was black from the mountain air, but now the glow of the flames made it turn to copper. His hair was thick and wavy and he had what we call a yak nose — the noble nose of a bull yak: broad and strong with a high broken bridge and a rounded end. And he had long and graceful hands — the most beautiful hands. He was the most beautiful man. He was also, as people say in English, a man of few words.

Without saying anything, he leaned to one side and reached for his canvas bag. First of all he took out three tea bricks and then a large bag of rice — a type of sweet rice that did not grow around Lake Lugu, for which, no doubt, he'd had to barter very hard. The tea and rice were for my mother. For Zhema he had a pink shawl with big red-and-white flowers, and for Ache, a Tibetan belt, and for little Howei, a cone of brown sugar. But apparently there was nothing for me, because he now closed his bag and leaned it against the wall, and he settled himself near the fireplace to roll a leaf of tobacco.

My father lit his cigarette and blew a few rings.

I laughed. I knew there had to be something for me and that he was teasing me. And I was right. Zhemi laughed, too, and pushed his cigarette to the corner of his mouth and again reached for his knapsack. And then he handed me the shoes.

Red corduroy shoes with black dots and a black binding. With white rubber soles. And fluffy pink cotton lining. Pink, soft, fluffy cotton.

They were the most beautiful shoes I had ever seen. And they were the only shoes I'd ever owned.

As I stood with my shoes in my hands, rapt, speechless, my mother dragged a small chair near the cooking stove. She told me to sit, and as I stood rooted to the ground, she pushed me down gently onto the chair before she ladled warm water into the blue enamel bowl for me to wash my feet. As I had never worn shoes before, my feet were very cracked from running over icy mud and snow, and it was hard to scrub the dirt away, and when at last my feet were clean, my skin had turned unnaturally white and soft and wrinkled.

My Ama's eyes misted over. "They're just like your uncle's feet," she said.

Of course, I knew what she meant to say, that my feet were like Zhemi's and that she so loved my father. And this was the sweetest thing my mother could have told me. These were the sweetest, the most loving words my mother was ever to say to me. To this day, when I recall my Ama saying this, about my feet being just like my father's feet, my heart aches, and I wish I had not wasted a lifetime of tears in my first three years, when I cried not knowing why.

I put my feet inside the shoes and wiggled my toes and closed my eyes.

My feet, hot and soft from the foot bath, soaked in the soft warmth of the shoes. This was the most comforting, melting feeling. Well, for a while. Because my soles and my ankles were so cracked from the cold and so raw from all the scrubbing, they began to itch, and itch, and itch, and soon I could not stop scratching.

"Best to take them off," my Ama said. "That way you won't be itchy anymore, and you won't get them dirty. You can save them for the New Year festival. Put them away and come and have your dinner."

Now, the pork soup really did smell good, but I was so

excited about my shoes, I could hardly eat anything. I barely swallowed a few mouthfuls before I ran out of the door, with my shoes in my hands, to show off to my friends. But Ama was right, I should not get the shoes dirty, and the little girls had to wash their hands before I let them touch them. And when they had squeezed their hands into my shoes and they had felt the warmth of the lining and they had put their noses to the white rubber soles, and we had agreed on who would get to borrow them and this time put them on their feet— after I had worn them at New Year—I went home to sleep.

That evening, and every night after it, when I climbed into bed, I put my shoes under the pillow. Then, as I curled up against Zhema, I fell asleep dreaming of the coming New Year, of chicken stew and thick slices of ham, and of the tap-tapping of my pretty little red shoes as I skipped onto the icy red earth, from courtyard to courtyard, and wished everyone a long and healthy life.

ONE MORNING I WOKE UP TO FIND my mother busy sweeping the dirt in the courtyard. My mouth immediately began to water. My Ama was sweeping away the dirt of the old year so that we could welcome the new one, and that meant New Year was only six days from now. On the twenty-ninth of the month, my Ama would cut slices of salted pork, and she would prepare rice and the flat bread we call *baba*. On the thirtieth, she would kill a chicken and Dujema would bring us goat meat. Then, on New Year's Eve, my Ama would invite the dog into the house for a human meal of rice and *baba* and vegetables and chicken and pork and goat. The dog would not waste his time with grateful tail wagging. While my Ama thanked him for giving us our human life, he would swallow and crunch and choke and crunch again, his stomach rapidly inflating like a blown-up pig bladder below his protruding ribs, then he would squash his muzzle into his empty metal plate and push it around the house until he finally settled in a corner with the plate between his front paws. And at last it would be our turn to sit near the fireplace and enjoy the feast.

Of course, there is a story about the Dog:

A long, long time ago, people and animals lived forever. But as eternity went on, there were more and more people and animals and less and less room for them to sleep and play, and less and less food for them to eat. So the animals and the people began to squabble and fight and eventually made so much noise that the Great Heaven could not stand it anymore.

The Great Heaven called all the animals together and told them that it had found a solution. From now on, aside from the goddesses and the gods, no one on the earth could live forever. Instead, every being was to have a mortal life, which meant that at the end of it, they would die. The Great Heaven, who did not want the responsibility of allocating life spans, had decided to call out a number of years and to leave it up to each animal to call back in response.

When the Great Heaven called one thousand years, the Wild Goose answered: "Yes! Me!" And when the Great Heaven called one hundred years, the Wild Duck answered: "Yes! Me!" And when the Great Heaven called out sixty years, the Dog said: "Yes!" But the Human Being was so slow and clumsy that it was left with only thirteen years.

Sorely disappointed at the prospect of such a short life, the Human Being went to complain to the Great Heaven. But the Great Heaven was not interested in complaints and suggested that the Human Being try to sort out its problems with the other animals. So the Human Being went pleading to all the animals, begging them to take its thirteen years in exchange for their own life span. Not surprisingly, no one was interested—until the Human Being asked the Dog, who agreed just because dogs have always loved people. But now the Human Being was so grateful that it promised to take care of the Dog forever. And this is why, every New Year's Eve, dogs are given a full human meal, in remembrance of the Dog's sacrifice.

ON NEW YEAR'S DAY we went to pay the customary visits to our neighbors, to offer good wishes of health and longevity. Under her goatskin cape, my Ama was wearing her red vest and a bright multicolored sash around her waist. My sister wore her scarf, and I wore my brand-new red shoes.

I felt so proud.

As we walked from house to house, I could not take my eyes off my feet. When we sat by the fireplace, snacking and drinking, all I could see, all I could feel, were my feet in the pretty, cozy red shoes.

But then, as the day grew old and darkened, my pretty shoes began to change color. Every yard had been swept clean of last year's dirt, but clean as the yards were, the red earth stained my soles. And everybody wanted to touch and feel how soft and how warm, and I could not pull back from all the hands blackened from the soot of the fires. When we came home late in the evening, the soles of my shoes were all brown, and the tops were streaked with black marks left by so many inquiring hands.

Everyone was very tired and full from too much food, and also quite drunk from all the Sulima wine, so they went straight to bed. But I did not want to go to sleep just yet—I was going to wear my shoes again the next day, and I wanted them to be clean and beautiful as new. I ladled some water into the enamel basin and washed and scrubbed my shoes until they were brand-new again, and I placed them against the fireplace to dry.

As I knew that would take some time, instead of going to bed with Zhema, I climbed up on the kang to sit in the warmth of the fire while I waited. But I was very tired, and before I knew it, I was asleep.

The smell of burning cotton woke me up.

I did not cry.

I just sat on my cracked heels and looked at the big ugly hole in my beautiful red shoe. The left shoe.

In the morning my Ama stuffed the lining with straw and patched the hole with black cotton, and when she was done, we set off to visit Lama Ruhi because, according to our custom, it is good luck to touch a lama's head on New Year. So I wore my red shoes again, but now all I could see was the black patch. And when my friends came to try their feet in my shoes, that was all they saw as well. That ugly black patch. They laughed. "Silly girl!" they cried, and they ran home.

I threw the red shoes in the pigsty.

Sometime after New Year, my father came back to visit us, with some yak meat and yak sausages. When he saw my naked feet, he asked:

"Didn't you like the shoes?"

"Don't talk about the shoes," my Ama said. "She's been sad for too long."

"They burned," I answered.

My father said: "Don't worry, I'll bring you another pair." But he never did.

For a while I tried my sister's old green cotton shoes. Shoes badly worn at the heels and patched with bark and leaves, and much too big for me, which soon became hard and viscous from the damp and the cold. I threw those away as well, by the side of the mountain path, and after that I walked barefoot again.

Two Chicken Legs and a Starving Man

Village life, in general, is uneventful. Tradition spins the eternal return of the seasons according to well-known expectations and well-worn habits. Every generation follows in the footsteps of the previous one, the routine of everyday life broken only by calamity—a hailstorm, a drought, a plague of locusts, an earthquake. Or a revolution. Sometimes also, but much, much more rarely, the rules are broken by stubborn individuals. And then there may even be a scandal. Now, my Ama had broken the rules by setting up her own house in Zuosuo, and she had also broken her mother's heart, but there had been no scandal. In the end, Grandmother had refused to fight and she had given in to my mother's will. Grandmother was a very wise woman.

In fact, it is very hard to make a scandal among our people. We live close to one another but we don't cultivate the stuff that makes for public outrage in other places. To begin with, Moso women are not sullied by sexual shame—for sex, as I have now discovered, is a much-favored source of disgrace in the world. But quite aside from this sexual freedom, which has proved so fascinating to revolutionaries, journalists, social scientists, public health officials, and in more recent years, international tourists, we Moso abide by rules of honor that forbid us the dubious pleasures of malicious gossip.

We must not speak ill of others or shout at people or discuss their private affairs. When we disapprove of someone, we must do so in halftones or use euphemisms or, at worst, mockery. Although we feel such passions, we must repress jealousy and envy, and we must always be prepared to ignore our differences for the sake of maintaining harmony. All this possibly sounds utopian, but it is absolutely true. In Moso eyes, no one is more ridiculous than a jealous lover, and short of committing a crime such as stealing, nothing is more dishonorable than a loud argument or a lack of generosity. So much so that nobody in Moso country today can recall either murder or beating or robbery, or a truly ugly fight between neighbors or jilted lovers. Under these circumstances, it should not be surprising that among us, people who develop bad tempers and fight with their own relatives are rare, although such was the fate the gods had intended for my mother's family. But my mother had not made a scandal. No. Scandal was to be my special destiny. But more of this later.

Growing up in Zuosuo, I had a lot of freedom. We children could roam at our own will and visit from house to house and village to village without our mothers' ever fearing for our safety. Every adult was responsible for every child, and every child in turn was respectful of every adult. Aside from dropping stones into the open bamboo pipes that brought running water into the village, there was little mischief for us to get into. There was nothing to break, nothing to steal, no one to insult — and if there was, we did not know it. We did not go to school but we were not idle. We could not read or write but we were not entirely uneducated. And while the boys played in the village streets and in the fields, waiting to turn into young men to begin learning from their uncles, we little girls already knew about work and responsibility. From the time we were perhaps five years old, we followed our mothers in the fields, our little baskets on our backs. Through example, our mothers provided us with all we needed to know.

My mother went in and out of the house like the wind. What I remember best about her was the swishing of her skirt. Her long skirt went *swish, swish* around her ankles — a black skirt on ordinary days and a white one on festival days. She was always working. Always busy. In and out of the fields. Sunflower fields, rice fields, cornfields. In and out of the house. Feeding the pigs and the chickens. And feeding us.

I must admit, I remember my mother's skirt better than her face. But then again, I remember very little of my early childhood aside from the rumblings of my hungry stomach and a few events: Grandmother's funeral and my red shoes — and the chicken legs and the starving man.

It happened when I was a little older, when I was already living with my uncle in the mountains. I had come home for a few weeks in autumn, when Uncle came to help with the house repairs and I helped with stripping the kernels from the ears of corn.

"Ama killed the big red rooster," Zhema told us as we cored the yellow corn into a basket. "We're eating chicken stew tonight."

"Why? Is there a special occasion?" I asked with some excitement, meaning to ask whether my father was coming to visit.

"No," Zhema said. "No special occasion."

"Is someone sick?" my brother Ache inquired in turn.

"No, no one is sick," Zhema answered, as she continued to husk the corn. "Do you see the Daba anywhere?" she added with a little laugh.

Ache made a face. There had to be a reason for Ama to

kill the rooster. It was not every day that we ate chicken or indeed meat of any kind. We killed chickens when we had guests, or as offerings to the gods and the ancestors during the healing rites. And then we needed to invite the Daba to conduct the sacrifice. The lamas are Buddhist and they cannot kill animals. They do not even eat meat.

"No," Zhema repeated. "No one's sick and there's nothing special. Ama said that the rooster was getting too old and if we didn't eat him soon, the meat would be too tough."

My sister was a big woman now. She wore a long skirt, and a turban around her head, and a thick gold bracelet on her wrist. She had her own bedroom. And her grown-up smugness, and the fact that she was always in my mother's confidence, were constant sources of irritation to me. But right at this moment, I was delighted at the thought of eating chicken.

"Zhema, will you let me have the skin?" I asked.

My sister grabbed another corncob and said, "I'll let you have the skin if you let me have the legs." And on second thought, she added, "I'll give you the bones back. What do you say?"

I said nothing. I needed to think about it. My sister was a big woman and she was often too smart for me.

Zhema laughed again. "It's funny that you like bones so much. Have you ever thought that maybe you were a dog in a previous life?"

But before I could think of something to say about Zhema's own past lives, Ache called our attention and pointed to the gates.

There was a man standing there, just outside our yard. He was wearing a pair of large black trousers and a black jacket, and over his shoulders, a felt cape. His head was wrapped in a gray turban, from the top of which his black hair escaped in a small tuft. He was of the Yi nationality and no one we had ever seen before, and he had no doubt come from a long way away. He seemed to be waiting for my sister and me to stop bickering.

"Hey! What are you doing here?" I called out.

But Zhema cut me off. "He's come here to beg. Don't talk to him."

I looked at the man. He was so thin, it seemed that his skin was all that was holding his face, which was otherwise black and dirty, and there was an expression of such deep sorrow in his eyes that I felt like I was looking into a dark pit — the sort of pit they had put Grandmother into. His eyes made me call out to him.

"Come in! Please come in!"

But he did not move, and he said nothing.

"Stop it, Namu," Zhema whispered. "He looks weird. Maybe he's sick, or mad. There is a ghost hanging about him."

"No, there isn't," I retorted. "He's just afraid of you."

Once more I turned toward the man. And now I thought that maybe he did not speak because he couldn't, because his lips were horribly cracked and bleeding and it would surely have hurt him to move them. But as I looked at his eyes again, I suddenly understood his desperate silence. He was hungry. Not just hungry for meat, but hungry. Really hungry.

"Do you want something to eat?" I asked, putting my fingers to my mouth in case he did not understand our language.

The man bowed his head slightly and lifted a foot to step through the gate but the effort was too much. He swayed and then he fell.

Zhema screamed and ran to him.

I ran inside the house. Near the cooking stove, on the floor, there was a whole pot of rice already cooked for our dinner, and there was the chicken stew. I grabbed a bowl and scooped rice into it, then I scooped some chicken stew, a little breast meat and a wing—and then a leg, and on second thought, the other leg. After that I sliced some salted pork—a thick slice of yellow fat. Outside, Zhema and Ache had helped the man onto a low chair.

"Please eat," I said, as I put the food on his lap.

My sister nodded encouragingly at first, but when she saw the two chicken legs and how much rice I had put into the bowl, she glared at me. Whether the man saw the angry expression on her face, I do not know. All I remember is that the smell of the food revived him almost immediately.

"Thank you. *Kashasha. Kashasha,*" he whispered through his bleeding lips.

Perhaps it hurt him to eat as well as to talk, because he ate everything very slowly. At least, such were my thoughts at the time, because I had never suffered enough to know that this is the way you must eat when you have been starved. Chewing forever on each tiny mouthful, the Yi man ate half the rice and half the chicken. And he left all the pork.

Zhema eyed the chicken leg he had left on the side of his dish. "Have you had enough now? Don't you like our *bocher?*" she asked a little rudely.

"Oh, yes, I like everything. Thank you. *Amisei,*" he answered, this time in Moso. "I want to keep this for my daughter. She's waiting for me at home." His voice was stronger now and his face had regained a more human expression. And although he was frightfully thin, he was striking. His nose was aquiline, and his eyes, in spite of their being sunken, seemed almost fiery. He wore a silver earring with a large piece of amber and a little bright red coral hanging beneath it. The man was a Black Yi, a member of the old aristocratic caste the People's Liberation Army had defeated in 1956.

Only the suffering of his starving daughter could have persuaded him to come to our village and ask for help, for Black Yi are the proudest people in the world.

"Oh!" Zhema exclaimed, suddenly ashamed at her callousness.

"We can give you more," I said. "Don't worry, eat everything!" And I ran into the house again.

When I came back with a bag of rice and a bamboo box filled with salted pork, Zhema had fetched water for the man to drink.

"Kashasha, kashasha," the man said as he grabbed at the copper ladle and drank eagerly.

But now, on seeing his dirty hands on our copper ladle, Zhema had gone pale and again she lost her heart. When she handed me the ladle, she whispered, "You better get it clean before Ama comes home."

So I went into the house and scrubbed the ladle. It took me a while to get the dirty, greasy imprints off, and when I returned to the yard, the man was gone. He had got back on his horse, with the bag of rice and the bamboo box and half his dinner.

Zhema looked straight into my eyes, and she did not need to speak for me to know what she meant. I had given away half of the rice and about half the chicken to one stranger, and five of us had to feed on what was left. And we ate rice only twice a week. The other days, we ate millet and corn. And we ate chicken only when we had a guest or when the Daba came to cure the sick. And of course, I'd given him the chicken legs as well — and on purpose.

"But this man, wasn't he a guest? Wasn't he sick?" I asked Zhema.

"What's Ama going to say when she comes home and sees that we have no dinner?" Zhema snapped.

Our Ama came home at dusk, carrying yet another basket filled with corncobs, on top of her head. She looked very tired but Zhema did not waste any time before she called out: "Ama! A dirty Yi man came here to beg and Namu gave him our dinner!"

Our Ama put her basket on the ground and said: "Yes, I heard. Their crops failed because of the hailstorms this summer." Straightening her vest and tightening her sash back around her waist, she added, "Strange to think that in my youth, when the Yi fell on hard times, they came to rob us. Now they come for help. The world really has turned over. But you did right, Namu. I hope you gave him some tea as well, and that you made sure he took plenty home with him."

At these words, my sister's face went bright red. Ama had not reprimanded Zhema directly, but by complimenting me at her expense, she had meant to teach both of us a lesson about generosity and hospitality. Of course, I felt triumphant. I had done something right, and my mother approved of me. What was more, she approved of me and disapproved of my big sister, who was always in her confidence and a grown-up woman.

Now, I was just a little girl who had not as yet learned the merit of humility (and to be honest, humility is an art I still have not entirely mastered), but pride and self-righteousness and sibling rivalry were not all there was to my triumph. Because my mother was always working, her approval was as rare as her attention. And when it came to me, her approval felt almost as good as being told that my feet were like my father's feet.

Into the Mountains

I was perhaps eight years old when my mother sent me to live in the mountains with my uncle. He had come to visit us in the fall, as he did every year, to help with the harvest and repair whatever needed fixing in the house.

Uncle lived in the mountains between Qiansuo and Zuosuo, where he took care of the yaks for the village people, just as Great-Uncle had done. This is a hard life, especially in winter. It is so cold at these altitudes that the waterfalls freeze on the side of the cliffs — as though time itself would stop. Herding is also a job with great responsibilities. In Grandmother's village, every family had at least one yak, and yaks were very expensive. We say that if someone loses a chicken, she will cry for half a day, but if she loses a yak, she will cry until she gets a new yak. Besides, the herdsman must not only make sure that the animals stay healthy but also deliver fresh butter to the villagers every lunar month. Butter is very important to us. It is a sacred cosmic thing, an alchemy of Heaven, Mountain, Sun, Water, and Earth. We use it to make tea, of course, but also to offer to the gods in our ceremonies, to fashion intricate sculptures for temple display, and to anoint the foreheads of newborn babies and the bodies of the dead.

Aside from being a responsible herdsman, my uncle was a very good carpenter who made furniture and repaired houses and knew how to carve and paint birds and clouds and lotus flowers in wooden doors and windows. All the doors and windows in our house were decorated with my uncle's colorful carvings, and I remember sitting quietly next to him, watching him work, fascinated by his little pots of paints. But until I went to live with him in the mountains, I had never once had a conversation with my uncle, or indeed heard him say very much more than a few words to anyone.

My uncle's silence was due to a great sadness he carried with him. Sometime before he became a herdsman, he had walked to the house of a woman whom he loved dearly and who loved him in return. In the summer, only a few weeks before she was to give birth to her first child, she set off with a group of villagers to collect wild mushrooms in the mountains. She slipped on the mud because she was wearing brand-new shoes and fell into the ravine.

After his lover died, my uncle never walked to another woman's house. He became very quiet, and after his brother disappeared on the road to Lhasa, he went to live with Great-Uncle in the mountains. When Great-Uncle, who suffered from rheumatism from years of living in cold and dampness, grew too old and creaky to herd the yaks, Uncle began working alone. In truth, my mother's brother liked living all by himself in his tent. He liked tending to the yaks, to his memories, and to his sadness, and he liked to have no one to talk to. But even a sad lonely man cannot take care of a herd of yaks without help.

Now, my sister Zhema could not have gone to live with Uncle. She was a grown woman and my mother needed her help—to lock up the animals at night and to tend to the fields and to cook and help take care of my little brothers. Besides, Zhema needed to sleep in her own bedroom. One day she would become pregnant and she would help grow my mother's family. As for my big brother, Ache, of course he could have gone to live with Uncle because he was not quite a man yet and not very useful at home, but Ache did not want to go and live in the mountains with only Uncle for company.

I did not mind going to live in the mountains. I liked Uncle. Above all, I liked the idea of living alone with someone who did not speak and who would not tell me what to do.

WE WALKED A WHOLE DAY before we reached the meadow where the tent was pitched. If he had done the journey on his own, Uncle would have been home much earlier. Our two little horses, with their supplies of rice and salted meat and my little bundle, were not overly loaded. But I was not used to riding a horse, and by midafternoon I was too sore to sit on the saddle, and I was still too young to walk very far or very fast. As well, since we rarely left our valley, I was not used to the altitude. In the high mountains, where you feel as though, if you could just stand a little higher, you could grasp at the stars, your breath shortens, and it is hard to walk and easy to feel dizzy.

The moon was shining round and full amid the myriad stars when we heard the soft thudding of copper bells dangling from the yaks' necks. We heard the bells, and then we smelled the smoke trailing from the tent.

"We're home," my uncle said. "You can eat and rest soon. Can you see your great-uncle?" And he pointed under the bright light of the moon at the dark shape of a man standing outside a circular tent between what seemed like two smallish cows but that, on closer look, turned out to be huge, hairy black dogs.

Although this was the first time I was to camp in the mountains, I knew what sleeping in a tent was like because in the summer we had camped at the foot of the mountain goddess Gamu. We had also stayed in a tent another time, when we had gone to visit Aunt Yufang after Grandmother's funeral. Moso tents are made of yak skin and are just like Mongol tents. The fireplace is a small pit in the middle of the tent, encircled by rocks. Like the fire in the house, however, it is sacred and we must never allow it to die out. Whenever we go out, we put the root of a tree in the middle of the fire and cover it with a thick pile of ash. If it is a very big root, it will burn so slowly that it will still be red-hot at the end of the day.

Although Great-Uncle had retired, he still liked on occasion to spend time in the mountains and he had been quite happy to come and watch over the herd while Uncle went to Zuosuo to get me. Great-Uncle had not seen me for some time. "You've grown," he said approvingly. And I smiled at him and looked sideways. Since he had caught me in the storeroom during Grandmother's funeral, I always felt somewhat sheepish around him, guilty and uncomfortable, as though he knew a dark secret about me — which, of course, he did.

Great-Uncle had already cooked our dinner, a gruel of corn and rice, and all Uncle had to do was to throw in some of the fresh vegetables we had brought with us from my mother's garden. As for me, I was so hungry I did not notice how bland it tasted. When their dinner was over, the two men brought out the wine and drank and spoke a few words, and I fell asleep.

Next morning Great-Uncle led me out of the tent to introduce me to the yaks, the horses, and the dogs. "If you see a wolf," he said as we walked through the pasture, "don't run. Just watch him until he turns and goes away. And if an insect bites you, just take the ash from your uncle's cigarette and rub the sting with it."

When we had reached the yaks, he showed me how to call out to them and how to give them salt to lick so they could produce more milk and where to go to fetch the water. Over the weeks, he explained, I would learn which pastures I could take the yaks to and which I could not. We then walked back to the tent, where Uncle said that he was going to accompany Great-Uncle up to the pass and that he would be back by noon. And thus, I was left in the high mountains with two huge dogs and a herd of yaks.

At first I sat quietly inside the tent and ate my breakfast of roast potatoes and butter tea. Then I untied and retied my little bundle, where my mother had put a cape and a blanket woven from coarse yak wool, a cotton towel to wash my face, some of my sister's old clothes, and the stalk of an opium poppy in case I got a stomachache or a headache. "Remember that you have to boil it first," Ama had said. "You can't just chew on it."

This inventory over, I sat staring at the fire for a while, feeling at a loss as to what to do next. Then I went outside.

Although I had walked on the mountain paths and our own house in Zuosuo was nestled at the foot of a tall hill, I had never before seen the mountains as I saw them that morning, as I stepped barefoot into the white, vapory dew rising from the grass. Red granite and evergreen forests towered over the meadow, and peaks like saw teeth pierced the blue sky, slicing through feathery clouds — ridge after ridge, and as far as I could see. The air was so pure, so still, so empty of familiar smells and sounds that I might have become frightened if I had not been overwhelmed by so much wild beauty. And if I had not been so curious. Calling the dogs over to my side, I retraced the steps I had taken with Great-Uncle toward the yaks' enclosure, where I put my hand out to a large hairy cow with a white triangle on her forehead. The cow wrapped her rough, pink tongue around my fingers, looking for salt. It was a strange sensation and I quickly pulled my hand back.

So much for the yaks, I thought, and I walked over to a bamboo enclosure around a vegetable garden where Uncle hung his laundry to dry. I surveyed the potato patch and then went to inspect the horses, who, like the yaks, were locked in a corral but with the added luxury of a stable, built of rough planking. I concluded with great comfort that my uncle's tent and the enclosures in the meadow were just like our house. Meanwhile, I stole some beans from a wooden trunk and brought them back to the tent to roast in the fire. When they were burned, I shelled them and ate them. And when Uncle came home, he found me lying on my side near the fireplace, holding my cramping belly in both hands.

"You see what happens if you steal the horse's food?" he said, laughing. "Don't worry, it's just gas!"

During the years I spent herding yaks with my uncle, I was never lonely and I was never bored. Of itself, life in the mountains was more varied than in the village. There was always something new, something unexpected to do — mostly on account of the animals, who seemed to have their own idea of where they should go and what they should eat — and there was always something beautiful to look at, a multitude of wildflowers, birds and rabbits and deer, and an ever changing sky. Besides, we were always on the move. Whenever the yaks had finished grazing on a pasture, we had to shift them to another. The pastures were all well established, with fenced enclosures where we could lock up the animals at night. We moved the horses and took our tent and pitched it again wherever the yaks ate. In springtime we did not always bother putting up the tent and just made our home inside a large tree trunk or in a cave.

In the warmer months, our day began with a silent breakfast of butter tea and roasted potatoes seasoned with chili pepper. Then I fed the yaks their salt lick. And since that was about the extent of my duties, I was free to roam around the pastures and the woods for the remainder of the day, until I got hungry again or the moon rose in the dusky sky. I picked flowers and looked for birds' eggs and collected the large tree leaves we used to wrap around the butter my uncle churned from the yaks' milk. I also gathered wild mushrooms; some we ate, and others I kept and dried to bring to my mother.

My Ama had told me that there were three types of beings in the world: the gods and ancestors who lived in the heavens, the people who lived on the earth in the middle, and others, who had done wrong things during their lifetime and who lived under the earth, where they swept the floors of hell. "And that's why in this world," she explained, "we need to turn the sweeping brushes upside down when we put them away." It never occurred to me that I could ever do such bad things in my life as to deserve sweeping the floors of hell, but when I could not think of anything to do, I would put my ear to the ground and try to listen to the people in the underworld. When I heard nothing, I had conversations with myself or I sang at the top of my lungs the songs I had heard from the people in the village — songs of love for my mother, and working songs, and in a softer voice so that Uncle would not hear, songs of love for my future lovers. And when I ventured too far from the camp and did not know how to get back, I sang to let Uncle know where to come and get me. Then, as the sun dipped behind the mountain peaks, we came home together. We locked the yaks into the enclosure and milked the cows, and we cooked dinner. My uncle was a terrible cook. He boiled everything. I missed my mother's cooking, but I always finished my bowl of food. I was always hungry.

Uncle teased me: "How will your mother make a Dabu out of you? You're so greedy, you'll eat everything before the rest of the family comes back from the fields."

I ignored him and helped myself to another potato.

But although he made fun of me, whenever we had meat, Uncle always put the biggest piece onto my plate. "You eat it," he would say.

And when I would put it back onto his plate, he gave it back to me: "Eat. I already had some."

When Uncle woke up in a good mood, he would say: "Madam, do you want to eat bird or rabbit today?" Then he would walk into the forest and set a trap. Sometimes I woke up to the smell of rabbit or bird already roasting outside on a campfire, and I ran out of the tent to my uncle, who'd hit me on the head and taunt me: "Sorry, today is bad luck. I only caught one bird. There's nothing for you."

I liked my uncle's teasing, perhaps because when he teased me, he talked to me. For he was a very silent man. So silent that after living with him for some time, I began to notice that in fact there were different silences about him. Some were just quiet, others were sad. My uncle was always very sad when he sat down to weave cane baskets, and I often wondered if he was thinking of the baskets he had made for his lover who had died in the mountains. But I never dared to ask him.

Sometimes, when he had drunk too much wine, Uncle talked about his dead brother who had gone to Tibet and never come back. "Your uncle could really ride a horse. Sometimes he rode backward! From the time he was little, he always loved horses. He painted horses, and he rode them."

But mostly when Uncle drank too much, he fell asleep without even wrapping himself in his blanket, and he kept me awake with his snoring.

On one of those nights, I was also kept awake by a terrible storm. I was terrified of storms — because I had heard a lot of stories from the old people in the village about trees and people being split in half by lightning. That night the forest was howling and our tent was shaking, pounded by rain and wind, but as I shook with terror under my blanket, Uncle slept on, dead to the world. The storm lit the walls of the tent and thunder roared in the nearby sky, but my uncle went on snoring and grinding his teeth. He had got so drunk that I could not wake him for anything, no matter how much I pushed and shoved him — until I thought of something. I took some dried chili from our supplies and broke off a little piece, which I pushed up his nostril.

He breathed in, made an awful coughing noise, and sat straight up, his hands to his nose, his face dark red and bewildered. His eyes streaming with tears and bulging out of their sockets, and frothing at the mouth, he coughed and groaned horribly and grabbed at his nose and blew out of his nostrils like an angry bull yak, but even as he managed to blow out the chili, his nose kept on burning and burning.

It never occurred to me to worry about him. I just thought it was funny, and I laughed uncontrollably. Meanwhile, Uncle looked at me through his tears and said nothing — but much later, when he had recovered, he grabbed me by the shoulders, turned me around, and kicked my backside straight out of the tent and into the thundering rain. I had trouble sitting for two days after that. When I went home and told this story to my mother, she said sternly: "Namu, you could have killed him!" Then I really did feel ashamed of myself, because I loved my uncle.

Except for the electrical storms, I was never really frightened of the wilderness—although I did fear snakes, and on my mother's advice, I always carried a piece of string to make a tourniquet in case a snake bit me. Not that we had ever known anyone to be bitten by a snake, and the snakes probably had more reason to be afraid of people than we had to fear them. On several occasions I had seen my mother cut a poisonous snake in half with her scythe while working in the vegetable garden or in the fields. But then again, it was not really the snake's bite that I feared most.

In our village there was a family whose house was set back at a short distance from the others. One of their daughters, Tsilidema, was a grown and very beautiful young woman, but no man ever walked to her house to visit her at night. Whenever we met anyone from that household, we kept away from them—and not only my family did this but all the other villagers. Tsilidema's people likewise kept away from us. Once, when I was returning from the fields with my sister Zhema and my mother, we passed Tsilidema and her sisters on the village street.

"You've been to Mother Lake?" my Ama asked pleasantly enough, although she kept going and stayed well clear of the girls' path.

"Yes," Tsilidema answered, averting her eyes, and in a voice so quiet we hardly heard her. She quickened her pace as though she were running from us, while her two sisters hastened behind her with their heads bent toward the ground.

Watching Tsilidema and her little sisters scurrying away, it occurred to me that of all the people in the village, they were the only ones who never came to our house for dinner. Then it occurred to me that we had never visited Tsilidema's family at New Year, and that I had never seen Tsilidema at any of our neighbors' houses. When we came home, I asked my mother why Tsilidema and her sisters were so shy.

"They're not shy," Ama answered matter-of-factly. "Their family has the Gu."

"What's the Gu?"

"The Gu is a very dangerous thing," my mother continued in the same tone, as she put her workbasket on the ground. "During the fifth lunar month, there are people who go into the mountains to collect snakes, centipedes, spiders, toads, sometimes bats—if they can catch them. They take all these dirty animals home and put them in a jar. Then they close the lid and all the poisonous things fight and eat each other until, at the end, only one is left. That one is the Gu, and it's the most poisonous thing in the world." She stopped talking and stoked the fire under the cooking stove.

"Then what?" I asked, my heart beating fast.

"Then what?" my mother repeated without interrupting her chore.

"What happens to the Gu? What does it do?"

"Well, it has to eat—just like everything else. Except that it eats only dirty things."

My big sister Zhema then joined in the conversation with the grisly details. "If a man owns the Gu, he feeds it the sweat of his armpits, and if a woman owns it, she feeds it her monthly blood."

"Oh, yuk!" I said.

"And that's not all," Zhema continued. "The Gu doesn't just eat dirty things. It has to give its poison to other people. If it doesn't make people sick, it will harm its own masters."

I protested, half believing these bad things and also a little bothered by the fact that once again my older sister knew something I didn't. "Tsilidema doesn't look like a bad person; I'm sure she wouldn't let the Gu make us sick."

But my Ama scoffed: "She can't do anything about it. The Gu cannot die and it is passed down the generations. Even if Tsilidema is the best person in the world. Even if she doesn't want the Gu anymore, she can't get rid of it. She's stuck with it forever and so are all her people and all their descendants."

Now, I felt very sorry for poor, beautiful Tsilidema, who was cursed with the horrible Gu and who had no one to talk to, no friends to invite her for dinner or a bowl of butter tea near the fireplace, no man to give her a belt in token of his admiration, but Ama's words and the gravity of her tone truly frightened me, and a terrible thought engulfed my sympathy. "So, Tsilidema's Gu could really get us?"

"Of course it could!" Ama cried out in alarm. "The Gu can get anyone. That's why we don't have anything to do with Tsilidema and her family. And that's why nobody ever invites people who have the Gu into their house. That's why only Gu people can talk with Gu people. Don't you remember when Dujema's older brother got sick a few months ago? Well, that was the Gu. A lot of people get sick. You don't even have to touch someone who has the Gu to get sick from it. All you have to do is eat while you're near them, or even swallow your saliva when they look at you. All of a sudden you smell something very strange, like cigarette smoke or sweat or a wild animal, and then you lose your appetite. The next day your stomach swells up and you can't eat anything except the thing you were eating at the time the Gu poisoned you. Then you can't stop eating that thing, you crave it and eat and eat and eat. You can get very sick."

"Can you die?"

"You could, but the lama will cure you. He gives you medicine and you have diarrhea for three days, then you are all right."

"What kind of Gu has Tsilidema's family?"

"Who knows?" my Ama answered bleakly. "You don't think they would show it to anybody, do you? But some people say that it's a snake."

And so it was that I learned to keep clear of poor, beauti-

ful Tsilidema and all her family, and to fear the evil magic of
snakes that could not die and that no one had ever seen.

IF LIFE IN THE MOUNTAINS was pleasant in the warmer
months, in the winter it was harsh, much harsher than it ever
was in the village. After the snow had covered the meadows,
I wore a goatskin coat and took to hugging the yaks to keep
warm. Meanwhile, because it was too cold to wash, my hair
became horribly matted and I was soon crawling with lice.
When I had scratched my head and neck and shoulders to a
bloody mess, my uncle sat me near the fireplace and shaved
my head.

"You are a good person with sweet blood, that's why they
like you so much," he said to cheer me up. And undoubtedly
I needed cheering. I was very unhappy about my shaved
head, for we Moso believe that a woman's hair is her beauty.
Uncle added: "Don't worry, the more you shave your hair as
a young girl, the more hair you will grow later!" He gave me
his Tibetan fox hat to keep my bald head warm, and I did feel
better. Besides, I had to agree that Uncle's lice control was a
better method than the white powder I had seen people use
in the village, after which the children would lose not only
their hair but the skin off their heads.

After he shaved my head, Uncle stoked the fire at night
and gave me his blanket, but still I could not keep warm, and
every day I woke up freezing and ran to the corral where the
yaks were huddling against each other. Now, I don't remember how the thought first entered my head, but perhaps it
came naturally, just from watching the steam rising from the
icy ground. At any rate, as soon as a yak began urinating, I
sat on the ground and placed my hands and then my feet
under the hot golden stream, paying special attention to the
little bumps that looked just like baby mice that the cold had

burned into my soles. Because they drink such huge amounts of water, yaks can pee for a very long time. The heat from the urine was heavenly, and so I would go from one yak to another. But then when my feet and legs dried out, they burned horribly and I hopped about on the cold ground, scratching and hollering in agony.

Yet, every morning, as soon as I opened my eyes, I wrapped my blanket around my stiff, shivering body and ran to the corral to put my feet under the yaks. I could not help myself. No amount of pain and no amount of scolding from my uncle, not even the goatskin boots he fashioned for me, could deter me from seeking out the blissful minutes of relief the yaks provided against the bitter cold.

Stories Around the Campfire

At night I sometimes looked at the moon and wondered what it would be like to be a grown woman, to be back in the village and to have lovers giving me beautiful colored belts. Whenever Uncle saw me looking into the sky, secretly dreaming of my future lovers, he said: "You can look at the moon, but you must not point with your finger or you will get your ears chopped off." I still don't know if he meant by this to teach me respect for the moon goddess or to protect me from the sorrows of love. During the day, however, when I looked into the sky, I wondered where the birds came from and where they went to, and what was on the other side of the mountains. Sometimes I even imagined becoming a man and joining the horse caravan to trade far-fetched stories in distant and marvelous places where people rode in cars and airplanes.

Yet, at this time, I had not truly begun to suffer from our extreme isolation from the world. And certainly we were not always in the mountains and we were not always alone. Twice a year my uncle took me home—for New Year, and then in the fall, when we went home to help my mother prepare for the winter months. And even in the mountains, we had visitors—Yi herdsmen leading their goats and woolly sheep yet higher up on the mountain, and the horsemen who passed our way on the road to market and who sometimes pitched their tents on our meadow. I especially loved the old horsemen who told stories of their youth, when Moso country was still ruled by native chiefs and tribesmen from all over traded their goods from China to India, and foreigners with white faces and blue eyes flew their planes above our mountains to fight the Japanese devils.

In actual fact, not so many of those foreigners had ever made it to Moso country. No American pilot had ever landed or crashed or parachuted from his airplane, and neither the foreign experts nor even the Christian missionaries, who forbade the tribal people to sing and dance and drink wine, had ever trekked across our mountains. No doubt the Yongning chief, who was a devout Buddhist and who loved drinking and dancing, would not have tolerated such strange doings in his realm. The missionaries might have tried their luck with the La feudal lord in Zuosuo, on the other side of the lake, but they could not get there—their only possible access being through Yongning. For the northern and the eastern trails all passed through hostile Yi territories, and the western road through dense forests where Tibetan bandits waited only for the opportunity to murder and plunder. And, in fact, the few white people who had so dared venture had been pushed off the cliffs or had met with yet more gruesome fates. One white man, however, had come to Moso country and spent much time among us. His name was Dr. Joseph Rock. He was a big, fat man with blue eyes and yellow hair and a fiery temperament and he had traveled all the way from America to become the dear friend of the Yongning feudal lord.

One evening, while sitting around the campfire, a young horseman boasted: "During the war with the Japanese, my father rode with Dr. Rock all the way from Dali to Lake Lugu. It took them almost two months because Dr. Rock stared at the plants for hours."

"What could he be looking at for so long?" my uncle asked.

"He was a botanist. He looked at everything like that."

An old horseman continued, "I knew him well. I was with him when he went to Gonggao Mountain, where the Yi lived. Rock was after a butterfly, and our chief had given him some tents and an escort of thirty men so that he could go wherever he wanted. When we were on our way back to Yongning, there was a terrible hailstorm. No one had ever seen anything like it before. The hail was so big it killed goats and sheep, and in no time it destroyed all the crops. Of course, the Yi chiefs blamed the blue-eyed devil for angering the mountain god. His eyes were like wolf eyes, they said. So they decided to cut his head off. Fortunately for Rock, a small Moso boy who was herding his goats in the mountain near the Yi villages heard the rumors and raised the alarm. As soon as our chief heard the news, he told us to take Rock back to Naxi country. Then the Yi made up for missing out on Rock's head by raiding our villages. They stole cattle and horses and as much grain as they could carry, and they burned some houses. After that they rode their horses over our fields and trampled our crops. Ah! It was a terrible thing. The next time Rock came to visit, he felt very sorry to see the harm he had caused. So he brought all this glass from America and gave it to our feudal lord to build a little palace on the island. You should have seen it! It was so beautiful. Everybody went to the chief's house to touch the glass. What a pity the Red Guards destroyed that little glass palace. What a shame! All that glass that had come from so far away! From America! And all of it smashed up!"

Once they began, the men could go on about Dr. Rock

right through the night. For Dr. Rock had done a great deal for the Moso: he had studied our culture and published books about it in English, he had given our chief a pair of binoculars, and he had cured the villagers of venereal disease by writing to America for penicillin. The Americans had sent the penicillin via India and over the Himalayas in a little plane that landed in Lijiang at the foot of the Jade Dragon Mountain, and then Dr. Rock had carried it all the way to Lake Lugu by horse caravan.

All these stories were so entertaining: they were scary and sad enough, and in the end, Rock and the Moso always won. But what kind of place was America, I wondered, where people have yellow hair and blue eyes? Everyone we knew, everyone we had ever seen, had black hair and brown eyes, even the Han Chinese. Although, now I thought about it, I remembered that when I was very little, someone who spoke Moso and dressed just like us, someone with yellow hair and white skin and pale, colorless eyes, had come to our village. My mother had said: "It's because he didn't get enough salt." But the horsemen laughed and said that he was surely one of the many blond-haired children Rock had fathered with Moso women and that it was a good thing—because in this way Dr. Rock would always live among us. Joseph Rock, who had lived and traveled in western China for the better part of thirty years, hauling a portable bathtub and far too much personal weight for the comfort of his horse, was truly a legend among the Moso people.

But the horsemen did not only bring us tales of times long gone. They also brought us news of the world and of the Cultural Revolution that was still raging beyond our mountains—which was how we learned of the mass meetings and the criticisms, of the Muslims who had rebelled in the northwest, of the lamas who had been imprisoned in Tibet, and of the former Communist heroes who had been purged in

Lijiang, and those who had committed suicide. Then one day the horsemen brought news of our very own world, and for months to come, the news got worse.

The government had sent special teams of soldiers and officials to our valleys to reeducate the people—because the Moso shared everything, including their lovers, which amounted to a form of primitive communism that was a health hazard and a blight on the face of modern China and that nowhere fitted in with the thought of our paramount leader, Mao Zedong.

In fact, the people had heard all this before. Almost every year since liberation, government officials had visited Yongning to harangue the people there on the dangers of sexual freedom and the benefits of monogamous marriage. Once, even, they had brought a portable generator and showed a movie of people dressed as Moso, people who were in the last stage of syphilis, who had gone mad and lost most of their faces—and the villagers had set the makeshift cinema on fire.

But now the officials had held meetings night after night where they harangued and criticized and interrogated. And they had not gone home. Instead they had ambushed men on their way to their lovers' houses, they had dragged couples out of their beds and exposed people naked to their own relatives' eyes. Then they had issued orders for the couples to build new houses that no one could afford to build but where the couples ought to live together like married people did everywhere else in China. Finally, they had refused to provide the certificates for extra grain, and for cloth for the children, unless their mothers told the officials the names of the fathers.

The Moso protested. They spoke up at meetings to explain their way of life and the customs of their ancestors. But the officials did not give up, and the people stopped protesting. The men stayed at home, no longer daring to walk to the women's houses at night. But still the officials did not give up. They waited for the women to make a decision about the planting and the harvesting, about the grain rations and the other things their children needed that the government provided. They waited a long time, until at last many people agreed to live as husband and wife and to participate in the government-sponsored marriage ceremonies, where they each got a cup of tea, a cigarette, pieces of candy, and a paper certificate.

"What shame," Uncle whispered.

The horseman squashed the tears under his tired eyelids.

As for me, I also pushed on my eyelids, although I cannot pretend that I understood how terrifying the events taking place in Yongning truly were. Whatever lay beyond our meadow was to me like the invisible and untouchable world of bygone times, the world of yellow-haired Americans and murderous Yi chiefs — whimsical places filled with strange beings, events I visited in my dreams that vanished as soon as I opened my eyes or when, very late in the night, the campfire died.

But that night, as I closed my eyes to the glow of the campfire and the government officials joined Dr. Rock and the Yi tribesmen in my childish imagination, I made believe that my father had really come to stay in our house forever, that Zhemi and my Ama were living under the same roof as man and wife. And now a deep sadness came over me — as I pictured Zhemi sitting near the hearth, no longer an honored guest, and yet, neither uncle nor brother but just a man living in my mother's house.

The Mountain Goddess

When the Great Cultural Revolution entered its tenth year, the lamasery and the pretty glass palace were gone; the lamas had been humiliated and their books burned; and the festivals were no more. The people too had changed. Many had married, and some had even abandoned their own traditional clothes — among them, my mother was now wearing trousers and a Chinese-style fur hat. But then Mao Zedong died and the winds of change soon blew over China. When they blew over Moso country, the people sighed with relief. Most left their wives and their husbands to live as they had always done, in their own mothers' houses. They were ready to make up for lost time, to do whatever they could to honor their gods and their ancestors, to dress up and dance and sing again.

When Uncle took me home in the summer, the village was bustling with activity. Banquet tables had been set up in the courtyards and people were arriving from different villages to compete in wrestling and horse-riding contests, to sing and dance and drink wine and tease each other about their accents:

"Your voice is beautiful, but your words are garbled!"

"Maybe your mother did not straighten your ears when you were little!"

With so many visitors and so much taunting, Ama thought she should remind us of the finer points of etiquette: "When you go out in public, you must behave. Make sure you don't fight with anyone and watch out for each other. When you meet an older person, you must show respect. If you see someone drunk, you must help him. If someone offers you food or drink, you must take it with both hands and say thank you." She told us over and over until she got too busy to notice that we had stopped listening.

That summer there was a lot to keep my mother busy, and us as well. She had decided that we would walk around Lake Lugu in honor of the mountain goddess, as we had always done until the Red Guards had upset everything. We would go to Yongning to sing and light sagebrush for Gamu Mountain, and we would also go to Qiansuo to visit her family. We had to leave things well organized for Dujema, who would take care of our chickens and pigs. We also had to pack food for ourselves and for anyone who cared to join us for a picnic, and we had to prepare the customary gifts of salted pork, tea bricks, cloth, and tobacco. Finally, we had to wash and mend our clothes because we should look our best during the festival, and also to show off to Aunt Yufang and Second Aunt and all the people of Qiansuo. And for this occasion, my mother took out her white skirt and wrapped her turban around her head.

And so my mother's skirt swished to and fro as she shouted orders left and right. Meanwhile, my little brothers ran around in circles and got in everybody's way, Ache went off to fetch some water and disappeared with his friends, and my big sister Zhema, who seemed to know what to do next, poured rice into sacks, sliced up the pork and boiled the eggs, and counted bamboo boxes. And I felt jealous—because Zhema was so grown-up, and she was so capable, and my mother was going to so much trouble on account of her dress, tying one colorful sash around her pretty waist and then another, adding a string of glass beads to her headdress, and a ribbon here and a flower there—while I was still a child and my hair was too short, and I had to content myself with a clean version of the linen tunic I wore every day. But I held my tongue and tried to make myself useful.

I was in the vegetable garden cutting up cilantro when Ama called out to me:

"Namu! Come over here. There're some people to see you."

"Who is it?" I asked incredulously because I was still a child and I had a visitor.

"It's a Yi man and his daughter," Ama answered. And she pulled the garden gate closed behind me and hurried me along.

He looked much better than the first time I had seen him, with his lips bleeding and his eyes dying, but I recognized him immediately. So he had come back, I thought in amazement. And this time he had come with his daughter, and two horses loaded with big bags of potatoes, wild mushrooms, and wheat flour. In another sack he had three wild hens. And now he was speaking with my mother in Yi, and I could not understand anything, but I heard my mother say my name a few times, and she was smiling and looking very happy.

As for his daughter, her name was Añumo. She seemed a little older than me. She was very proud but also very shy. No girl in our village, except for Tsilidema and her unfortunate Gu family, was this shy, but then when she smiled, she had a pretty dimple in her right cheek, and when she curtsied, she did so in the most graceful manner. As for me, I felt very proud at being curtsied to, as I knew that all this politeness and all the gifts had come to us on account of my generosity. But I was a long way from guessing what was coming next. Not even in the horsemen's stories had I heard of such a thing as the Yi man requested, when he explained with grave dignity that he wanted me to become his daughter's blood sister. Now, I surely did not understand what he meant for us to do, and I cannot say today that I would have done things differently if I had understood, but I do know that I was enjoying myself so much at the center of attention that I accepted his offer without even raising a question.

The man asked my mother for a bowl and some water and salt. When she came back, he grabbed one of his hens and drew his knife and cut its throat, and as the poor animal flapped and twitched, he poured her blood into the bowl. After that he stirred in the water and the salt, and he told Añumo to drink and then to hand the bowl over to me.

I had never put anything in my mouth that had been killed and was not cooked, and I took the bowl with as much reluctance as was possible under the circumstances — because I knew that it was much too late to say no, unless I never wanted to show my face again to anyone in the world. The smell almost made me puke, and I held off for a moment. In the end I closed my eyes and held my breath, and I drank the chicken blood. Añumo and I became sisters.

My Ama took the bowl from my hand, and while Zhema took the hen away to pluck and ready for lunch, she invited the Yi man to follow her into the house to drink some tea. I stayed outside with Añumo, wiping my lips with my hands, and my hands on my shirt, and then my tongue on my lips, and then my lips on my sleeve. But as the briny taste faded, I began to feel rather special at having a Yi sister. She looked somewhat different from us Moso. She had black hair like we had, but large brown eyes and slightly darker skin, long eyelashes and a straight and narrow nose, and beautiful white teeth. I touched her eyelashes over and over. We held hands and smiled at each other. Ama brought us some sweet dumplings filled with raw sugar. Añumo took a bite and her face lit up. She loved the sugar, so I emptied the inside of my dumpling and gave it to her. I loved my mountain sister.

At lunchtime Ama served us chicken stew and my brothers and I ate with our mouths wide open as we listened to her speaking with the Yi man in his language. Actually, we could not believe our ears, and so much so that we began to laugh uncontrollably — until Ama took us aside and explained in a stern voice that many words in Moso and Yi sounded the same and had completely different meanings. *"Kasha nosha opa nozha"* meant "Please don't be shy, and eat all you can!" and not "Please, you may eat my ass."

When the Yi were about to leave, my mother packed some slices of salted pork and some rice and bricks of tea, and she gave my mountain sister a scarf and said: "This is a present from Namu." We accompanied them to the last house in the village with all the regard owed to honored guests. I held Añumo's hand and swung on her arm and I wished I could have spoken to her but I did not dare. I did not want to offend anyone by speaking the wrong Yi words. I also wished Añumo could have stayed with us forever, or at least that she could have come with us to Yongning for the mountain festival, but my mother said that Añumo had to go back to her own home and live with her own family, and that she was not that sort of real sister.

WE LEFT QIANSUO EARLY IN THE MORNING. We loaded our little horses and began our walk along the shore of Mother Lake. When the sun was high up in the sky, we hiked on Gamu Mountain amid the spruces and rhododendron and peonies. We came to a nice picnic area, where we met up with other families already engaged in the celebrations. There we lit piles of sagebrush, and the women took off their turbans and the men removed their felt hats, and we all kowtowed to the mother goddess.

The full name of our mountain goddess is Segge Gamu — the White Lioness — and in fact, from Yongning plain she does look just like a crouching lion, with her front paws resting on the lakeshore. From the lake you see her face, broad and square, and if you lower your eyes, you see her placid reflection mirrored in the water. From the top of Gamu's head, you can see all of the Yongning plain and all the other mountains, and immediately below, the lake, bluer than the sky, and the little islands covered in spruce and pine trees. Somewhere on the mountainside lies a great treasure of gold and precious jewels that was buried many centuries ago by one of our feudal lords, but no one has ever found it, and probably no one ever will. Then, right at the crest of Gamu, there is the entrance to a huge cave where women come in the hope of conceiving children. This cave is the womb of the goddess — because Gamu is not only a lioness, she is also a woman and the mother of the Moso people.

Every summer, on the twenty-fifth day of the seventh lunar month, our Gamu must go to Lhasa to play games with the gods of Tibet, and the ancient mountain festival, with all the dancing and singing and praying and drinking, was meant to encourage her to win. For Gamu is wrathful as well as loving, and if she were to lose, there would be terrible weather and the crops would fail, the animals and the people would become sick, and they would have no offspring. Thankfully, Gamu is very intelligent and she almost always wins, even without the festival. And naturally, she is also very beautiful and has many lovers, as well as a special companion whose name is Azhapula, who is the mountain god of Qiansuo. Oh, but poor Azhapula! Life with beautiful Gamu can be so difficult that he cannot always control his temper. For example, when he caught her making love with Cezhe, a young man she had only just met, he became so furious that he castrated him. Even today you can see there is a spike missing at the top of Mount Cezhe.

Sometimes, when Azhapula has had enough, he threatens to leave Gamu and to go look for a new woman, but then she pleads with him and tells him that she loves him, and he always stays. That was how, a long, long time ago, they had a terrible fight and Azhapula, crazy with jealousy, jumped on his horse and galloped away. As could be expected, Gamu could not bear it and she ran after him to stop him. When she caught up to his horse, she reached for his vest, just managing to grasp it, and then she held Azhapula back. The god and the goddess tugged and pulled all through the night until the sun rose on the horizon, when, under the light of heaven, they were turned into mountains. They are still here today, and Gamu still holds on to Azhapula's vest across the deep ravine that separates them, to remind the Moso that men must always return to their mothers' houses at the first light of dawn and that our mother goddess and her lover Azhapula should not have made such a scandal.

MY MOTHER WAS READYING HERSELF for a third kowtow when she caught sight of Zhema and stopped in amazement. My big sister was bowing from her waist, with her hands joined together in front of her mouth. "Where have you learned to kowtow like the Han Chinese?" Ama asked, and she told my sister to bow properly, with her forehead all the way to the ground and her hands joined together first on her brow, then touching her mouth, and then her heart. Afterward we all had to kowtow again, three times, and in the correct fashion. Then Ama joined in the singing:

Gamu, we have been busy for a year,
Today is a very special day and we have come to thank you,
I have brought some small dishes and wine.
I know these are not enough to show my appreciation,
But these are given in all sincerity.
Thank you, Gamu, for your protection.
My family and our village had a peaceful year.
Thank you, Gamu, for the good weather,
We had a very good harvest.
Everyone is healthy.
Thank you, Gamu, for the year starting,
Please protect my family,
Please protect the people of our village.
This is my first daughter, Zhema.
She has come to kowtow to you.
And here is my daughter Namu
And my sons Ache, Howei, and Homi,
And my last-born, Jiama.
They have all come to kowtow to you.

And again we kowtowed and we prayed, and kowtowed one last time before we spread our blankets around the campfire and sat to eat our picnic lunch with the other families.

In the afternoon we continued our walk to Yongning town under the gaze of the lion goddess crouching impassively above us, square and imposing, dreaming of her lovers and of the times when thousands of villagers gathered at her feet to worship her. Or perhaps that was what my Ama was doing—dreaming of the days before the Red Guards had broken everything up.

In those days the people would have gathered on the side of the mountain for a whole week of dancing, singing, and praying. As far as the eye could see, the Yongning plain would have been covered with tents—yellow, black, white,

and blue—some of them painted with beautiful flower de-
signs. And amid the spiraling smoke of smoldering sagebrush, amid drunken men, and women bright as flowers,
hundreds of lamas in brilliant yellow would have performed
the ceremonies for the goddess. Their faces glowing, showing
that nothing in the world could be better, they would have
chanted sutras in deep vibrating voices and blown their long
brass trumpets into the heavens.

In those days, when my mother was still young and much
of her life awaited her, the people really knew how to have
fun and how to honor their gods. Arm in arm, the women
sang to each other about how bad the men were, and the men
sang back and teased the women, and the women replied,
and their songs grew ever more witty and ever more daring.
Every night the people danced in big circles around the bonfires. They danced the hoeing and threshing dances, or the
weaving dance, where men and women touched knees and
made turns, which was my Ama's favorite. And when they
did not dance or sing, they went to the hot springs to find
lovers. The women washed each other's backs, and the men
sat in the health-giving water, drinking wine, until one of
them announced that his cup was empty and the woman who
liked the gleam in his eyes got up and fetched him some more.
Then, as she poured the wine for him, he told her under
which tree and under which cluster of stars she would find
him later in the night. She, of course, would say nothing, but
soon afterward she would leave the water, and he would follow her.

BY THE TIME WE ARRIVED in Yongning town, the sky had
grown dark and rain was pouring so hard that the streets
looked like mountain streams and we had to hitch our skirts
and trousers above our knees to wade through the brown

water flooding the road. When at last we found our relatives, we bid a hurried good night to the other families and gladly settled around the fire to dry up and gossip and enjoy ourselves for the rest of the evening.

The next morning, as is usual in this season, the weather was hot and sunny again, and I followed Zhema and my cousins into town. There was so much excitement in the air, and the market street was bustling with people, almost all Moso in festival dress but also Yi men in gray turbans and black felt capes, Yi women in large black hats and multicolored skirts, and Tibetan horsemen in embroidered caps, their long knives hitched conspicuously to their waists. My sister and cousins strolled up and down the street, and I followed behind them as they casually avoided the puddles and the pigs and chickens who were going about their own business, delighting in the grubs coming out of the ground and the refuse from the market stalls.

Every now and then we stopped to greet friends and relatives, or to look sideways at someone of interest, or to peer over the counters of the small wooden shops where Naxi women in revolutionary caps gossiped and sold everything you could ever dream of owning—blue-rimmed enamel basins, pink-and-white thermos flasks, brass ladles, iron pots, rolls of blue cloth, leather belts, and Tibetan locks. Then I followed my sister and the other grown women as they moved from stall to stall, with their long skirts hovering over the steaming, muddy ground, and as they commented on the freshness of the vegetables and the fat on the chickens, and as they chatted with the watchmaker and joked with the shoemaker polishing a horseman's boots, and when they gave their prettiest smiles to the young Moso men who had caught up with them.

Oh! I so wanted to be a grown woman! I so wanted to wear a long skirt that would sweep the ground before my feet and to have men smile at me, and to have men sing for me and dance with me — I so wanted to be like my sisters and my cousins and our neighbor Dujema, to be a big woman, beautiful and powerful, and to have many lovers. And then I also thought of falling in love and of finding just one boy for myself as my Ama had with Zhemi. But then, I thought, if I fell in love, he should be from Qiansuo, so that he could be just like my father and because whenever my mother was with my father, she always reverted to the speech of her girlhood. Oh, yes! All I wanted was to be a grown woman with my own boyfriend from Qiansuo.

Now, I did try my best to look grown-up. I felt the vegetables and smelled the eggs, and I sat next to my sister and the other women and listened in on their conversations, but they all showed so little interest in me that eventually I gave up in disgust and went off to play with my little brother Howei and the rest of the children.

For the remainder of the day, we went running in and out of the pools at the hot springs, throwing stones at each other. The next day we spent most of the afternoon collecting cold ash from the bonfires and wrapping it into leaves to make grenades. In the evening we went out to play war. But while I was looking to ambush Howei, I found a couple making love in the dark.

"*Che sso!* Naughty boy!" they shouted in my direction.

Of course, they never thought that a girl would do anything so bad as throw an ash grenade at them. They never suspected that a girl with all her hair shaved off could be jealous of the good time they were having.

But perhaps the mountain goddess did.

WHEN I WAS BACK LIVING in the tent with Uncle, I woke up one morning with a backache. It lasted two days. I thought that maybe I had hurt myself riding on the yak. And then, because the weather was unusually hot, I thought that perhaps a dip in one of the mountain springs near our meadow would do me good. I loved bathing, although I could not swim, and I was very careful never to go into the water above my waist because the pools are sometimes very deep and dangerous.

But the water did not ease my back pain. To the contrary, and my stomach now began to hurt as well, and I thought that perhaps the water was too cold. When I came out, I found blood running down my legs, and I thought that I had been bitten by leeches. But then I realized that the blood was not coming from my legs but from inside me, and I quickly dressed and ran back to our camp and went into the stable to take a closer look at myself. When I found nothing, I knew that it was woman's blood. I should have been relieved, but when I lifted my face and saw Uncle's horse looking straight at me, I knew I had done something terrible because you are not supposed to show this dirty thing to the horses and the yaks. Moso people must always show a lot of respect to yaks and horses. Today I can still see the horse's eyes, and I still shudder at the thought.

And of course, I could not show the dirty thing to my uncle either, so I sat on the grass and waited for him to leave before going back into the tent. But then, when I was inside the tent, I didn't know what to do, so I put the black goatskin on the floor, and I sat on it. Every now and then I got up and sneaked outside to wash myself, and then I went back to the goatskin, stepping backward and rubbing dirt and ash into the ground to clean up the spotting I left in my tracks. When I heard Uncle coming back at the end of the afternoon, I quickly wrapped the goatskin around my waist and I did not get up for the rest of the evening. Uncle said nothing, and he asked no questions. Perhaps he knew, and perhaps he didn't.

Either way, this was not the sort of thing a man could discuss with his sister's daughter.

The next day Uncle had to go to the village. He would leave early in the morning with the three horses loaded with pads of butter, and he would not be back until the evening with our supply of vegetables, rice, and corn, and salt for the yaks. Now, because I had spent years living with my uncle, I had only the vaguest notion about women's blood, but I knew I had to do something, and I spent a great deal of the evening thinking my problem over. The next morning, as soon as Uncle was gone, I tore off one of my shirts and took out the sewing kit, and I made up a pad and a pair of suspenders that went over my shoulders and crossed on my chest. It wasn't the most comfortable thing, but it was better than sitting on the goatskin all day not daring to move.

The blood lasted a whole week. And it came again, every month, at about the same time as Uncle took the butter to the villagers. During all this time, I said nothing. I never told anyone, not even my Ama when I went home for New Year. But my sister found the pad in my little bundle. She knew right away what it was for and she went to tell about the suspenders to all her girlfriends, and everyone laughed at me. After that I did not talk to Zhema for a week, but she talked to my mother, and then my Ama knew that I was probably about thirteen years old and ready to come back to live in the village to become a grown woman.

My Skirt Ceremony

When Uncle came home from his butter delivery, he handed me the rice cakes my Ama had cooked and said, "Next time I deliver the butter, you'll come with me. Your mother has already talked with the lamas about your Skirt Ceremony."

At these words my heart leaped in my chest, but although I wanted to jump for joy, I only nodded my head. I could not possibly show my happiness to Uncle. I did not want to make him think I was happy to leave him. Yet, for the rest of the day, I could not help thinking of my ceremony — of all the beautiful clothes and the silver jewelry and the presents the neighbors would bring me, and how I would go dancing and how the boys would talk to me. I tried so hard to suppress my joy, and my poor Uncle tried so hard not to show his sadness, until, later in the evening, after his usual cup of wine, his eyes suddenly filled with tears. And then I felt lonely. So lonely. So much happiness, and no friend to talk to, no one to tease and pinch me and run after me. No one but Uncle, who would soon be fast asleep and snoring, and then the yaks, who would be stomping their hooves on the ground, and the horses snorting and the dogs scratching at their fleas — all of it keeping me awake into the long night.

The first thing that came to my mind when I woke next morning was: "Twenty-nine days before the next butter delivery" — and I began counting to twenty-nine, and then I started again. When we had finished breakfast, I took the yaks to graze on the side of the mountain path, where I could look down into the valley, just in case my Ama had decided to send for me earlier. I did this for a few days, until we ran out of grass and I had to take the animals to another pasture. But that evening I thought, "All Uncle needs are ten pads of butter; if I get more milk, we will have the butter sooner and we will go to the village earlier." And I pulled hard on the cow's teats to try to get more milk. The cow lifted her back leg, turned her head, and looked at me with surprise — so I stopped pulling and stroked her side to make her feel better. Animals can look into your soul and they always know when you are being bad to them, and I knew I should be kind to animals because of my karma.

Before dinner I placed five potatoes near the fireplace, one for each of five days, and after dinner I took one potato away. When four more days had gone by, I put another five potatoes in the same place. Uncle looked at the potatoes and said, "Don't worry, it will pass soon enough." But it did not and my heart itched with impatience.

But perhaps when you want something badly enough, you can make it happen. Because the night I would have removed the eleventh potato, when Uncle and I were sitting near the fire eating our corn soup, the dogs began barking from the corral and then we heard the hooves of horses coming up near the tent. It was my brother Ache. He had come to get me. It was harvest time and my Ama did not want to wait until the end of the month. She needed help in the house.

Now I could not eat. And as soon as Ache and Uncle had finished their soup, I got up to clean their dishes, and then I cleaned them again. That night I don't think I slept at all.

The next morning Uncle tied my little bundle on the horse, and then he took the leaves that were drying on top of the tent and wrapped up some milk curd. "Here, take this," he said, avoiding my eyes as he handed me the curd. "And when you're home, be good and listen to your mother." After that he turned around and picked up the broom to sweep the tent — because we should never sweep the floor after a person leaves, since that would mean we are sweeping away the memory of their presence. When he was done with sweeping, he lit some sagebrush a few feet away from the entrance of the tent, and as he stood watching us get ready, he took hold of his prayer beads and began chanting softly to himself.

We said good-bye, nodding to each other, our eyes shining with tears. There were no embraces or kisses because this is not the way we do things.

I felt so sorry for my lonely uncle. But we had not gone more than a few hundred yards on the mountain trail when an irrepressible feeling of happiness welled inside my chest. And now I could not wait to get home. I was so impatient I could not even sit on the horse. So I got down on the ground and handed the reins over to my brother. Then I ran and skipped and ran, and I shouted for joy.

When we arrived home in the late afternoon, the streets were empty except for a few old people taking care of babies. Everyone else was out in the fields. But in our house, we did not have any old people to take care of the little children, so my Ama was in the courtyard, chopping firewood, and my little sister, Jiama, was sitting at a safe distance building a miniature mud house. On seeing us entering the yard, she ran to Ache and ignored me.

"Hey, Ama!" I called to my mother.

My mother looked up from the pile of wood and smiled. "You're here already!"

"She ran all the way!" Ache said, laughing.

He passed Jiama over to me so that he could take care of the horses, but she wriggled and I put her down.

"Sit down, Namu," my mother said, pointing to a little wooden chair on the porch. "You must be very tired." She went inside to fetch some hot water for me to bathe my feet. When I was all cleaned up, she handed me an old pair of canvas shoes. Zhema's shoes.

"Where is Zhema?" I asked, as I put the shoes on and then took them off again.

"In the sunflower fields," my mother answered.

I was so happy to be home. I tried coaxing my little sister to come for a tour of the house with me — after Uncle's tent, our house always seemed so big, the vegetable garden so full — but Jiama ran back to Ama and I decided to go look for my big sister. I found her, bent over her rake, working much too hard to notice me. I crept up behind her, very quietly, to play a game I sometimes played with the yaks. When I was just about touching her, I whispered *boo!* into her ear. She jumped and turned around — and glared at me.

My big sister Zhema was very quiet and clever, and she was a good girl. When my mother went visiting, she always took Zhema with her because she was never any trouble. All the men loved her too. Everyone spoke nicely about my sister; nobody ever had anything bad to say about her. But maybe she was too quiet for me. When I whispered in her ear, she jumped. It was very easy to scare my sister: although she was older than me, she wasn't very brave.

Zhema softened her eyes, wiped her dusty forehead, and smiled somewhat slyly. "So, you're back already! Are you sure you're old enough to become a grown woman?"

MY INITIATION CEREMONY was to take place during the New Year festival because this is when the Skirts and

Trousers Ceremonies always take place. In the meantime, we had to finish the harvest, and after the harvest, we had to fertilize the fields, and after fertilizing the fields, we had to slaughter the pigs.

Twice a year we kill the pigs, once in November and then just before New Year, and at least three pigs in total. Two pigs of three hundred pounds each can provide a family with meat for a year, and one pig must be saved for gifts and offerings, for funerals and any other special event. We Moso waste no part of the pig. After the animals have been bled, the legs are cut off and the bones and innards removed, and the cavities are filled with chili and salt. Then the pig is sewn back up. We call these salted pigs *bocher*. We keep them piled on top of each other on a bench in the main room of the house, and traditionally, the greater the number of *bocher*, the wealthier the family. Aside from making *bocher*, we also debone the legs and fill them with salt and chili and make them into ham. As for the bones, we hang them from the rafters to smoke and make soups for old people and children. The fat we boil down to pour into bladders and make cooking lard, and with the blood and the leftover meat, we make delicious sausages.

Butchering and salting pigs is a great deal of work, so people always send the children from house to house to ask for their neighbors' help. As a child, I loved doing this. We would stand outside people's courtyards and shout at the top of our lungs, and people would let us in and give us soup. Thanks to the time I had spent in the high mountains, singing and shouting in the rarefied air, I could scream louder than any of the other children.

While the men butchered the pigs, the women cooked and fermented wine. Every day, in every courtyard, a spread of the most fragrant dishes was served on long tables covered with pine needles. This was a time to show off. A really capable woman can fill a bowl of rice with a single ladle scoop, and a woman's reputation may go a long way beyond the village. My mother had earned herself a reputation for making the best blood sausage in the village, and she always kept it for my big sister. In the evening she boiled the sausage, and when it had cooled down, she put it in Zhema's bamboo box for her to take to the fields the next day.

Thinking back as far as I can remember, I am quite sure that I always coveted a piece of the blood sausage, and yet I never dared ask Ama. Then one year, when I was home from the mountain, something terrible happened to Zhema's sausage.

Every evening, as I watched the blood sausage disappear under the lid of Zhema's lunch box, I drooled. And every morning I gawked at Zhema selfishly sauntering down the village street with the sausage in her lunch box. After a few days, all I could think of was that sausage. So one night, when everybody was asleep, I crept out of bed, stole the sausage from the lunch box, and replaced it with a piece of my own poop I had spent the afternoon drying in the sun and fashioning into the correct shape. The next day I shared the blood sausage with my little brother Howei. We sat at the bottom of the stairs, right under Zhema's bedroom, and nothing ever tasted so good. My big sister came home from the fields around noon, screaming and crying, and when Ama found out what I had done, she laughed and laughed, and that evening she made sure to give me a piece of sausage. And Zhema screamed again and said that she would never, ever eat blood sausage again. But she did.

THIS YEAR IT DID NOT MATTER TO ME who got to eat the blood sausage. Because this year was the year of my Skirt Ceremony.

As soon as the pig slaughtering was over, my Ama and my

sister set out to clean the house and prepare the customary foods and drinks. At a Skirt and Trousers Ceremony, three types of drinks must be served: butter tea, rice wine, and our own Sulima wine, which we brew from corn, millet, and honey. Every guest must be served these drinks in small bowls placed on a tray covered with pine needles and popcorn. This was a lot of work, and toward the end of the week, our neighbor Dujema also came to help, to ferment the wine and make rice cakes.

Now, I had wished for this moment for so long, I should have been very happy. Certainly it was comfortable to sit around our fireplace and to eat my mother's cooking instead of my uncle's. It was so exciting to think that soon I would be one of the grown women and that I would be dishing out food to my brothers and my little sister. But I felt strangely out of place.

Since my last visit, everything and everyone had changed a little. Some old person had died, some baby had been born. A baby had learned to walk and talk. Of course, every year when I came home, something had changed. But in all the time I had spent with Uncle in the mountain, I had come home only for a few days each year—never long enough to give in to the daily routine of village life. And now that I was home for good, now that every morning I tied my workbasket on my back and followed my mother and sister to the fields, now—when I looked at my mother's shadow dancing on our log walls as she went between the fireplaces busying herself for my coming-of-age ceremony—I found myself missing the walls of Uncle's tent.

One late afternoon, when I was hanging about with some village girls, trying to find something of interest to say, one of them asked: "Will you go back to the mountains after your ceremony?"

"I'm not going back anymore," I answered. But I understood that they had grown used to my living away, that they were used to my not being one of them.

They were right. I was not one of them. I had not grown up as they had with their mothers and aunts and sisters; I had not grown up playing with girls. I had grown up with my silent uncle in a world of hairy yaks and vapory dew, and in remote mysterious lands that lay beyond our mountains and where blue-eyed people lived.

In the week preceding my ceremony, Ama washed my hair every day and she rubbed yak butter into it to make it shine. Traditionally Moso women lengthen their hair with extensions fashioned from the hair of a yak's tail and silk threads, and also colored ribbons. The hair and the extensions should be very long, so that the whole thing falls way below the buttocks. But because my uncle had kept my hair so short on account of the lice, my Ama could not attach the extensions, and Dujema suggested that they make me a wig. Besides taking care of my hair, my mother examined my hands and my face and ears. "Don't forget to rub butter into your skin after you bathe," she told me several times a day, whenever she finished with a chore and she happened to look in my direction, for my skin was very brown and rough from spending too much time in the high mountain air. One afternoon, when my brothers were out of the house and I was left alone with my mother, she taught me the way a woman should sit to show that she had self-respect and how a woman should walk to show herself off. And no doubt, on the day of my ceremony, my mother wanted to show me off—but all this admonishing and prodding and inspecting made me think of Uncle when he took care of the yaks and the horses.

Uncle arrived from the mountain on New Year's Eve. My brother Ache helped him put up the prayer flags over the roof and over the gates of the house and in the yard. When the flags were up, Ama called Uncle to help her haul a large sack of corn from the storeroom to the foot of the Mother Column. Then, together with Ache, they pulled the sewn-up pig down from the bench and pushed it along the floor to rest level with the corn sack. And when I saw the pig and the sack of corn on the floor all set for the next day's events, I could hardly contain my excitement.

That evening, the last evening of my childhood, my mother said: "Make sure you get a good night's sleep, you'll need all your energy tomorrow. You're going to do a lot of kowtowing!" And as I curled up next to my little sister, Jiama, I thought with trepidation that this was my last night in the storeroom, that tomorrow I would be sleeping in my own room, with my own bed, my own fireplace, and my own door, which I would open to whomever I pleased.

Zhema woke me before cockcrow. "Namu, you must get up now, you have to be ready at sunrise." I opened my eyes immediately. I did not mind that I had not slept enough or that I must leave the warmth of the little bed where Jiama was still sound asleep, her little hands joined under her chin.

In the main room, Ama was putting the finishing touches on some trays, and Uncle, who was quietly sipping from a bowl of butter tea, invited me to sit next to him and have a quick drink. But my mother told me to come out into the courtyard, where she took off her headdress and kowtowed three times toward the sunlight, pink and orange and yet barely visible on the jagged horizon. Then I too kowtowed to the rising sun. The ceremony had begun. I had only just stood up when the lamas walked into our courtyard, followed by our neighbors bearing gifts for me and offerings for the fire god. We kowtowed to the lamas, and Ama invited everyone inside the house, where the holy men took their place on the kang around the fireplace, and the guests sat at the lower hearth. Uncle lit incense sticks and sagebrush and added wood to the fire, and the lamas began chanting in a low drone interrupted every now and then by the blowing of the shell conch.

"Good fortune! *Cheche zheke!*" the guests said as they stepped through the door. *"Amisei, amisei!* Thank you, thank you!" my mother answered, as she handed each person a tray with the three bowls of wine and tea and directed them to take a seat near the hearth. Perhaps sixty or seventy people came — all of them our neighbors, all of them dressed up in the Moso traditional costume, the women in long skirts and pretty, colorful shirts lined with gold thread, and the men in Tibetan dress.

When my mother's friend Cilatsuo came in, everybody was already seated and happily sipping wine and tea. Cilatsuo handed me a scarf. I was a little surprised, because everyone else had placed their gifts in a big basket for me to open later. Still, I thanked her, and she smiled and walked off to chat with the rest of the party. Once she was out of earshot, my Ama told me that she had asked Cilatsuo to help me change into my adult clothes.

This came as a shock to me. "Why her? Why not you?" I asked. Everyone I knew, including my own sister Zhema, had her mother officiating at her ceremony.

But my mother replied, "Sometimes it's better if a friend helps you change."

"But why?"

Ama looked into my eyes and said firmly, "She was also born in a horse year, so there's no problem. She has a perfect face, and very good fortune. She will be better for you."

I looked at my mother's face and I could not see anything wrong with it. Her face had been good enough for my sister's ceremony, why wasn't it enough for me? Why was she giving me away now that I was about to be reborn?

But her mouth was tight and her eyes determined, and

there was no moving her. I was confused and hurt but also at a loss for what to say, and with all these people around, it was not the place or time to have an argument. Cilatsuo would help me change into my adult clothes and I would get some of her good fortune.

When Cilatsuo came back to stand by my side, I kowtowed to her, and she took me by the hand and walked me toward the Mother Column, where I waited by the side of the pig and the corn and a bundle of brand-new clothes neatly piled on the kang.

Meanwhile, my Ama handed Zhema a tray heaped with sunflower seeds, pears, and walnuts to pass around, and she took another for herself. Her cheeks flushed and her eyes shining, Ama smiled and joked with everyone. Five lamas, and so much food and so many guests! My mother was truly showing off. And as I looked at her gliding among the guests, so proud, so happy, wanting to give away all the food we had in the house, my heart ached from all the sacrifices and the hard work that had gone into this ceremony, an event my mother meant to be remembered by all the villagers and that was not only about her pride but was also my very own special day. My heart beat a little faster, and at last I felt the heat of joy rising in my cheeks.

When she had taken care of the guests, Ama put away her tray. She called the dog into the house, making him stay next to me. She told the story of how, a long time ago, the Dog had exchanged his own life of sixty years for the people's thirteen years, and she thanked our dog and gave him human food. Uncle lit more sagebrush and the room filled with smoke. And when the lamas had finished praying for our dog, they began to pray for me to have long life, wealth, and many children, and they blew the conch to call the gods so that they would descend from heaven and witness my ceremony.

This was the moment for Cilatsuo to take my hand and help me step up and place one foot on the pig and the other on the sack of corn. Now I was ready to give up my old life.

Cilatsuo took off my blue linen shirt and I stood naked as I had been at my birth, in front of all our neighbors and my own relatives, in the golden glow of the fires and the thick scented haze of sagebrush smoke. I felt so beautiful and so perfect, and I thought of the heavenly goddess who, at the beginning of time, had descended to the shore of our lake on a beam of moonlight, where she had mothered our Moso race.

Dujema called out: "Do you believe that this crying baby turned out so beautiful? Your mother is so fortunate not to have given you away!"

Everyone laughed and cheered and offered more comments, including old Guso, who said: "Latso, your family has the most beautiful daughters. I am old, but it's good to see that the younger generation is so blessed." And he began to sing, in a broken voice, of the beauty of Moso women and the strength of Moso men.

When the cheering and the laughing had quieted, Cilatsuo threw my old shirt into the fire and my mother chanted:

Before Buddha we are burning these old clothes,
We are burning Namu's old fate.
Today Namu is reborn.
Please protect her that she may be healthy,
And that she may prosper, and that she may have
    many children and grandchildren.

As she finished her chanting, Ama reached out for the new set of clothes she had prepared for me. First she handed Cilatsuo a pink shirt bordered with black-and-gold trim. Then, as Cilatsuo helped me get my arms into the sleeves and she closed the buttons, Ama took the white skirt, all bundled up like a sausage, and shook it. It opened in one swoop like a summer cloud, and everyone went, *"Oooooh!"*

All the while, as she was dressing me, Cilatsuo commented, "Look at those eyes, they are like stars in the sky. Look at this face, it is round as the moon. Look at her breasts, they are like ripe peaches." And she spoke of my waist, my buttocks, my thighs, while I felt at the same time embarrassed and proud. She wrapped a multicolored belt around my waist and attached a silver chain on my shirt, just above the belt, to signify that perhaps one day I would run the household. If I ever became Dabu, the key of the granary would hang from the chain. Then she placed the wig with all the silk threads and hair extensions on my head.

Everyone was stunned. They said, "Oh! She's so pretty!"

The transformation was complete. I was a woman, I was brand-new, and I was beautiful.

My mother was glowing. She was looking at me from head to toe, as though she could not believe her own eyes. She was not saying anything. She was not moving. Meeting my eyes, she shivered slightly, startled as though suddenly waking from a dream, and for a moment she looked confused. Then she slid her jade bracelet from her wrist with great difficulty because it had been there forever, and she kissed it, touched her forehead with it, and put it on my left wrist. "Namu, you will have good fortune," she said, her eyes filling with tears, her hands trembling. I said nothing, but I loved her with all my heart. The bracelet had been her grandmother's, and my Ama had worn it ever since her own skirt ceremony.

My eyes stinging from the smoke and emotion, I took Cilatsuo's hand and stepped down from the pig. I kowtowed to my mother and again to Cilatsuo, and to each person in the room. Finally, I kowtowed to the lamas, three times. My Ama was right. That was a lot of kowtowing. Lama Ruhi touched my head with his prayer book three times, leafing the pages over my forehead for their wisdom to penetrate my mind.

After receiving the lamas' blessing, I turned around toward the little crowd, and I saw my father standing with Dujema near the stove.

"Uncle! You came!" I said, laughing with surprise.

He had wanted to welcome the New Year with his own family in Qiansuo, and although he had set off really early, he had arrived at the end of the ceremony. He gave me a big smile and handed me a colorful woolen scarf. "This is for you," he said in his quiet voice. "Your aunt wove it especially."

I took the scarf and thanked him and went off to thank all the other guests and to make small talk. Then I walked outside, my face hot and flushed with the pride of my womanhood, into the sunlit courtyard while the older women followed me, and behind them, the rest of the guests. The women stopped halfway, and everyone watched as I went up the stairs to my *babahuago*, my flower room.

I went in and shut the door behind me. My big sister was sitting on my bed, waiting for me, and soon her friends were knocking at the little window and we let them in. They were in a happy mood. "Namu, don't let too many men into your room!" they joked. "Too much love is bad for your eyes," another warned. "Actually, too much love makes it harder to get pregnant," someone corrected her. And another pretended to look inside my shirt to see if I was ready for love. "Are your nipples pink?" she asked. She was very funny and everyone laughed. At last I was a grown woman; I was just like my sister and her friends, and it all felt so good and so embarrassing.

Downstairs the guests had seated themselves at the tables in the courtyard — the lamas were at the head of the banquet, and next to them the old uncles and the old women, and then the children. My mother and the younger women did not have time to sit down. They were too busy bringing out the dumplings, the grilled meat, the omelets, the vegetables, tea, and wine.

The rest of the day was spent chatting, singing, eating, and drinking. When the last of the guests left, it was high time to go to bed, and I followed my sister Zhema up the stairs. On the balcony she stood for a moment as she was about to enter her room, gave me a big smile, and waved me good night. Then I opened my own bedroom door.

I placed the candle on the little chest of drawers and sat on my bed — a plank bed with a small cotton mattress and a brand-new, thick cotton quilt. I took off my wig and, turning it over and over in my hands, examined every ribbon, every silk thread and strand of yak hair. And then I lay down under the comforter without undressing. It felt strange to be sleeping alone — without my little sister curled up against me or Uncle snoring on the other side of the fireplace. It felt strange and wonderful, and a little unnerving. I surveyed the plank ceiling above me, and then I sat up and looked at the plank walls around the room. For a while I made animal shadows on the wall by moving my hands in front of the candle. But the night was so quiet and I was so tired.

I had only just blown out the candle when the dog suddenly gave a sharp bark at the foot of the stairs. I sat straight up, my heart beating very fast. Someone had come into the courtyard — someone the dog knew well because he soon stopped barking. And now I heard footsteps on the stairs. I held the comforter around my neck and strained my eyes in the darkness, looking toward the dark shape of the door. The footsteps came closer, and my heart beat faster and harder. But the lover passed my door and shuffled toward my sister's bedroom.

I breathed a sigh of relief and then, putting my hands to my chest to check my heartbeat, I burst out laughing.

I should have known better of course. A grown woman never received lovers on the night of her ceremony. Not because there was a rule against it but because her womanhood was so new she had not had time to sing the courtship songs with anybody. As for me, I told myself as I lay my head back on the pillow, there was little chance of my attracting a lover for some time yet. I knew nothing of what girls learn when they spend all their time gossiping in the fields. I had a long skirt and my own bedroom, but I still had everything to learn about being a woman. Before I could find a lover who wanted to sing with me, I had to learn to joke and to do something about meeting men's eyes. I had to learn to walk the way my mother had showed me and to sit like a self-respecting woman. And perhaps also, I needed to learn to speak in a sweeter voice.

In the meantime, I thought to myself as I inhaled the sweet smell of my brand-new bedding, I was perfectly happy to have beautiful new clothes and a jade bracelet and to look forward to having so many things to learn. I dragged the quilt over my head and tried not to listen to the whispers and giggles coming from my sister's room.

The next day my brother came to knock on my door. "Namu, we're about to eat breakfast. Are you going to get up?"

I opened my eyes. Sunlight was casting a golden glow on the timber walls of my flower room, making it so cheerful and pretty, and when I came downstairs, I had trouble adjusting to the darkness inside. Everyone was already seated around the upper hearth, and my mother was pouring butter tea into their bowls. She lifted her head and greeted me with a smile while she put down the teapot and wiped her hands on her skirt, and then rubbed mechanically at her left wrist, looking for her bracelet. She would do that a lot over the next few days, so much so that I almost felt like taking the bracelet off my arm and giving it back to her.

Still, for the remainder of the New Year festival, my mother was very happy, perhaps as happy as I was. That same afternoon she said, "Namu, you must sort out your presents. Zhema will tell you who gave you what, and you can return something to them and thank them." So Zhema and I spent some time taking an inventory of my gifts, while my mother and Dujema finished cleaning and tidying up from the day before.

With every gift I thought, I am a new person. I am a skirt woman. I had nothing, and now I have everything. And I did have so much — cotton scarves, silver earrings, plastic mirrors, a yak-wool rug, two wooden trays, a bunch of silk threads to weave in my hair, at least three shoulder bags . . . and a bag of salt. I thought my mother had misplaced the salt.

"Ami, here's your salt!" I said.

"This is not my salt," my Ama answered. "It came from the Azha family. They've had some difficulties lately and they had nothing else to give you."

A Knock on My Bedroom Door

One of our relatives in Luo Shui had just given birth to a baby daughter and my mother was filling up the bamboo boxes to bring to her. "Thirty eggs, fermented glutinous rice, a longevity charm for the baby, and some brick tea. Namu, why don't you come with me while Zhema takes care of Jiama and your brothers?" I had been a woman for over a year by now, and I felt rather proud that my Ama wanted me to go visiting with her. For that was usually Zhema's privilege.

At the lakeshore we pushed our canoe onto the water. My mother stepped in and I sat behind her, and we began paddling. The sky was a pure blue, and aside from the whispery clouds floating above the head of the mountain goddess, it was empty. The lake too was empty. Ours was the only boat on the water, and the only sound came from the soft clapping of our oars. I had not heard such silence for a long time, since I had left Uncle in the mountains and come back to live at home, and I felt an irresistible urge to sing. So I began to sing one of our working songs.

My mother's back softened and she slowed her paddling. She was listening to me, and I imagined that she was surprised and pleased by my voice, but when I had finished, she held her oar out of the water and said without turning around to look at me: "Namu, if a man sang to you, would you know how to sing back to him?"

"Of course," I answered, looking beyond her head toward the lakeshore. "Of course I would know."

Suddenly I no longer felt like singing. Instead I felt queasy. And perhaps Ama felt my discomfort, because she began paddling again—until we had gone a long way from shore, when she stopped without warning and drew her oar into the boat. Then she turned around and looked at me.

"Namu, stop! I am going to teach you to sing."

My mother had a beautiful voice and a sharp wit but the intensity in her dark eyes immediately warned me that I was not going to enjoy this lesson. As soon as she began singing, I recognized the tune—the lovers' tune.

Mother Lake is wide and deep,
Too wide for the wild duck to fly across it.

My Ama was improvising a lovers' duet for my benefit. She had sung the opening couplet and now she was pausing, waiting for me to answer. When I did not, she sang back to herself.

There is no point in fearing the size of the lake,
Just rock the boat from side to side.

And again she paused, and still I did not sing back to her, and still she went on singing:

I did not intend to go fishing,
But the fish has eyes of gold,

I had not thought of going hunting,
But the deer horns are too precious.

If you are the transparent water of the lake,
I would gladly change into a fish to probe your heart.

Then Ama stopped again. "Namu, why don't you sing back to me? Didn't you say that you knew how to sing?"

But I could not sing back. It was not that I didn't know how to sing. I had spent so much time singing to my imaginary lovers in the mountains. But this was my mother. I could not sing back to my own mother. I could not even look at her. I felt so embarrassed. I turned my eyes away and stared at the water. Ama clicked her tongue with impatience but she did not force me. Instead she went on with her own songs.

After some time, when I realized that my Ama was no longer singing for me but for the lovers of her youth, I finally dared look at her. There was such tenderness in her face, such joy, and she looked so beautiful, radiant. I felt awed. When she stopped, we sat for a moment without speaking, rocked by the soft clapping of the waves against the canoe, feeling awkward. This show of intimacy was so unusual, so out of our common experience. And suddenly I could not wait to get to the other side of the lake. I plunged my oar back into the water, but my Ama was not ready to go anywhere just yet.

"Wait, Namu," she commanded quietly, and as I pulled the oar back into the boat, she asked, looking straight into my eyes, "Do you put out the little fire in your bedroom in the morning?"

"I've never lit the fire," I answered in a whisper, looking sideways.

Ama sighed in a way that meant, How can you be so hopeless, and then she said, "One day you will have to light the fire, Namu." And she explained how the fire should not be too hot or too low but give a beautiful light, to make you relax and soften your body. "You have to be relaxed. If you're relaxed, then he will also relax. He will take his time with you. It's always better when a man takes his time, you know. And you must please yourself first. He will always be pleased to please you." She reached over toward me and touched a pimple on my cheek. "Making love is very good for the skin."

I could not bear it. I felt exposed, naked, and as I looked at the water all around me — trapped. "I know, I know, I know," I repeated while staring straight ahead toward the village of Luo Shui on the other side of the lake. But the shore was a long way off and there was still plenty of time to talk. And now I understood why my mother had not taken my brothers and sisters along with us.

AFTER THAT BOAT TRIP, I knew how I should light the fire in my bedroom, and I knew that I should please myself to please him, but still I did not wish for a man to come tapping on my window at night. Fortunately, the men never looked at me, or perhaps they did but I never looked at them. I, who had spent so much of my childhood in the company of men, could no longer look at men. I, who had so wished to become a grown woman, to show off the belts tied at my waist, just wanted to be left alone. At night, when I stared at the cold fireplace in my bedroom, and then at the bottle of Sulima wine waiting to be opened, I had only one thought — that I did not want to open my door to anyone. And this thought was all that kept me from sleeping at night.

As the months went by, however, other thoughts began keeping me awake. A woman was supposed to have lovers. A woman was supposed to have children. And I was a woman. And my mother had a dream, a grand ambition, to rear a large family, just like my grandmother had. My mother needed grandchildren, and since my sister Zhema had not been able to conceive, she had pinned her hopes on me. As I lay awake turning these thoughts over, I wondered why I had no desire for love and why I was such an ungrateful daughter. Sometimes I also wondered if perhaps I was not simply ugly. Or if there was something wrong with my body and that unlike other women I just did not need love. And then I would ask myself over and over: What will the neighbors say if no lover ever knocks on my door? Will my mother lose face? And what will I do with my life if I never let a man into my room? And what if I were to meet the fate of Zhecinamu?

Zhecinamu was a beautiful girl from our village. When she bathed at the lake, the men hid in the trees to watch her long black hair flow down her back like a waterfall. When she danced, the men could not take their eyes off her, but her eyes were cold and proud. So proud. She looked down at her suitors and while she smiled with her red lips and her perfect white teeth, her eyes said: You're not good enough for me. Not one of you is good enough for me. And she would take their courtship belts with a laugh and never wear them. When word of her coldness had spread as far as Tibet, men from all over began coming to our village to court her — not only Moso but Tibetans and Yi and even a few Han officials. Meanwhile, our own men took bets to see which of the newcomers would win her favor. But no one ever did. No matter how well they dressed, no matter how well they sang, how clever or how beautiful they were or how far they had traveled or what precious things they brought with them, Zhecinamu refused to open her door.

Time passed and the village boys grew bored with their betting game. They began to feel resentful and eventually became very annoyed at Zhecinamu for making them wait for nothing, until one day one of them thought he would play a little trick on her.

"I know why she won't open her door," he said to his

friends. "Last night I crept up to her window and I saw her, on her bed. She was naked and she was . . . oh, yes, so beautiful. But there was a huge snake with her. It was coiled around her waist with its head between her breasts. And she was asleep."

So the word spread that Zhecinamu had reared a Gu. It began as a silly prank, then it became a rumor, and soon enough everyone believed that it was true, that Zhecinamu did not want to take lovers because she had the evil Gu magic.

When Zhecinamu went to bathe at the lake, she no longer heard whistling. When she walked in the village street, she no longer felt the eyes of the men burning into her skin. No one brought her gifts, no one sang for her in the mountains. At night the dogs no longer barked in her deserted courtyard. No one came tapping on her window.

One afternoon Zhecinamu told her mother that she was going to the mountain to collect firewood. She put the ax in her basket and tied the basket on her back, securing the rope across her chest. She walked up the mountain path into the forest, and when she grew tired, she put her basket down. She slid the rope out of the basket, swung it over a high branch, and placed her basket at the foot of the tree. Then she climbed on top of it and tied the rope around her neck, and she jumped.

In the months that followed, every morning before sunrise, the villagers woke to crying and wailing coming from the forest. It was Zhecinamu's mother calling to the lonely ghost of her proud daughter. And now all the boys in the village cried for Zhecinamu, but it was too late.

ANOTHER NEW YEAR HAD PASSED. The end of winter was nearing but the nights were still very cold. That evening

I had gone to bed fully dressed but had not as yet garnered enough heat to fall asleep, when the dog suddenly barked in the courtyard. I sat up and listened. Sure enough, there was a shuffle of footsteps, and someone was coming up the stairs. But this time the footsteps could not be for Zhema, because her lover was already with her, and they were still whispering and giggling on the other side of the partition. And if the footsteps were not for Zhema, they had to be for me. I jumped out of bed to make sure the door was closed properly. Whoever it was had reached the balcony, but the shuffling was hesitant, disoriented, and very light. Much too light for a man and much too hesitant for a lover. I held my breath and listened. No, it could not be a man looking for love — lovers always know where they are going, even the first time; it just would not do to knock on the wrong window. But certainly whoever it was had come for me.

There was a whisper, and then someone asked in Yi, "Namu . . . Namu, are you here?"

"Añumo? Is that you?"

It was. It was my Yi sister, Añumo. I called her into my room and lit the candle. She was sweating and out of breath. Her skirt was covered in mud, her square hat had half fallen off her head. She dropped on my bed, almost falling over, exhausted.

"So, you came back after all! Is your husband a very bad man?"

IT HAD BEEN JUST OVER A WEEK AGO when I had last seen her. She was on her way to Muli with her wedding escort — her father and her cousins and about ten other men. They had stopped to greet us and tell us the good news.

That afternoon she looked magnificent. Besides her own colorful skirt, she had three other skirts tied to the side of her waist—part of the bride-price her husband's family had given for her. And with all these skirts around her, she seemed to be sitting in a sea of colors. She was wearing a beautiful red bodice and her chest was covered with silver jewelry. Large, flat silver earrings hung on each side of her proud face, reflecting the glow of the fire. As she brought her bowl of tea to her lips, I became fascinated by the traditional tattoo on her left hand, nine dots arranged in a square. I had not noticed this tattoo when we had become blood sisters.

"Did it hurt?" I asked.

"At first. But it healed very fast. Do you think it's beautiful?"

I rubbed the back of my hand. Not wanting to hurt her feelings, I said, "Yes, it's beautiful." But I knew I did not sound convincing. Añumo took another sip of tea and we were quiet for a while. She was staring at the fire, and her eyes looked dark and worried.

"You don't seem happy," I said to her.

She turned to gaze at the men who were standing near the stove, drinking rice wine and laughing, and she answered in a low tone. "I've never been to his village before. I have never even seen him."

I felt so sorry for Añumo. I knew that Yi people had very different customs from ours, but I could not understand how anybody could leave her own house to marry a man she hardly knew. For my part, I was terrified that a man would come knocking at my window at night, but no one and nothing could ever force me to open my door if I did not want to—not even the love or the pride of my own mother. How could my sister Añumo be made to go to live in another village, in someone else's family?

Añumo thought she could explain. "One of my father's relatives came to our house when my mother was pregnant with me. He touched my mother's stomach and said, If this is a girl, she will be for my son. . . . That was how the match was decided, and now I must go."

When the wedding party was ready to leave, I took Añumo's hand: "If you're not happy, you can come and stay with us anytime." She nodded, obviously unconvinced, and then she set off on horseback, a sad colorful girl among twenty men dressed in black capes.

And now she had come back! And there she was lying on my bed, out of breath, her skirt muddy and her feet bleeding. Was her husband such a bad man? Did she hate her in-laws? What had happened? I hurried downstairs to wake my mother and tell her that Añumo had run away from her husband. But as my Ama got up, she said, "Namu, there's nothing to worry about. This is the Yi people's custom: the harder a woman runs from her husband, the more she shows that she is strong and capable and that she comes from a good family. The men will soon follow after her, and if they find her, they will carry her back on their shoulders like a sack of potatoes. But if she manages to run all the way back to her father's house before they get to her, she will have won everyone's respect."

When I brought Añumo into the main room, my mother was already stoking the fire to boil the kettle for some tea. She welcomed Añumo with a nod, and then we sat down to listen to her story. She had been running for two days without eating, stopping only at night to sleep. It had taken her longer than she had thought to get to our house, and when night had fallen, she had become scared. This morning she had lost her shoes and her feet were very dirty and bleeding, and now there was a big splinter under her sole.

My mother took some kindling from the fire and passed it to me to hold above Añumo's injured foot so that she could take a look at it. She wiped the dirt off with a wet cloth and went to fetch a needle from her sewing basket to take out the splinter. Blowing gently over the wound to calm the pain, she worked the needle into the bleeding flesh. Añumo was hurting terribly. Her face was covered in sweat and tears rolled down from her eyes, but she did not say anything. She did not complain.

I wished Añumo had been a real sister and that I could have protected her. I wanted her to stay with us.

Ama held the splinter to the light and exclaimed, "Look at this! It's as big as a tree trunk! How could you run with that thing in your foot? You're lucky it did not get infected." Then she told me to put the kindling away and pour hot water in the washbasin.

When the water was ready, I moved to take Añumo's feet, but she pulled back from me. "No, no, I would not let you wash my feet." And she put her feet into the bowl herself. Meanwhile, Ama went to look for a pair of her own shoes to give to her, and then she warmed up some leftover stew.

Añumo ate as though she had been starving, and I could not help commenting, "You eat like your father did the first time!" And Ama slapped me on the back of the head. I immediately understood why. Still, I kept staring at Añumo because the Yi have a very peculiar way of eating by placing food in their cheeks while they still are taking more into their mouths, until their cheeks seem very full and round like squirrels' cheeks. When she had finished eating, she came into my room and we went to sleep next to each other. She fell asleep right away because she was so tired. I too was very tired, but I found it difficult to sleep. First of all because the events of the night had disturbed me, and then because of the acrid smell that emanated from Añumo's hair. Following the custom of her people, my blood sister had not washed her hair or her face for a very long time.

When she joined us for breakfast the next morning, I had already warmed up the water to wash her hair. Before she had a chance to sit and drink a bowl of tea, I handed her the washbasin. "Here, come outside with me and let me wash your hair. I could not sleep all night."

This time my mother did not slap me. Añumo was horribly embarrassed but she obliged me and followed me into the courtyard carrying our enamel basin. When I had finished drying her hair with the toweling cloth, my Ama said, "You have such long and silky hair, Añumo. Would you like me to comb it for you?"

Añumo smiled and my mother combed her beautiful hair and braided it into two parts as was the correct way for a married woman. Then Ama carefully cleaned her comb, placing the loose hair in the little basket under the porch with the rest of our hair, because we believe that unless we store every loose strand of hair, the birds will use them to make their nests and give us headaches.

Later in the morning, when I picked up my basket to go and do some weeding in the fields, Añumo prepared to come with me but my mother would not let her go because of her foot. "You can't go anywhere with this," she told her. "And you need to rest. You have a long way to run before you get back to your father's house."

When I came back from the fields sometime after noon, Añumo was standing at the stove, working side by side with my mother. They were making tofu and taking turns at stirring and scooping the thick white foam rising above the bean stew. I could not help thinking that they looked like mother and daughter, and again I felt so sorry that Añumo was not a real sister to me. I did not want her to leave, and told her as much.

"But I can't stay with you, Namu," she said a little sadly.

"I'm a married woman. What would my husband say? And my father?"

"Well, if you stay here with us, you won't have to worry about husbands or fathers, will you?"

Añumo held her breath for a while and then she burst out laughing. For my part, I did not think it was very funny, and I continued arguing, trying to convince her to stay with us, until the dog cut the discussion short, barking furiously. And just as my mother went out to see what was happening, Zhema rushed into the room and went straight to the pantry. "Quick, Namu, they're here! She has to run," she ordered in a low voice, as she took out some barley cookies and quickly cut a thick slice of ham, which she wrapped in a cloth.

Añumo had sprung to her feet, ready to run, but she did not know which way to escape and so she stood in the middle of the room, her eyes wild and darting toward every corner, like a trapped animal.

"Wait! At least put the shoes on properly. Be careful of your foot," I pleaded, my voice breaking and my eyes burning.

She looked down at her feet and bent over to pull the canvas shoes over her heels, and I helped her tie the laces. Meanwhile, Zhema had grabbed her felt cape and wrapped it around her shoulders. She pushed the food into her arms and, taking her by the hand, quickly led her through the storeroom and out of the house and into the vegetable garden, where we helped her over the mud wall.

The men, a party of six, had come into the courtyard, and my mother was talking with them, doing her best to waste their time. "Yes, she must be quite a long way away by now. She left yesterday. But you must be so tired, why don't you stay for dinner and sleep here overnight?"

The men looked at each other and hesitated. They were

very tired and they could do with something to drink. So they came into our house and wasted more time, but they would not stay for dinner.

After they left, I suddenly felt angry at my mother. "Why didn't you say something to them? Why didn't you keep them here longer? Why didn't we keep *her* here? You're an older woman, the men would listen to you!"

My mother shook her head impatiently. "This is a Yi custom. She has to run back home. What are you so upset about?"

Well, I knew it was a Yi custom, but Añumo was my sister, and I knew better than anyone how dangerous the mountain was and how late in the afternoon already, and I could not bear to think of how frightening it must be to run alone through the night. I was far from knowing then that only a few months from now, I too would be running alone in the mountains.

Meanwhile, from that evening on, whenever I heard a dog barking in the night, I no longer feared that a man might be coming to knock at my window. Instead, I hoped it was Añumo returning to stay with us after all. But we never saw her again.

A Song and a Trip to the City

Not long after Añumo left us, we received other visitors. I had been at the lakeshore all day with my girlfriends, turning over the earth to prepare for the spring planting. And now the sun was beginning its descent behind the mountain and the birds were growing quiet. It was time to walk home. We were almost at the village when we heard the children laughing and calling out: *"Letsesei!* Guests are coming! *Letsesei!"*

Outsiders were so rare. Except for government officials and the paramedics who chased after the children with vaccination needles, no one ever came to our village. In those days the only motor vehicles that crossed our mountains were the log trucks that sputtered up the hills and then rolled down the dirt tracks, freewheeling over potholes, their engines cut off to save fuel. But even these dirt tracks were a long way from Zuosuo. To get to our village, you had to come on foot or on horseback.

Before we even saw their faces, just from the way they held the leads of their horses, we knew that only one of the four guests was Moso. When we met up with them, we recognized our neighbor Yisso, a big man with a thick head of black wavy hair and laughing eyes. As for the three Han Chinese, we had never seen them before. One was quite old, with white hair, and evidently the leader, because he was doing most of the talking.

"*Ni hao!*" the children called out in the few Chinese words they had managed to acquire at the local school.

"*Ni hao! Ni hao,*" the officials answered, with big kindly smiles on their faces.

Being grown women, we only looked and nodded our heads and pretended not to be excited, but we followed them for a little while down the path until we had made sure that they were going to Yisso's house. When we turned back, we could not contain our curiosity. "Maybe they're surveyors," Erchema said. "Do you remember the surveyors who brought all that candy?"

"Well, I hope these guests have brought some candy too," I joined in emphatically, because I had never eaten candy wrapped in paper, and because I didn't remember the surveyors who had come when I was still living with Uncle in the mountains.

The news that there were guests staying at Yisso's house spread from door to door like wildfire, and before we had sat down for dinner, we had already found out that they were not surveyors but cadres from the Cultural Bureau in Yanyuan county who had come to record Moso songs. We also knew their names. The leader, the old man with the white hair, was Mr. Li. The younger ones were Zhang and Zhu, though we were not sure as yet which was Zhang and which was Zhu.

"They heard that our village has the best singers," Dujema said with unrestrained pride.

And I thought, Yes, that's true, we have Latsoma and Zhatsonamu, and I can sing louder than anyone else. I asked

Ama, "Why don't they come here to stay with us? Why do they have to stay with Yisso?"

"Yisso speaks Chinese," she replied rather gruffly. Then she muttered, "What use can Moso songs be to the Han anyway?"

My Ama was stirring a big pot of stew. There was a deep scowl in the middle of her forehead and her mouth was all tight. She was in a bad mood because Zhema had come home late to help with the dinner and because, since the Cultural Revolution, nobody in our village ever felt very enthusiastic about Han officials, even if all they wanted was to collect our songs.

Nonetheless, over the next two days, whatever their mothers and uncles thought about Han officials, the children followed Mr. Li and Zhang and Zhu everywhere, running back and forth from house to house to give the latest news. As for us, the young people, we gave up our work in the fields and listened to the children's every word.

The first morning, Yisso had taken the Han by canoe to the island of Lewube and they had climbed up the hill to visit the little Buddhist temple that had escaped the Red Guards' fury. There, standing under heaven, the Han had squinted in the bright sunlight and turned in every direction, pointing above the lake toward Gamu Mountain and then beyond the jagged horizon to places of interest to them. "Kunming is in this direction!" "No, no! It's over there!" "Aya! Over there is Chengdu!" In the afternoon the Han had gone to Zhatsonamu's house and she had sung the goddess song for them. And in the evening, the Han had tea with old Guso. There was a big crowd of people in the house, and Guso was telling the story of the rabbit who got the better of the tiger. Of course Yisso was translating! How else could the Han know what he was saying? On the second morning, a little boy called out, "I saw the guests suck on little brushes and foam at the mouth!" This time I could no longer repress my curiosity; I had to run after him to see for myself. I had never seen anyone brushing his teeth.

In the afternoon the children ran ahead of Yisso and the cadres from the Cultural Bureau, who were making their way to our house.

"They're here!" Homi ran in to tell my Ama. "They're in the courtyard!"

My Ama wiped her hands on her trousers and glared from behind the cooking stove toward the front door, where Yisso and the guests were stepping through, squinting in the darkness and stumbling on the dog, who sprang out of their way after nipping Mr. Zhu on the leg. I shooed the dog outside.

"It's nothing, it's nothing. Don't worry!" Mr. Li said to me while Mr. Zhu rubbed his leg.

Mr. Li had brought us a pack of tailored cigarettes, brick tea, and rice wine, and my mother, seeing that these people knew the proper way to behave, at last softened her stance, and placed their gifts on the ancestors' altar.

Soon we were all sitting at the fireplace, Zhu still tapping his leg and the others brushing the dust off their trousers, then peeling their apples with a knife in Han fashion, and drinking black tea because no one expected Han Chinese to like butter tea. Zhang had tried to entice Jiama and Homi and the other children to play, but they were too shy. When he went to touch them, they giggled and twisted their bodies sideways, and suddenly they shrieked and ran outside looking for their mothers. Jiama then grabbed hold of Ama's vest and Homi took my hand.

Meanwhile, Mr. Li had explained to my mother that he wished to hear as many people sing as possible and that he wanted to organize a big dance in someone's courtyard. To my delight, Ama answered, "We can do it here." And when Yisso suggested bringing more firewood for the bonfire, she said firmly, "No need, we have enough."

I could have jumped for joy, but instead I asked Yisso, "Do they have any candy wrapped in paper?"

Ama turned about and fired an astonished look in my direction. Pulling me to her side, she said sternly, "Namu, come and help me over here!" "Over here" was in the courtyard. "Where have you learned to beg from guests? You're a grown woman! Just as well they can't understand what you're saying!"

That evening the villagers made their way to our house, bearing pine torches to light their path. The Han were already standing near the bonfire, talking among themselves, Mr. Li looking like a leader, Zhang holding a black plastic box, while Zhu, who had evidently got over the dog bite, was demonstrating a dance step. As the villagers walked into the courtyard, Mr. Li and Zhang and Zhu bared their brushed teeth, smiling from ear to ear, calling out, "Welcome! Welcome!" in Chinese. And soon we were all standing in a tight circle around the fire—watching with wide-open eyes, feeling much too curious to have anything to say, until an old woman commented between two drags on her clay pipe, "You wonder how they can ride horses with those flat butts," and everybody laughed.

Zhang put the black box on the ground, and Yisso translated that Mr. Li wished to hear all of us sing and that someone had to start. Now, among our people, if you can walk you can dance, and if you can dance you can sing, so we were not short of singers. But we thought that, to begin with, they should hear someone special, so we turned to Achimi because she was an old lady and she could sing about our old stories. Jiaci accompanied her on the bamboo flute and Achimi sang a sad and hopeful song about saying good-bye to the horsemen who were taking the caravan to Tibet. After Achimi, women and men of all ages stepped into the circle, one after the other. I followed my friend Erchema. When all those who wanted to sing had had a turn, we waited to be told what to do next, all the while watching Mr. Li's every move and trying to guess what he was saying to the others. Then Zhang nodded his head and pressed on the black box, and we heard Jiaci's flute and Achimi's voice coming out of the box.

"Ah! What is this thing?" the people shouted. "What is this black box?" And they moved as one body toward the box.

"Don't push! Don't push!" Mr. Li cried.

"Do that again!" the people answered. "Touch that box again!"

So Zhang touched the box, and when Jiaci again heard himself play, he said: "This box learns very fast, it only listened to me once and now it can already do it!" Everyone laughed. Yisso translated for the Han and they laughed too. Then he turned to the rest of us and spoke in the superior tone of one who has traveled the world. "It's called a tape recorder," he said, using the Chinese word. "These things are made in Japan."

"Where's Japan?" someone asked.

There was a pause. For aside from Dr. Rock, who was a ghost from a fabled country called America, our people knew only two types of foreigners: the English, who were in India and Tibet, and the Japanese, who had made war on China. But no one had ever bothered to think of where Japan was.

So Yisso spoke up again. "Japan is an island in the east."

And old Guso, who could not take his eyes off the tape recorder, shook his head. "Well, that's no good. You can't ride a horse to an island." And again everybody laughed.

For the rest of the evening, we sang and the Han recorded our songs and then played them back to us until, very late in the night, the tape recorder began emitting whiny tremolos and Mr. Li explained that he wanted to save the rest of his batteries for the next day. Besides, he and his colleagues were very tired. So we wished them a peaceful night and watched them disappear behind Yisso, who was carrying the wondrous tape recorder under his arm. We did not move. We sat around the fire talking about the black box for a long time.

THE HAN STAYED THREE DAYS. On their last afternoon, Yisso once again brought them to our house. They had something important to discuss with my mother—Mr. Li wanted to take me back with him to Yanyuan to take part in a singing contest. He had chosen three of us; the other two were our best singers, Latsoma and Zhatsonamu. Mr. Li would take care of all our expenses and "if the girls win a prize, they will bring back a little money." And above everything else, of course, if we won a prize, we would bring fame to our village and our Moso people. And yes, Mr. Li was quite sure that we were good enough to win a prize. Did my mother agree to let me go?

At first I could not believe it. But as Yisso kept on talking and my sister Zhema and my friend Erchema and the others turned toward me, smiling with admiration and a little envy, I had to trust that I was not just wishing for this but that it really was happening—I was going to travel with Latsoma and Zhatsonamu to the city; we were going to take part in a singing contest in Yanyuan, and Yisso would accompany us because we did not speak Chinese and we were very young and we knew nothing about the world. Now, I had no idea why anyone would want to sing Moso songs in the city, but just the same I was overjoyed. Ever since I had gone to live with Uncle, I had watched the birds fly over the mountain peaks and wondered what lay beyond. I had watched the horsemen with the caravans and I had listened to their stories about the world outside. And now it was my turn. I was going to see the world. I was going to see all the marvels the men talked about. I was going to see the cars and the trucks and the movies and the airplanes. I was going to see the "oil road" that was so slick and shiny, Zhema's lover had once told me, you could admire your reflection in it.

Over the next few hours, I grew every bit as impatient as when I had said good-bye to Uncle. In the meantime, my mother dispatched my sister to the neighbors to borrow the things I needed for the trip, and soon they had assembled three different outfits in beautiful bright colors, with matching jewelry. My Ama said, "When you leave your home, you must look your best, you don't want your people to lose face. And remember the old proverb 'There are no white eagles, and there are no good Han people.' So don't leave the other girls. You must stay together wherever you go. You must be just like eyes and eyebrows!"

Zhema added, "Yes, you must be like the fingers of one hand! Inseparable. And please, make sure you bring me back some white socks."

The village girls also wished for something: "Can you bring us some scarves?" And they handed me a box of wild mushrooms to trade for their goods.

But my Ama scoffed: "Namu is not going to trade anybody's mushrooms. You silly girls! She's not going to the market! She's going to win a singing contest!"

I gazed at my mother, and I thought, yes, I am going to win a contest and bring fame to my family and to my village, and everyone will be proud of me!

When we set off the next morning, all our neighbors had assembled to accompany us to the edge of the village and wish us good luck. We were like the caravans of old—ten horses and nine people, for Yisso had decided he would need two helpers to take care of the horses when we arrived at the cement factory, the first stage on the famed oil road, where the cars were to pick us up.

Now, according to Moso custom, we must never ride horses within the boundaries of the village in case we should meet an older person, as it is considered a great insult for a young person to stand above an older one. But we had barely passed the last house when my mother told me to get on my horse, and while I stood above her on my little pony, she took the reins and led me forward to show how proud she was of me. After a few steps, she stopped and handed me the reins and walked back to where the other villagers were standing, waving us off. Several times I turned to see her standing on the road, following me with her eyes and warming my heart with her pride, until the trail curved and I lost her.

THE TREK TO THE CEMENT FACTORY took five days, during which we spent as much time walking alongside the horses as riding on their backs. We passed through Moso villages, and then through Pumi and Yi villages, where Mr. Li impressed us with his ability to speak the local language. Wherever we knew people, we took advantage of local hospitality to eat and sleep indoors — but on the third night, we made a fire outside and piled up pine needles for mattresses and slept under the stars in the mountain. Generally speaking, Moso women do not like to travel very far from their villages because of the wild animals, and also because in the old days, before the Communist liberation, the mountains were filled with dangerous people and bandits. That night, when we slept outside, Latsoma and Zhatsonamu grumbled that it was too cold and they missed their beds. But young Zhu said, "Hey! What are you complaining about? This is the best there is! Look at the sky . . . this is an all-star hotel!" And I thought, I am going to see what a hotel looks like.

Next day, in the early afternoon, the path turned, revealing on the opposite hillside the colored strips of cultivated fields and a typical Yi village with a half dozen houses built far apart from one another, with yellow earthen walls and roofs made of long planks held down by big boulders arranged in neat rows, and each house enclosed by a tallish fence made of interwoven wooden sticks. Yisso announced that he had an old friend in this village and that we could stay the night. "That way, you'll get a good rest."

"That won't be too soon!" Latsoma griped, as she wiped the sweat from her face.

From where we were standing, the village looked very close and we could even smell the smoke from the wood fires, but we knew we should not rejoice too soon. In high mountains, the peaks are so tall and the valleys so deep, it takes a long time for the road to wind down from one hillside across to the next. As an old Moso proverb tells, "A man and a woman may sing to each other from the peaks of two mountains, but they will need to carry food for three days if they want to meet halfway."

Thankfully it took a few hours rather than three days for us to reach the stick fences, where, as usually happens in mountain villages, we were greeted by savage-looking dogs barking at us furiously. As no one came to our rescue, we bent down to pick up some stones, and the dogs, snarling and growling and with their hackles up, retreated to a safer distance. After the dogs the children came out, barefoot and curious, and before long we found ourselves in the house of Yisso's friend — a tall man with a face black from soot and years of accumulated dirt, and small glowing eyes. His name was Jibu.

Jibu invited us to sit at the place of honor, between the

sooty back wall of the house and the fireplace, which consisted of a circular pit in the earth floor and which produced what struck us as a great deal of smoke. There he left us in the company of his wife, who offered us roasted potatoes and then gathered her long skirt underneath her to take her place, as mistress of the house, on the left-hand side of the hearth, while her daughter poured us rice wine and hot tea. Like my Yi sister, Añumo, Jibu's daughter had a beautiful smile and beautiful white teeth.

Mr. Li was raising a toast when Jibu came back in, leading on a short rope a sheep that stared at us through the thick smoke and bleated in discomfort. I thought the poor animal probably needed salt, but before I had time to say anything, Jibu had smashed a heavy stick over its head and was hauling it out of the house, stunned or dead, across his shoulder. Within minutes he had come back, holding the sheep's liver in his bloodied hands.

Zhatsonamu raised her hand to her mouth as though she were about to gag. Latsoma and I stared at the man's hands and then looked at each other. We had never seen anyone kill an animal in such cruel and cold-blooded fashion.

Jibu then prepared to roast the liver over the fireplace, and Yisso explained that this was the local custom, that in Jibu's village the proper way to treat respected guests was to show them the animal they were about to eat and then kill it and give them the liver. Furthermore, to truly show respect, the animal had to be four legged — it couldn't be a chicken or a duck. Not wishing to offend anyone, I asked no more questions, and when Jibu handed me a piece of the liver, I took it and thanked him, but I swallowed it whole without chewing.

While Jibu respectfully went about handing us pieces of freshly killed liver, his wife and daughter dragged a large iron pot over the hearth and filled it with water, and when the liver was finally disposed of, Jibu went out again, to hack the sheep into several large pieces, which he then threw into the pot. And at the sight of these pieces of meat and bones dropping into the water, the three Cultural Bureau officials turned a little green.

The aroma of mutton stew soon pervaded the room, seemingly attracting Jibu's relatives, who began streaming in, bearing wine and the local brew of beer. The house took on a festive atmosphere, with much drinking and singing, dancing and laughing, and by the end of the evening, there was nothing left of the sheep but the bones the dogs were fighting over. And that, Yisso explained, was also the custom of the Yi people, who, whenever they killed an animal, ate the whole thing in one sitting.

It was very late into the night when the last of the guests tottered back to their houses and our hosts to their beds. We spread our cotton quilts straight onto the earth floor next to the fire, and I fell asleep as soon as I closed my eyes. We woke very early next morning, feeling stiff and scratching wildly at our legs, and Latsoma, who could barely open her eyes, complained that she would have preferred the all-star hotel. "Well, maybe the fleas don't like mutton stew," Yisso said, laughing. We went out and relieved ourselves in the fields and then washed our faces in the courtyard while Mr. Li and Zhang and Zhu were foaming at the mouth, diligently working their toothbrushes, and the village children, who for their part had not washed since New Year, looked on, puzzled and wordless.

The morning ablutions over, we were again seated around the fire, the daughter of the house serving us tea, still smiling with her beautiful smile, while her mother sat herself at a low table to prepare corn and buckwheat cakes for our breakfast. "You girls are so fortunate to go to the city!" Mrs. Jibu repeated over and over as she kneaded her dough and occasionally blew her nose into her fingers. But we all agreed, even Mr. Li agreed, that her corn cakes were the best we had ever eaten. Mr. Li said that several times as we waved good-bye to Jibu and his family.

One more hillside to descend and we finally reached the cement factory, a huge brick building with a tin roof. It stood in a great dusty quarry that had been carved out of the forest. Workers in blue overalls and dusty caps milled about. It was a strange and ugly sight—and a marvelous sight as well. Ah! And here were the trucks I had so wanted to see! Noisy and spewing bad odors but nevertheless rolling up and down on the road under their own steam. And there also was the oil road.

We had heard so much about this oil road from the horsemen, but now that we were standing on it, we were so surprised. It was hard and black and dull—where had all the oil gone?

On seeing the three of us touching and smelling the road, Yisso stared as though he were seeing us for the first time in his life. "What are you talking about? What are you doing?" He burst out laughing. "This is not the same oil as we cook with!"

Crestfallen, we moved off to the side of the road and squatted on our heels to wait for Mr. Li, who was arranging our transport to Yanyuan. Then we heard a loud engine noise as a Jeep came toward us, hopping and bumping on the uneven road and across the potholes like a monstrous green rabbit. It stopped right in front of us.

We looked at it and then at each other. There were seven of us. "This thing must have a huge belly!" Latsoma said.

"This is a car. It doesn't have a belly, it has seats," Yisso replied. "But we're not all going to get into it. Mr. Li and the others are waiting for another car."

The driver got out and opened the back of the car for us to stash our bundles. We obeyed him dutifully and then climbed in, leaving Yisso to close the doors behind us and get into the front seat. We touched the canvas seats and the glass windows and wound the windows up and down and tapped our feet on the floor. We changed seats, several times, to try out which suited us best. Naturally, we all wanted a window, but someone had to sit in the middle and we quickly agreed we would take turns. Latsoma then volunteered to sit between us. When we were finally settled, the driver turned the key in the ignition and we took off with a jerk, hitting our heads together and laughing wildly, and as the car built up speed, we hung out the windows and held our faces to the wind, staring at the trees and the precipice whizzing below us, and we screeched in delighted terror. To this day I can recall the exhilaration, the sheer thrill of the ride — until we had gone a few kilometers on the mountain road, falling over each other to the left and then to the right, and then to the right and left, and again, and I suddenly stopped laughing and said: "I want to throw up."

We all threw up.

Yisso told the driver to stop.

While the driver mopped up the floor of the car with an old rag, we did our best to clean ourselves, but we could not get rid of the smell on our clothes. "Oh, this is disgusting," Latsoma cried. "Now the smell is enough to make me sick again!" And Yisso, who had apparently thought of everything, took some fresh ginger out of his bag and broke off a piece for each of us to chew on. "That will stop you from feeling sick," he said. But it didn't. We threw up until all we could do was dry retch and our heads felt like they would explode, and at last we could no longer open our eyes — until about five hours later when we arrived in Yanyuan and the car finally stopped.

"That's it," Yisso said. "It's all over now!"

I opened my eyes and looked at the city.

The City

I should have found it ugly. The guest house was a squat gray concrete building three stories high, with large glass windows in metal frames, and underneath, white and blue shirts and dark trousers and flesh-colored underwear hung on square metal racks, billowing in the breeze like prayer flags gone awry. The yard was an uneven patch of dirty broken concrete surrounded by buildings and a brick wall with tall iron gates. A gray, dusty haze covered everything, including a half dozen geraniums growing in pots and a poor excuse of a shrub meant to decorate the entrance. Latsoma and Zhatsonamu found it ugly. But I did not.

The tall rectangular building took my breath away. I thought of all the glass Dr. Rock had brought from America and imagined that this must have been how the little glass palace on our island had looked. I tapped my feet on the dirty hard ground and touched it. Curiously, no dirt rubbed off, and I thought, if we had this sort of floor in our courtyard, it would not get muddy and would be a lot easier to sweep. The worn-out local buses parked alongside our Jeep, the people going about their business, milling back and forth between the buildings, the loud unfamiliar noises, and perhaps also the fact that my ears were still ringing with the vibrations of the car engine and my head and stomach had not yet settled from the motion sickness—all of it transported me into a strange and wonderful space, marvelously unreal, as the world beyond our mountains ought to be. And that world, to me, was immediately beautiful.

Latsoma climbed out of the car holding her stomach. "If I had known it was going to be this horrible, I would never have come! When we go home, I am not riding in this car! I'd rather walk all the way!"

"Me, too," Zhatsonamu joined in. "I'll never ride in a car again!"

They looked at the surroundings. They said nothing, but the expression of disappointment and shock on their faces spoke plenty.

Latsoma tried shaking the dust from her soiled clothes and she leaned back against the car with a dejected expression on her face. "We look horrible. . . ."

We did. We looked terrible. We were so dirty, covered in red dust, and our clothes reeked of vomit. And we had left our mothers' houses so beautiful. . . .

"Come, you'll feel better soon," Yisso bravely cheered us on, as he pointed toward a building at the end of the yard. "Let's go to the canteen and get you some sour cabbage. That will settle your stomachs."

By now we had our doubts about Yisso's remedies, but the sour cabbage worked better than the ginger. When we felt a little better, Yisso led us to a sink with water faucets. He poured water into an enamel pan and we washed our faces and hands and slowly woke up to the world, but then we could not stop ourselves from turning the water on and off.

When he'd had enough of us playing with the water, Yisso told us to pick up our bundles and follow him inside the guest house. It was only then that we noticed Mr. Li and Zhang and Zhu had not arrived.

"Hey! Where are the other three?" Latsoma asked.

"They went home. We'll see them at dinner."

I looked above the brick wall at the protruding concrete buildings beyond—so people had homes here in the city. And I wondered what Mr. Li's house looked like.

The foyer of the guest house was a square room, large enough for people to stand about chatting and laughing, almost as large as the main room of our house. There were a lot of people in this hotel, most of them dressed in minority costumes—Yi, Tibetans, Miao, Lisu—all of them strangers, people who did not speak our language and whom we had never seen before, people who were neither relatives nor friends of relatives and who had come to participate in the singing contest. To the left was the reception booth, with a boxed window beyond which the service woman was taking a nap, her head resting on her arms folded on the service desk. Leaning all the way into the window, Yisso woke her by tapping gently on her shoulder.

She lifted her head and snapped rudely, "What? What do you want?"

And we could not believe our own eyes or ears, for no one in Moso country would ever dream of barking at a guest. But Yisso looked unfazed, and whatever passed between him and the service woman, she eventually came around the corner, holding a set of keys, her spirits up somewhat, because she was smiling—the sort of kindly smile that, I would discover later, is often displayed by city people in their dealings with country folk.

She was wearing a white blouse and black pants, and her hair was pinned back into a bun. There was no cap or shawl on her head, and her lips were painted bright red. Her feet *click-clack*ed on the smooth concrete floor as she stepped ahead of us in her high-heel shoes.

"Hey, Yisso!" Zhatsonamu whispered. "How can she walk on these little sticks?"

"All the city girls can do that," Yisso answered. "They think those shoes are pretty."

"Well, I think they look strange and ugly," Latsoma said.

I didn't say anything but I liked the woman's shoes. I also liked the way the woman walked in them, with her hips swaying prettily from side to side. Most of all, I liked her painted lips. Her mouth looked like a red azalea flower.

She took us upstairs to the second floor, where she unlocked a door to a square room with a smooth cement floor. The walls were painted green halfway up, and the rest was all white. There were four beds, arranged neatly at each corner, covered by a pink cotton spread with a flower motif. Each bed had two pillows, also pink, bordered by frilly trims. At one end of the room was a small wooden table and a chair, and on the table, four bright red enamel thermos flasks with white flowers and a blue enamel basin with pink flowers that looked just like the enamel basin we had at home. On the floor beside the table was a green plastic wastebasket. Sunlight poured in through the large metal window and the effect was perfect. I had never seen anything so beautiful, so colorful, or as bright and cool as this room. We stepped in, carrying our bundles in our arms, and then stopped in our tracks, overwhelmed by so much luxury, so much cleanliness, not daring to tread on the floor or to put our things down.

The service woman pushed past, budging me out of her way with her hip. She slapped the beds and lifted the thermos flasks and pointed to the wastebasket, all the while shouting in Chinese, evidently in the belief that if she yelled loudly enough, we would overcome all language barriers. When she was satisfied that we knew where everything was, she told Yisso where we would find the showers and warned that we needed to call her whenever we wished to get into our rooms and that she did not want to be bothered after eleven o'clock at night. Then she left us and Yisso followed her into the corridor.

Well, no Moso woman would ever shout like this and slap furniture! But then again, we were not in Moso country anymore, we were in the city. We tried the beds, sitting on them and bouncing a little, and then lying down, and then we discovered the white sheets inside. We had never seen sheets before, but we had a good idea that we needed a wash before we dared sleep between them.

The showers were in an outhouse across the street — another brick building, dank and black, with slimy walls glumly lit by a single electric bulb hanging from the low ceiling. On the wall nearest the entrance were a series of hooks with clothes and towels hanging, and only a few feet from those, women were standing on slippery wooden slats, scrubbing themselves under some metal pipes that spouted a jet of hot water when you aligned a little handle in the direction of the tubing. Ah! Turning that little handle was the most beautiful experience! At home, we were at least two days' walk away from the hot springs in Yongning, so we washed ourselves out of the enamel basin, or else we bathed in the cold water of the lake. And now we had not washed for days. The water ran deliciously hot and black off our bodies and our hair. We stayed in the shower room, soaping ourselves over and over under the steaming warm water, for such a long time that when we came out, squeaky clean, having forgotten all about the car ride and looking magnificent in our Moso costumes, the sun was beginning to set.

Yisso was waiting for us in the yard, sitting on a bench, smoking a cigarette. "Did you enjoy yourselves in there?" he asked, laughing.

"Yes, we did! We really enjoyed ourselves!" we answered in one voice, laughing back.

"Do you want to go for a stroll in the streets before dinner?"

"Yes! Yes! We do!"

And on Yisso's instructions, we ran to the guest house to give our dirty clothes to the service woman and ran straight out again, laughing with joy and entirely amazed at the fact that someone we didn't even know was going to wash our clothes.

Everything to us was so new, wonderful, astonishing—from the electrical switch that lit the neon tube in the middle of the ceiling in our bedroom, which we turned on and off over and over, to the soft wheezing of the bicycles, the din of the trucks and tractors on the street, and the people bullying each other. It was not as though we were entirely ignorant of the world, but what we knew, we had pictured in imagination, we had learned by hearsay, through others' stories— some of them tall stories, as we had found out when we had touched the "oil road." And now that we were touching and smelling and hearing and seeing for ourselves, we were not only setting things right in our own minds but discovering other things we knew nothing about, like bedsheets and hot showers and, almost as soon as we had stepped outside for our first stroll in the city, toilets. In Zuosuo we didn't have toilets. But here, in the city, there were no fields to go to and no dogs or pigs to clean up after you. Instead there were concrete blocks where you had to squat hurriedly over a narrow slit in the floor between two low walls, closing your nose to the stench and your eyes to the pit below, and then you rushed outside, back into the strangely acrid city air, and then the wonderful streets and the shops, lit magically by naked electric bulbs, where you could buy everything you'd ever dreamed of owning and at least as many things none of us could even identify—shops not built of rough planking with a countertop for you to lean on but brick buildings with concrete floors, with wide-open entrances where you could walk all the way in. And there were so many people, and all of them strangers. Nationality people in colorful dress, and Han people; Han women who did not wear turbans or caps on their heads or braided hair but wore their hair cut short, just below their ears. "Are you sure they're women?" "Yes, look, they're wearing those little stick shoes!"

"And what about them?"

Outside a shop, there were two young Han women whose curly hair made me think of the sheep the Yi herded in the high mountains. They were sucking on pink sticks.

"It's ice cream," one said in Chinese.

Icecreem, we repeated. Icecreem. What's icecreem? She tried to explain but there was no point. So she walked into the shop and returned with three sticks.

I loved the ice cream so much I did not bother licking but chewed on it instead and ate the whole thing in no time. Then I chewed on the wooden stick while I watched my girlfriends lick theirs, and then lick the sweet melted goo off their fingers, and I thought of how my little brothers and Jiama would love this ice cream.

When we got back to the guest house, the dining room had been set up with twenty or so big round tables and was brightly lit by fake brass chandeliers. It was filled with people all dressed in colorful ethnic costumes. Latsoma, who prided herself on her knowledge of ethnic dress, identified the Tibetans, Naxi, Yi, Pumi, Miao, and Lisu, and Yisso pointed out the Bai, Dai, Zhuang, and Hani. All these people had come to Yanyuan to take part in the singing contest.

Some were already seated, and others were moving between the tables looking for their friends. I spotted a few faces we had passed in the corridor, and also Mr. Li and his colleagues, who were looking very clean and were waiting for us at our designated table.

"So, you're feeling better? I heard you got very carsick," Mr. Li said as he took out a little brown bottle from his pocket and emptied a few pills into his hands to hand over to us. It was traditional Chinese medicine, he explained. "Something to clear your throat and energize your qi."

We swallowed the pills and then drank some tea that tasted like hot water to us. But if we could not help wishing for our butter tea, the food was splendid. We had never seen such a variety of dishes. The rice especially was so white and fluffy.

Mr. Li explained that Chinese rice was steamed, not boiled like our rice, and that was why it was so sweet. "Good food?" he asked, turning to me directly, perhaps impressed by my gluttony.

"Yes, very good food," I answered him in Chinese. And I dished myself a fourth helping of rice.

"Very good," Mr. Li continued. "You need to eat well and get a good rest so you can be strong and practice tomorrow."

"Practice, what for?" Zhatsonamu asked. "All we have to do is sing!"

Yisso translated and Mr. Li laughed out loud. "Well, at least you can make the most of a good night's sleep, don't you think?" He paused for a while, still smiling, and again addressing me directly, he said, "Do you like your room, Namu?"

"Yes, the bed is very comfortable, thank you," I answered him, once more using Chinese and feeling very proud of myself for doing so.

"Good, good," Mr. Li said, and he picked up a little piece of meat with his chopsticks.

Zhatsonamu turned to Yisso. "Can you ask him why the bedrooms have no fireplaces?"

"Oh, yes, ask him! Ask him how people light their fires at night!" Latsoma giggled.

Of course, Yisso knew what they meant—that it was hard to imagine yourself whispering to your lover under the bleary light of the neon tubing. He smiled and shook his head. "I'm not asking him that."

"Come on, Yisso, ask him!" Latsoma put on her prettiest smile.

So Yisso asked Mr. Li, who answered matter-of-factly: "It's difficult to get wood in the city." And when we burst out laughing, he continued in earnest, "Besides, if you were to light a fire in these rooms, everything would turn black and you'd suffocate."

Even without a fire, my girlfriends slept very well that night. It was so good not to sleep on the floor and not to be bothered by fleas. The beds were so comfortable, and the sheets and the covers smelled like the soap we had used in the shower.

THE NIGHT OF THE SINGING CONTEST, Mr. Li said, "Don't be nervous. Everything will be fine. There's no need to be afraid." We laughed, of course. We were not afraid, we were going to sing! What was there to be nervous about? But Mr. Li looked nervous. He wiped his face with his handkerchief, and he told us over and over as he led us through the big function room to the backstage area that when the hostess called our names, all we needed to do was walk to the middle of the stage.

We were the first to be called. And when I stepped onto the stage, I understood what Mr. Li was worried about. It was easy enough to answer to my name, but I took only a few steps before I was blinded by the stage lights and all I could do was stop and wait for the hostess to take me by the hand and lead me to where my girlfriends were standing, their eyes blinking and their faces glowing in unearthly fashion. Gradually I began to make out the faces in the darkened audience before us, and my heart missed a beat. It was the first time in my life that I was going to sing in front of people I did not know, and there were so many of them. And I was afraid.

When the clapping had quieted, the hostess introduced us as "three Moso girls from the Country of Daughters," and we sang and the audience clapped again. And we could tell by the clapping that the people had loved our song. I turned around and looked for Mr. Li, who was standing behind the curtain, a big smile on his face. He nodded for us to sing again, and we sang another song, and again the audience loved it. We were about to begin a third song, but the hostess walked up to us and congratulated us and ushered us out. For the rest of the evening, we sat in the wings listening to the other nationality people, some of them performing with a full orchestra, their songs as varied and colorful as their costumes. I was entranced. I had never imagined that the world was filled with so many songs.

The hostess broke the spell, thanking the performers and telling the audience that the music was over — it was time to announce the prizes. Mr. Li then walked up on the stage and said something, and before we had time to ask Yisso to translate, we had been called and pushed up on the stage toward him, and we were shaking hands and smiling back. The hostess, also smiling, handed each of us a red diploma and a red envelope. Meanwhile, the audience had stood up, applauding us. My girlfriends waved and bowed and made toward the back of the stage, and the hostess gently pushed me in their direction. I didn't want to leave just yet. These strangers could not get enough of me.

Next day, when we walked in the streets, people we did not know called out to us and smiled at us. Zhatsonamu and Latsoma hardly seemed to notice. When we had opened our red envelopes, we had discovered that they each contained fifty yuan. We had never seen so much money, and my girlfriends were so excited they could not wait to spend it on gifts for their mothers and their boyfriends. In those days you could buy a lot of things with fifty yuan. For my part, although I was very happy with the money, I especially loved being famous, and I could think of only one thing: I want to see more of the world.

My wish was granted that same afternoon when Mr. Li and Yisso came into our room to announce that we were not going back to Zuosuo as planned. Mr. Li had enrolled us in another contest in Xichang—eight hours away by car, and we had to leave early the next morning. My girlfriends sat back on their beds, almost in tears. I was overjoyed.

Xichang is a much bigger city than Yanyuan. The tallest building in Yanyuan had four stories, the tallest building in Xichang had twelve. The hotel in Xichang also had a red carpet and toilets on the floors that flushed most of the time. The morning after we arrived, Mr. Li took us on a tour of the city and said, "Now I'm going to show you the railway station and a train." And gazing at the giant centipede, it occurred to me that the farther away from Zuosuo we traveled, the more marvelous the cities became. . . . I would love to ride in this train.

Back at the hotel, the TV people were waiting for us. They were carrying a thing on a stick and what we assumed was a big tape recorder. "It's a video camera," the cameraman said. "And that's a microphone," he added, pointing at the thing on the stick. Then he pointed at the glass box in our bedroom. "And that's the TV" — and that annoyed us a bit because we had already worked it out for ourselves and learned to switch it on and off.

When the TV people were done with making us sing and dance and laugh in front of the video camera, the cameraman hooked his machine into the back of the television and turned on the screen. There was a little explosion, and our faces suddenly lit up on the screen. Awestruck, we watched ourselves laughing and singing and smiling on the television. We looked at ourselves inside the TV and then we looked at each other inside the room, and then again we looked at ourselves in the TV. I thought we were so pretty. But on seeing how the TV had captured her face and her songs and her laughter, Latsoma said: "Can this thing steal our souls?"

At the Center of the World

In Xichang we won first prize again. But this time we did not get any money, although Xichang was a much bigger city than Yanyuan, so big we were sure we would earn at least a hundred yuan each. But all we got was a red diploma — and we had our photo taken.

The day after the contest, we were driven to the local airport and a journalist took a photo of us standing in front of a plane. That was the first photo ever taken of us, and it was also the first plane we had ever seen. After the photo session, we watched the planes take off and land. How could a thing like this, made of metal, fly like a bird? And what was it like inside a plane? Was it like riding in a car? Did it make you throw up? No, the journalist said. It didn't. You could eat in an airplane and walk around. I had always wanted to fly beyond our mountains, like the birds that came and went with the seasons. And now that I was seeing with my own eyes that not only birds but people could fly, I wanted to fly and see the world. Zhatsonamu and Latsoma only wanted to fly home.

In the evening there was a lot of talk between Mr. Li and the Xichang organizers, and it was about us. I could not understand any of it, but I stayed with them, hanging on their every gesture, every now and then pestering Yisso for some information. When at last they were done with talking, Yisso said that fifteen people had been chosen to represent Sichuan province in a national competition in Beijing and that I was one of them. When I went up to our room and told Zhatsonamu and Latsoma that I was going to Beijing, the place where the Panchen Lama lived and Mao Zedong slept, and they were going home, they jumped for joy. They could not wait to go home to their mothers and their boyfriends.

Yisso was also going home, and so was Mr. Li. From tomorrow, Mr. Luo of the Xichang Cultural Bureau would be the leader. Yisso would inform my mother, and since I knew enough Yi to get by and I was already making some progress in Chinese, neither Yisso nor Mr. Li could foresee any problems.

"NAMU, SINGING IN BEIJING is not going to be as easy as singing in Xichang," Mr. Luo warned me. For a start, I was to perform with the famous Tibetan opera singer Nankadroma — one Moso song and a Tibetan and a Yi song, and with a full-size traditional Chinese orchestra. Now, for Nankadroma and the others, who were all professional singers, learning new songs and singing with an orchestra were routine work, but not so for me. As Mr. Luo saw it, I sang as one walked or danced, I had only ever sung to the accompaniment of the bamboo flute and I knew only a few tunes. For Moso songs, like almost all the music of the ethnic people of western China and unlike Chinese or Western music, consisted of improvised poetry sung to a few set and standard tunes. And how many tunes did Moso people have? Mr. Luo asked. Six or seven? Ten? One tune to sing of our love for our mothers, another to farewell the horsemen leaving with the caravan, another for funerals, another to sing for our lovers, and finally, the working songs, whose simple rhythms express the movements of people laboring in the fields.

From Xichang we went to Chengdu, where we stayed at the guest house of the Provincial Cultural Bureau and began daily rehearsals the following morning, and Mr. Luo's assessment of my musical capacities proved correct. I found it very difficult to learn new melodies and almost impossible to sing with the orchestra. No matter how much I tried, I could not count beats. I just could not come in on time — until the *erhu* player suggested tapping his foot when it was my turn to come in. To everyone's relief, it worked. But then, as though the orchestra were not enough, Mr. Luo had also arranged for a professional voice teacher to coach us. I did my best not to appear reticent, but I just could not bring myself to contort my face as I needed to in order to make my voice come out louder and clearer. Moso women sing very high and very loudly and because they sing in falsetto, they can always sing and smile at the same time. To pull an ugly face in order to sing better seemed to defeat the purpose. But perhaps more frustrating than anything, especially for those around me, was that although I learned quickly, by imitation, I forgot everything almost as fast — most likely because I had never learned anything in any formal setting. Nevertheless, after two weeks the rehearsals were over, and the next day we were on the train to Beijing, traveling in second-class sleepers.

For three days and two nights, the giant centipede chugged through the mountains and alongside great rivers, crossing through small villages and big cities, stopping at the railway stations filled with noisy people and noisier vendors. Some of the singers complained that the journey was too long but I kept my face glued to the window, and for three days I watched China go by. When I grew tired of looking outside, I practiced speaking Chinese. At night we slept on the narrow sleeper bunks and I dreamed of stage lights and pink ice cream. I dreamed with my eyes closed but I was not sleeping.

Beijing is a very big city, much bigger than Chengdu, perhaps even bigger than all of Moso country. From the moment the train drew into the station, I felt its sheer size. And as we stepped off the train onto the platform, I felt terrified. I reached for Mr. Luo's hand. "You don't need to grab me so hard!" he said, pulling away. "Look at what you've done!" And I looked at the scratches I had left on his hand.

Nankadroma took my arm and we made our way through the surge and swell of a human sea to the gigantic hallway, where a woman's voice boomed melodiously over the general uproar, "This is Beijing railway station, Beijing is our great capital city, Beijing is the capital of the People's Republic of China." Although I could not make out the words, it sounded like a soft song to me. I found it calming and I began to sing in imitation of the woman, a soft singsong in gibberish that made everybody laugh.

In the hall we were met by the organizers, who led us outside to the minibuses waiting to take us to our hotel. The hotel in Beijing was bigger than the hotel in Xichang. It not only had a red carpet but there were bedrooms with attached bathrooms with tiled walls and bathtubs and toilets that flushed every time you pushed on the handle. I shared such a bedroom with the famous Tibetan opera singer Nankadroma.

Nankadroma was beautiful, tall, and strong, with very dark skin. Her hair was thick and black, her eyebrows likewise, and her eyes, trained in the movements and expressions of Tibetan opera, had the power to silence or entrance. Nankadroma always seemed absorbed in her own thoughts; she talked slowly and sparingly, and whenever she spoke, everyone listened. I admired her very much, and I was so proud to share a hotel room with her. I watched every move she made, and then I copied her facial expressions, the waving of her hands, and the swaying of her hips. And I followed her everywhere. I even followed her into the bathroom when she was preparing to take a bath, which was how I discovered another thing besides airplanes and trains and ice cream.

"What is this?" I asked in Chinese.

"It's a bra. Don't worry, you don't need one." She laughed as she waved me out of the door.

Outside the hotel there were grand avenues, and on the avenues the people walked and talked as though they owned China. My wonderment was total. I had seen many marvelous things already in Yanyuan and Xichang and Chengdu, but nothing compared with Beijing. Beijing was enormous, stately, beautiful, overwhelming. Here I was not just enjoying myself, I was awestruck. "You're so happy," Nankadroma said, "you sleep with a smile on your face!"

The organizers had arranged daily outings for us to visit important sites—the Great Wall, the Forbidden Palace, Tiananmen Square, Mao Zedong's apartments, and the mausoleum where the great helmsman lay embalmed in his glass sarcophagus. The state of my political and historical education was such that on seeing the giant portrait of Mao in Tiananmen Square, I was only struck by the mole on his chin—because my mother had a mole at exactly the same place. I could not believe it! Years later my mother would come and visit me in Beijing, and she would also notice Mao's mole. It would become such a source of pride to her.

THE NIGHT OF THE CONTEST, I stepped onto the stage trembling with fear and anticipation. Nankadroma smiled at the audience, huge and darkened before us, and I smiled too. Then she smiled at me and the orchestra played the first notes. That night, under the heat of the stage lights, I remembered everything, every Tibetan and Yi word and what I should do with my face and when I should come in. I sang with all my heart, and at the end of the evening, Nankadroma and I had won first prize along with the rest of the Sichuan group.

The next day we were given our red diplomas and pushed on and off a huge stage in the People's Great Hall, where all manner of officials made speeches I could not understand and hundreds of people in the audience applauded the speeches. But this time we did get some money — wrapped, not in a simple red envelope, but like a precious gift, in the most beautiful rice paper. And it was a lot of money, Mr. Luo told me, two hundred yuan. A fortune.

My first thoughts were to count the money and buy truly expensive things for my family, but I could not bear the idea of tearing up the beautiful red paper. At home we never wrapped any gifts, and I so wanted my mother to see this paper. To everyone's amusement, I spent all evening mulling this over. It was not until we had gone back to our hotel room and we were ready to go to bed that, in the end, I decided not to open the money. Nankadroma then looked a little concerned and said I needed to watch out for thieves. The next morning I woke up to find her sewing a special pocket in my undershirt to keep my money safe.

"Little Namu, what did you decide to do with your money?" Mr. Luo asked as he counted our train tickets in the hotel foyer.

"I'm going to let my mother open it."

And he patted me on the back, and all the singers agreed with him that this was the best decision. They were all so kind and they had been so patient. I was the youngest and the least experienced by far, but I was everybody's favorite. In particular, I was Nankadroma's favorite. As I sat next to her on the bottom bunk of our second-class train carriage, I looked at her beautiful face, my heart welling with love for her and pride for myself. I was thinking, "I traveled to the center of the world to sing with the famous Nankadroma, and we won." But when the train shook and slowly began chugging out of Beijing railway station, I forgot about Nankadroma and the little red bundle of money pushing against my waist, and I just felt sad to be leaving.

A Village on the Edge of Time

The train ride to Chengdu took three days and two nights, during which I kept my face glued to the window and watched China go by in reverse. My eyes were still hungry for the world, and yet sometimes, instead of seeing the villages and the mountains, I saw Lake Lugu and our own Goddess Gamu. And when I closed my eyes at night, I did not dream of pink ice cream but of roasted potatoes and butter tea. I also dreamed of my mother's face as she opened the little red bundle, and then I dreamed of all the places I had seen and of all the other places I had yet to see.

From the train window I watched China go by. Fields upon fields, and meandering rivers, and mountains lost in cloudy heavens, grimy cities and earthbound villages, peasants walking in groups with hoes and rakes on their shoulders, peasants working alone in fields planted right up to the edge of the railroad track and littered with the garbage thrown out the train windows. In my travels I had discovered that there were two types of people in the world: city people, who ate in restaurants and took showers and went to the cinema, and peasants, who worked in the fields. We Moso were of the second type.

On the third day, when we reached Sichuan, the train passed through flooded fields and stranded villages, small islands wrecked in a sea of yellow water. Peasants waded through the dirty water holding their children and their belongings above their heads. Waded to where? There was water as far as the eye could see. Then I saw a small woman carrying a little child on one shoulder and a suitcase on the other. The water was almost up to her chin. If she stepped in a hole, she would certainly go under. One of the singers put his hand on my shoulder. "Don't worry, the People's Liberation Army will rescue them." The others nodded their heads and pulled away from the windows, and after some time, they went back to their games of cards, their books, their tea and cigarettes. But as the train chugged toward Chengdu, I could see no sign of the People's Liberation Army.

In Chengdu we were driven to the Jinjiang Hotel, where the director of the Sichuan Cultural Bureau welcomed us to a banquet organized in our honor because we had won first prize in Beijing. People from the Sichuan Television Network had also been invited, as well as writers from various local and provincial newspapers. In the dining room, the huge round tables were covered with dishes.

The director made an interminable speech. I could not understand any of it. But even if I could have, I would not have listened. As I stared vacantly at the official's mouth opening and smiling over tobacco-stained teeth, all I could see were people standing in dirty water up to their chests. All I could think was that not very far from this banquet room, a small woman was crying out under the black sky, a suitcase on one shoulder and on the other a little child who was clinging to her hair. I had never seen a flood. And surely if there ever was a flood in Zuosuo, surely we would help each other. How could the director put a smile on his face? How could any of us put food in our mouths? I could not eat and I could not speak for the rest of the evening. I could not understand these people. I missed my mother and Zhema and my brothers and I was glad they were safe in Zuosuo. For the first time since I had left, I missed my home and my people.

The next two days were spent giving interviews. Once again I saw myself on the television, and then in the local newspaper, the *Sichuan Daily*. There was a huge photograph of me on the front page. Nankadroma read the headline: A GOLDEN PHOENIX RISES FROM THE MOUNTAIN VALLEY. I took the page, folded it, and packed it carefully with the other things I was to give my mother. It would make her very happy, very proud, I thought with a sad sort of joy. Because I did feel sad. Because I could not forget the misery I had witnessed from the train window, and because the time had come to say good-bye.

Except for those who lived in Chengdu, everyone was going home. Nankadroma was also leaving. On that last afternoon, I found her sitting on her bed, alone in our hotel room. She was crying. I thought she was unhappy because we had to say good-bye, but she pointed to a letter lying in front of her on the bed. As I could not read, I asked her, "What is it? What's wrong?"

Nankadroma looked at me as though I were supposed to know the answer, and seeing that I did not, she said, "It's written in red. Don't you see?"

"Yes, I see." But I was puzzled. "Is red bad?"

Red was a beautiful color. It was the color of azalea flowers and of my mother's vest at festival times. It was the color I had so enjoyed painting on my lips when we had sung on the stage. Why was Nankadroma afraid of red?

Owing to my limited Chinese, Nankadroma found it difficult to explain that the letter was from her lover's wife, that the wife was Chinese and terribly jealous and that she now

wanted Nankadroma dead—which was why she had written the letter in red ink. In China red ink was a curse. Indeed,
it was not until a few years later, when I was a student at the
Music Conservatory in Shanghai, that I truly understood the
terror that red ink could inspire. Strolling in the streets with
my teacher and classmates, I came across a large poster with
the photographs of two young men and, listed under each
picture, their names, their ages, where they had grown up,
and last, the words *homosexual criminals.* Each list had been
ticked off with a large red stroke. I asked my teacher what it
all meant, as this was the first time I had seen the word *homosexual.* Then I asked him about the red strokes and he answered that the men had been executed. Everything inside
me turned to ice.

Now Nankadroma had dried her tears and she was desperate to talk to her lover, and as there was no telephone in
the hotel, we had to go to the post office. There I waited for
her outside the glass booth, and while she shouted down the
telephone and cried, I ate a red bean ice cream. I was terrified. I remembered the stories about the Yi chiefs who had
wanted to chop off Dr. Rock's head, but those were stories. I
had never before heard of anyone who had cursed someone
to die.

When Nankadroma came out of the telephone booth, her
mouth was set in a sad but resolute expression. She did not
want to go back to the hotel. She wanted to take a walk and
calm herself. So we walked on the streets for a while until she
said: "Are you hungry, Namu?" and she smiled weakly. "Of
course, you're always hungry. Come, I know a nice place."
And I followed Nankadroma down a few narrow streets to a
small restaurant famous for its duck stew.

We sat ourselves close to the street, on square stools at a
square table. Nankadroma drew closer to me and lit a cigarette. She asked me what I wanted to drink.

"Tea," I answered.

"You've never drunk wine?" she asked, pointing to a bottle of Erguotuo standing on a dusty shelf.

"Not Chinese wine."

"Try it," she ordered me.

I did not know that Erguotuo was a very cheap and very nasty liquor, but even if I had, I would not have dared refuse her. She looked so sad and I did not want to upset her more. Nankadroma called on the restaurant owner to bring her the bottle of Erguotuo. She poured two small glasses and drank hers straight down.

"Go on!" she said, pushing the other glass in front of me. "Bottoms up!"

I took a sip and immediately felt the fire in my throat and the heat rising in my cheeks. This Chinese wine was nothing like our Sulima wine. Meanwhile, Nankadroma helped herself to another glass and downed that one as well. I watched her, feeling at the same time fascinated and afraid.

Nankadroma was so beautiful and she was so famous. Why was she crying for a man? Why did she allow a man to cause her so much trouble? Nankadroma could have anyone she wanted. Why did she need to love a man who had such a nasty wife? It now struck me that marriage was a great source of misery and that love was a very complicated thing outside our Moso country. But, of course, I had known this before going to Beijing. All Moso knew this about marriage. Watching Nankadroma drink her second glass of Erguotuo, I thought of my Yi sister, Añumo, who had run away from her husband, and then I remembered other stories, and one in particular, about a young Naxi couple who had taken their lives in nearby Lijiang.

For all those who believed that love suicide had died with the advent of the Communist Revolution, this was shocking news.

The Naxi were not like the Han Chinese, who, in the days before Communism, had kept their women indoors. In Lijiang girls skipped arm in arm up and down the streets, singing at the top of their voices, teasing the boys. There it was the men who stayed at home, who played cards and smoked tobacco or opium, and who looked after the babies, while the women butchered animals and built houses and went to market. Naxi women carried huge loads on their backs and worked in the fields from morning to night. They were short and squat and strong as mules, and they took orders from no one. But until the Communists reformed their marriage rules, when it came to love, the Naxi were bound by a cruel tradition whereby Naxi girls were promised in marriage at their birth, always to a cousin on their mother's side, and the rule was so strict that only death could undo a betrothal arrangement. When young people who were pledged to others fell in love, they were honor-bound to commit suicide.

Then, years after the Communists had given the Naxi free-choice marriage, it had happened again. A young couple had committed suicide. For months they had met in secret in the fields and in the pine forest until one day the girl's stomach had grown too round to hide under her blue tunic and they had walked into the mountain according to the old custom. It had happened very early one morning, while everybody was still asleep. They had left the village, dressed in their best clothes, carrying a food hamper, and they had gone into the forest, looking for a beautiful picnic spot in a clearing where they could live happy loving days — until they ran out of food and wine and they hanged themselves from a tree.

When my Ama had heard about it, her eyes had shone with tears, and Dujema had whispered, "No Moso woman would ever hang herself for a man."

I wanted to tell this story to Nankadroma. I wanted to

tell her about the Naxi lovers and about my sister Añumo, and of how simple love could be in my village if you were not afraid to open your door. But I did not have enough Chinese words. I wanted to say, "In my village, when women are in love, their faces shine like the sun; your face looks like you've attended a funeral."

Nankadroma downed another glass and asked, "Do you know what the Chinese say about women? They say that beauty is a woman's misfortune." And she told me her story.

Nankadroma came from Mianing county in the Tibetan part of Sichuan. She was one of three daughters and the most beautiful—which caused her much trouble because everywhere she went, women were jealous of her and men pestered and bullied her. Where Nankadroma lived, men did not always court women with clever songs and pretty belts. Instead they threw stones and shouted ugly things, and when the women turned to shout back, they laughed at them. When Nankadroma was about sixteen, she was walking down the street when two boys ran up to her and tried to grab at her breasts. She was fighting them off the best she could when another man came along and chased the boys away. She didn't know who he was and she never saw him again, until many years later, when they met by chance at the local bus station. She was a famous singer by then, touring with the Tibetan Opera, and he was working for the local Cultural Bureau. They were about to get on the same bus. They recognized each other immediately and fell in love before the end of the tour. Unfortunately, in the years since he had rescued her on the streets, the man had married, and most unfortunate of all, he had married a Chinese woman. If his wife had been Tibetan, they could have come to some arrangement, but a Chinese woman would never tolerate a rival nor grant a divorce.

"Why didn't he marry a Tibetan?" I asked.

"She was a beautiful woman, and he loved her when he married her. How could he know that we would meet again? How could he know that she would turn out so mean-spirited?" Nankadroma lit another cigarette and then filled up her glass. By this time I had stopped counting the glasses, but the bottle was more than half empty. "Anyhow, it's all over. I'm going to break it off," she continued, tears suddenly flooding her eyes again. "I'm getting more miserable every day, and now I even have to fear for my life. I can't believe this!"

When the bottle was empty, Nankadroma wanted to go back to the hotel. It was very late and the only other customers were men yelling and playing a drunken betting game. But Nankadroma was herself so drunk that when she stood up, she knocked the glasses off the table, and I had to hold her up while the restaurant owner sent a waitress to call a rickshaw.

My throat was on fire and I had a bad taste in my mouth, but I was not sure that it was all due to the cheap wine. Nankadroma's story had unnerved me. I had been very jealous of my own sister at times, but the worst thing I had ever done was to steal the blood sausage from her lunch box. A truly terrible story that had my mother laughing for weeks. I had never wished to curse or do serious harm to anyone. And I had never heard of women fighting over a man. As I helped Nankadroma lurch into the rickshaw, I felt relieved that my mother and my sister and my little brothers lived in Zuosuo, where everyone took care of each other, where there were no floods, and where people could love without fear of jealousy or punishment.

Nankadroma leaned on my shoulder, and I stroked her thick, silky hair. I felt very close to her, as I had felt sleeping near Añumo that night, happy in the thought that I was of some comfort. When we were back in our room, I helped her take off her shoes and clothes and put her to bed. I kissed her on the cheek, as though I were her mother.

The next morning she was still drunk, or at least she had a hangover. I gave her a glass of water and said good-bye. She mumbled something but I am not sure that she really noticed I was going. I did not see her again for many years after that, and during that time, I often wondered if she had broken up with her lover and found a man worthy of her.

IT HAD BEEN ARRANGED that I would return to Yanyuan, where I could join some horsemen and make my way home to Zuosuo. The bustling county town that had taken my breath away only a few weeks before looked very small now, and the colorful bedroom at the local guest house was wanting a carpet. Early in the morning, I went to the Horsemen's Hotel, where I found Jiashe, a horseman from our village, and four others. They had already saddled the horses, fifteen altogether, loaded with salt, sugar, tea, iron sickles, and rolls of cotton cloth, and within the hour we had set off on the seven-day journey.

I did not feel the fatigue. I hardly saw the mountains, or even noticed that I needed a bath. My thoughts were with Nankadroma, and even as we walked up to the last ridge before Lake Lugu comes into view, all I could see were the places I had been.

"Going to Beijing has made you very quiet," Jiashe teased.

But it was my village that had gone quiet. So quiet. Mother Lake was of the purest blue, perfectly still, a perfect mirror for the mountain goddess to gaze endlessly at her own reflection. The sky above was large and empty but for the threads of white smoke escaping from the roofs of the houses, which soon lost themselves in the boundless sky. Here was perfect, unspoiled beauty . . . *eternal peace*—the meaning of the name Yongning, our Moso capital. I could not help thinking that the outside world knew nothing about it and that my people had truly been forgotten.

The horse bells announced our return a long way before we entered the village, and soon the children were running toward us, shouting in excitement, and behind them my mother came running to meet me, carrying Jiama on her back, her face white with flour. She had been cooking. And she was smiling from ear to ear and her face was shining as though it were a holiday.

"You've come back! I knew you were coming back! This morning the magpie called and I knew you were coming!"

Not knowing what to do with herself, she handed Jiama over to me and untied my bag from the horse. Then we walked home side by side, Jiama on my back and my bundle on my mother's. And it did feel good to be home at last with my mother and my little sister and Zhema and my brothers, all of us sitting around the fireplace, drinking butter tea, laughing and marveling at my stories.

That same evening, my Ama invited the whole village to our courtyard to celebrate my return and to thank the horsemen who had brought me home safely. There was a lot of dancing and singing and joking. It was just like that other evening, when Mr. Li and Zhang and Zhu had played their tape recorder, when the future was still unknown, a mystery, an adventure waiting for a heroine, but tonight the villagers were feasting the heroine's return. And the adventure was over. Old Datso, who had once traveled as far as India, stood up to speak. "Everybody listen! We must welcome Namu, who has returned from Beijing. She won prizes and is the pride of the Moso people. I am old and I will never go to Beijing. So let's be quiet, and let's listen to what she has to say! Because I want to hear."

But he sounded so formal, so like a government official, that instead of being quiet, everyone laughed. Undaunted, Datso took my hand and demanded that I make a speech. So I stood up and sang and said a few words, and I brought out the little red bundle I had carried under my clothes all the way back from Beijing. I asked my mother to open it, but her pride was now filling her with shyness, and she only shook her head and pushed the little bundle away from her, telling me that I had to open it myself.

"Two hundred yuan," I said, holding the wad of notes for everyone to see.

The villagers gasped. They all wanted to touch the money. "It's from Beijing," they whispered, as they passed the bundle around, touching their foreheads with it to bring themselves some luck.

After the money, I showed the newspaper. No one could read but everybody liked the photograph. Seeing this, I went to my bedroom to fetch the postcards I had bought in Beijing, and the newspaper photograph of Nankadroma. I talked a lot about Nankadroma.

"Why didn't you ask her to come back here with you?" my Ama said.

"I don't think she would like it here. It would be too quiet for her," I answered, already thinking that perhaps it was even too quiet for me.

Ama said nothing more about Nankadroma. She was much too happy to appreciate the meaning of my comment. Besides, people had got bored listening to my stories and everyone was talking and laughing again, and she wanted to join in the general mirth and to listen to Numbu, who had stood up to make yet another speech.

"As you all know," Numbu said in the same formal tone Datso had used and that had made everyone laugh, "a vacancy has opened at our elementary school. Well, it has been decided that Namu will cook and clean for the teachers. She will earn fifteen yuan a month."

This time nobody laughed. They cheered and nodded their heads in approval, and my mother was glowing. This was one of very few paying jobs in our village and every mother had held hopes for her daughters. Only a month or so before, I would have been among the least likely candidates, but now everything had changed. Now I was a star in my village and it seemed only natural that I should be given such a coveted position. The trouble was, I did not want to be a star in my little village, I wanted to be a star in the big world.

Love and Duty

For a few days after I returned from Beijing, I basked in my special status. I did no work and woke up very late, sauntering leisurely into the kitchen to find my mother already through with many of the house chores and Zhema absent, gone to the fields. I sat near the fireplace, drank butter tea, and ate roasted potatoes. I played with little Homi and Jiama. No one seemed to mind. I was a star and I needed to rest from my travels. Besides, I would soon start working at the school. Then late one morning, when I had finished breakfast, Ama asked me to go and dig a taro root from the garden.

When I came back into the kitchen, she threw the root into a pot and told me that I was going to make glue to stick my newspaper photograph on the pantry door. Ama needed me to watch over the taro because it had to boil for a while and she had too many other things to do. She was still talking when Geko came in with barley cookies and a bottle of wine his mother had given him for our family. Geko lived a few gates down from our house. He was about twenty years old, very tall, with a handsome, manly face and thick, wavy hair. There was a general agreement that he was the best-looking young man in the village. Ama greeted him and told him to sit near the fireplace, and while she placed his offerings on the ancestors' altar, she asked me to serve him some tea. And while I was pouring the tea, she suddenly excused herself, taking Homi and Jiama with her and leaving the two of us alone in the house. I didn't know where to put myself, and I was furious. It was obvious that my Ama had arranged the visit.

Meanwhile, Geko gave me a long look and took out a cigarette.

"How was Beijing?" he asked, rounding his lips and blowing smoke rings up in the air. "I thought you might never come back. I watched you when you left."

I pretended to take interest in the taro root boiling in the pot.

He blew more smoke, through his nose this time, and moved off the kang to come and stand by my side and look at the taro. "Did you like the outside world, Namu?" he asked.

"Yes, I liked it a lot," I replied coldly.

His face darkened, but he was not to be so easily put off. "Could I come and have a drink with you tonight?"

"I've never lit the fire in my flower room," I answered as I turned toward him and stared very hard into his eyes — which among us is a very rude way to look at somebody. "I prefer to sit near the fireplace, down here in the kitchen."

"What a waste," he countered.

And then he smiled, a very sweet, disarming smile that caught me entirely by surprise, so much so that I could not think of what to say next and blurted out, "I don't know why you should want to drink wine in my flower room. There are plenty of other girls in the village. Besides, I heard that you have a friend in Luo Shui."

Geko burst out laughing. He had expected something a

little less straightforward. "Oh, I don't see her very often. It's too tiring rowing the boat all the way across the lake at night."

"Well, who cares anyhow!" I snapped. I was so annoyed at myself for my lack of wit and playfulness. But somehow I did care. I didn't like the thought that he had so many girl-friends. And that also surprised me, because I had never thought anything special about Geko. In fact, I had never thought anything at all about him.

We both went quiet and watched the taro root boil away until the wordless tension, growing heavy with expectations and restraint, brought us much too close for comfort, and I began to talk again, about Nankadroma and how she had fallen in love, and how her lover had a nasty jealous wife who had cursed her with a red letter, and how I had left Nankadroma brokenhearted and drunk in the hotel room. Nankadroma's story was a very sad love story and Geko was all ears, but I could tell from the expression on his face that he was not sure I was flirting.

The taro had boiled enough by now. I ladled the glue into a little bowl and with a small paintbrush smeared it on the door of the pantry. Geko then placed my picture over the glue, carefully positioning it to make sure it was straight. He smoothed it flat, brushing his hands over my paper face, slowly, very softly, and I felt a little short of breath. His hands were long and graceful, like my father's hands. He was stand-ing so close to me and acting as though he could not even see me, but there was a sweet smell coming from his breath and his skin. When he was satisfied that the glue would hold, he took a couple of steps back and said, "Look! You're very pretty." Then he turned to me and asked with a big smile, "Do you want to go walking near Mother Lake?" And I said yes.

Now, outside festival times, couples do not usually walk around Lake Lugu in broad daylight, but the few people we saw on our way did not seem to mind. They simply looked at us and waved, and they smiled. Perhaps they were happy to think that at last someone was going to knock on my bedroom window.

I liked walking side by side with Geko. I liked talking with him as well. I told him more stories about my travels, and about the singing contests and the people I had met. Geko listened as though he were drinking my words, until I started to talk about Nankadroma again, and he said, "You had such a good time in the outside world. Did you really want to come back? Maybe you left your heart with your friend Nankadroma."

Suddenly I no longer felt like walking with him. All the softness, all the pleasure I had in his company had vanished. He had seen right through me, and he had seen right. *I had left my heart with Nankadroma.* And I did not want to come back, but I was back, and there was nothing I could do about that, was there?

"Yes, I did. I wanted to come back," I snapped. "I wanted to come back . . . just for you. Because your mother and my mother arranged everything. But now I've changed my mind. I don't want you! I don't even like you."

His eyes flashed, and then he burst out laughing. "What do you mean, you don't want me? Hey! I don't want you either. Who do you think you are? Do you think you're too good for me?" He stopped laughing and took both my hands in his. "Tonight, I'll come and knock on your window. You'll see, after you've been with me, you will never want to leave, ever!"

That night I waited for him. I waited, determined not to open my door. But he didn't come. I wondered if he had paddled across the lake to his girlfriend's house in Luo Shui or if he had gone to visit someone else and who that might be, or if he really thought I had left my heart with Nankadroma. Whatever, he never came. Not that night nor the following nights. And at the end of it, I was disappointed.

My mother too was disappointed. She was very fond of Geko, and he was such a good match. Geko was the best-looking boy in the village and every girl wished to love him. It seemed so right that the two of us should fall in love now that I too was a star in the village. When Ama understood that things had not gone well between me and Geko, she became very nervous. Perhaps she could see in my eyes something that reminded her of her own girlhood. Something that had made her leave her mother's house. At every opportunity, she mentioned Geko and how good-looking and kind he was, and how all the girls were chasing after him. And when she was not talking about Geko, she was talking about my girlfriends who were pregnant or already mothers.

Every night I lay on my bed and thought of him. My Ama was right. He was the best I could get. And if I did not get him, there were plenty of others who would. I did feel so ungrateful. My mother wanted to raise a big family more than anything in the world; why was I so resistant? "Namu, you have a good body," Ama had told me that morning. "You could have ten children." Ah! She was exaggerating. Nobody could have ten children anymore, unless you were willing to have all your pigs and horses and goats confiscated by the government. The new law limited all women to three children, a special rule because we were minority people. For their part, the Han Chinese could have only one child.

I remembered the smell of his breath and I burned to be close to him. But when I pictured myself with children clinging to my skirt, my thoughts again turned to Nankadroma—

how beautiful and sad she was — and the red letter, because even the curse of a red letter seemed more interesting than anything in my village. No, I did not want even three children hanging on to my skirt. What I wanted was to be a famous and beautiful singer — like Nankadroma. What I wanted was to be just like Nankadroma. I wanted to look like a woman with a broken heart.

But I was just a girl who, for a moment, had brought fame to her people, and who was about to be rewarded with a fifteen-yuan-a-month job, cooking for the teachers at the school — the only school in our village.

Sometimes I liked the idea of working at the school. I especially liked the idea of earning money. Although fifteen yuan a month seemed so little when compared with the two hundred I had earned in Beijing, it was more than many families made. Cash was so hard to come by in those days. Even the horsemen who took local produce to market did not always make much money, often resorting to barter, and there were no horsemen in our family. Also, I felt proud to cook for the teachers. Teachers were learned men, a bit like lamas, and I rather fancied the idea of cooking for them. The whole village agreed on this, cooking for teachers was a great responsibility and a great honor, not only for me, but for my mother and our family.

The morning of my first day at work, Ama made butter tea and served me as though I were an aristocrat. This job meant so much to her. From the time she had settled in Zuosuo, my Ama had worked hard to earn people's respect, and now that her third daughter had brought fame to the village and was about to cook for the teachers, she had more reason than ever to be proud of herself. Meanwhile, I felt undeserving and my heart ached. I had woken up thinking about Beijing again, and that morning I was not only thinking of the places and the people I had left behind, I was thinking of leaving home.

My mother accompanied me to the school. It was already summer and the weather was hot and humid, and the walk not a very pleasant one, as the school was some way into the valley, halfway between several villages. It stood in a quiet place, and from the path it looked particularly ugly, consisting of two single-story buildings, with no other decoration than a simple wooden porch. The walls were of rammed earth and had never been rendered. One wing housed five classrooms and the other the teachers' rooms and the kitchen, *my* kitchen. Ama said the school was ugly because it was built in Han Chinese style. I thought it was ugly because everything in our valley was ugly, but I kept my opinion to myself.

My Ama wanted to make sure I did everything right. So she did all the work. She lit the fire and showed me how to cook a few dishes I already knew how to prepare. Then she showed me how to sweep the floor and wash the dishes and other things I had been doing ever since I was a little girl, which came as easily to me as walking. Finally she told me over and over that when everything was ready, I should go find the teachers one by one in each room and very politely call them to eat. "And don't forget to serve them with both hands. Show some respect."

Three of the teachers were Yi and the other two were Han Chinese. None spoke Moso or even standard Mandarin, only the Sichuan dialect—which was certainly a handicap as far as the children's education was concerned, but it was not a problem for me. I was there to serve, not to talk. My mother cooked the teachers' lunch and while they were slurping their soup, proceeded to inform them that I was a good girl but very young and inexperienced and, please, not to take it too seriously if I made a mistake. I am not sure how seriously they took my Ama or even how much of her broken Chinese they understood, but she really annoyed me. I did not want to be treated like a child. I was a grown woman. I had traveled the world all the way to Beijing. I had switched a television set on and off and sat in taxis and earned more money in a single night than the teachers made in six months! Surely I could manage to cook and clean without anyone's doubting my skills. But perhaps she really annoyed me because I knew, deep in my heart, that I did not want to be cooking and cleaning for the teachers, that I was doing this work only to please her.

When the teachers were done with lunch, Ama wanted to wash the dishes, but I pointed out to her that the sky was darkening and she should hurry home before the rain broke. When my mother left, I felt relieved and very sad. I watched her running home, her body looking so small in her Chinese-style trousers. She was worried about me and she was worried about what was going on at home, what Homi and Jiama might be up to. She had worked so hard to raise her family. She was still working so hard.

I finished cleaning the dishes and looked around the kitchen. My heart sank. It was too big, too dark. Too ugly as well. There was nothing in it aside from a low wooden table and six little stools, the cooking stove, and a plank bed in a dark corner. My new bed.

Before going to sleep that night and every night afterward, I dragged a heavy piece of wood and blocked the door with it. Although it was the most unlikely thing in the world, I was terrified that someone would break in, in the middle of the night. In fact, I was so scared, that first night, that I could not bear even to try out the bed my Ama had made up for me just a few hours before. I sat in the light of the woodstove and took out Nankadroma's picture. I was quite convinced that

Nankadroma was the only person in the world who could have understood me.

MY WORKDAY BEGAN BEFORE SUNRISE. I woke up, put on my nylon slacks and a sweater, and lifted my workbasket onto my back to go collect firewood in the mountain. On the way back, I washed my face in the cold stream, and by the time the sun was up, I was in the kitchen, stirring hot embers and stoking the fire. The stove was an enormous brick box with a brick chimney that went through the roof. On top were three ceramic pots, going from large to small, and underneath was an opening where I added wood to the fire and blew and blew until my face was covered in soot and there was a big bright flame underneath each pot. The pots had come by horseback all the way from Lijiang and they were very precious. The largest was for cooking vegetables and meat and for frying flat bread and Tibetan rice cakes; the middle-size one was to boil water for tea; and the smallest was also for water, for the teachers to wash. The teachers only needed to wash their faces.

In the morning, with the fire going under the three pots, I could have everything ready in the correct sequence and at the right time. A little before the rice cakes were done, I ladled hot water into five enamel basins, which I brought to the teachers' rooms — running back and forth five times. While the teachers dressed, I set the table and served their tea and rice cakes. While they ate breakfast, I fed the chickens and the pig. When they had finished breakfast, I washed the dishes. And while the teachers were in their classrooms, I weeded the garden and cut garlic and cilantro and the other vegetables needed for lunch. I prepared the lunch — two vegetable dishes, one meat dish, and one soup — and when lunch was ready, I walked up to each classroom and called out, "Teacher, lunch is ready!" Then the teachers came and sat at the table near the fireplace and ate their lunch. They never talked to me, because I was too busy and I did not speak enough of the Sichuan dialect to have a conversation.

In fact, I hardly ever spoke to anyone. I sometimes talked with the children, because they spoke Moso, but they were almost never at school. On a good day there would be at least one child in each classroom. There was far too much work to do at home, with feeding the chickens and cutting grass for the pigs, for children to waste their time sitting on a bench in a bookless classroom, listening to teachers who spoke a language they could not understand. Sometimes when there were no children at all in the classrooms, the teachers played chess or read, or they went for a hike in the mountains and came back with baskets filled with wild mushrooms.

Occasionally, when I badly needed company, I ran home for a quick bowl of tea. I always took something for my mother, some leftover food or cooking oil, and everybody was always so happy to see me. Then I ran back to the school and to my lonely work. But it was a good thing I had no one to talk to—because I could not possibly have shared my thoughts with anybody. They would have thought I had gone mad. "Who do you think you are? You're a woman, you belong in the house, to the village. Your power is in the house. Your duty is to keep the house, to be polite to old people, and to serve food to the men." Only men could leave their mothers' houses, and even they never left just to fulfill their personal ambitions. They left to trade and sell goods and bring back money for their mothers and sisters. Or they left to study the Buddhist scriptures and they came back as lamas, holy men who served the spiritual needs of their families.

I had been working at the school for only a month and all

I cared for was to keep myself busy. When the usual chores were not enough to fill my day, I swept the yard over and over again. Or I went into the mountain to chop some extra wood for the fire. Or I bathed in a mountain pool. Sitting in the icy water, I thought of my Ama and Geko and tried to forget that I wanted to leave, and when I came out and dried myself, I tried to think up a plan for my escape. And the next morning, when I woke to find myself in the big, dark, empty kitchen, I remembered not to scream at the teachers.

A Scandal

I saw Geko one more time. He came to visit me at the school one afternoon and found me washing dishes.

"My mother asked me to bring you this," he said quietly, handing me some rice cakes.

I looked at the rice cakes and thanked him, and asked him to put them on the table. While I finished the dishes, Geko sat on one of the little chairs and watched me work while he smoked a cigarette.

"Do you like it here?" he asked.

"Yes," I said. I tidied up the last of the dishes and poured two bowls of butter tea. Then I drew up a chair to sit opposite him at the table. We tried to make small talk but we did not have a lot to say to each other. Or perhaps we did but we did not know where to start. When he put down his empty bowl, I told him that there was no kindling left and I had to collect some wood. I did not really want him to go home, but I could not bear the silence any longer.

"There's nothing left around here," he replied. "You need to go way up into the mountain."

"Yes, I know that."

"I'll come and help you," he then suggested, and I did not refuse him.

We set off for the long hike into the forest, Geko carrying the ax over his shoulder and me carrying my workbasket on my back. The walk, or perhaps the mountain air, did us both good, because Geko recovered his ability to speak. Now he could not stop joking and I could not help laughing at his jokes, and at every opportunity, he picked some wild fruit to give to me or a flower to put into my hair.

Higher up in the mountain, we came across a big pine tree with dead branches dragging onto the ground, which Geko cut down and chopped into kindling. When he was done, the sun was beginning its descent and the sky was growing gray, and I began to worry about the coming rain and the teachers' dinner. We loaded my basket and hurried down the mountain trail toward the school, but my basket was so heavy, and we were both so hot and tired, we decided to make a small detour and stop at one of the mountain pools.

Geko helped me put my basket down on the grass, and while he lit a cigarette, I stepped into the pool up to my knees and washed my face and arms. When I turned around to talk to him, he was lying back on his elbows, gazing in my direction, and I was suddenly struck by the handsome way he drew on the cigarette and the fullness of his lips and the roundness of the circles he was blowing in the air. My heart raced in my chest and the heat rose in my neck and face. I swiftly turned away, aware of my body burning, afraid he would smell the sweat on my body, and I lowered myself all the way into the water. But even then I wanted him to come closer to me, to touch me.

"Namu," he called out, laughing. "Don't walk too far into the pool. It might be very deep."

"Don't you know how to swim? Couldn't you rescue me?"

But when I came out of the water with my wet clothes clinging to my body, he stopped laughing. "Look," he said, "you've grown funny. One of your breasts is bigger than the other."

I knew he was trying to joke because he was embarrassed, but this time I did not find him funny. I felt ashamed, and disappointed in him. "You dog," I snapped.

Turning my back on him, I went to sit in the sun at a safe distance. I was angry with him, but my heart was still beating wildly and I did not dare look at his face. I tried to think of Nankadroma and what she would have done. But all I could think of were his hands and his lips and the smoke rings he was blowing with his cigarette. And all I felt was the fire melting my body. "Come to me," I said softly, staring straight ahead into nothingness. "Why don't you come to me?"

Geko came to me, or rather he pounced on me—embracing me, grabbing my breasts, squeezing me so hard it hurt, and kissing me with his tongue, and I could taste the smoke on his breath and his tongue was strong and sweet and my mouth was dry. I felt drunk from wanting. His hands were grabbing at my clothes and they felt rough on my skin, a mountain man's touch, and I wanted his hands so much. He pulled me onto the grass and whispered, "You small torment. I was going mad." He kissed my face over and over, and I closed my eyes, enraptured, clasping blindly at his body. On feeling my arms tightening around him, he laughed. "You'll see, you'll be so happy, you'll never want to leave again."

I remembered Latsoma and Zhatsonamu, who had so wanted to go home to be with their boyfriends. "Once you've tasted a man's body," Latsoma had said, "you just want more and more. You don't belong to yourself. You're just like the old people when they smoked opium." Oh, she was so right. And Geko was right too. All I wanted was to taste more and more of him, and if I tasted more, I would never leave him. . . . And then as he pulled himself over me, my mother's words — you have a good body, Namu, you could have ten children. . . .

I released my arms and opened my eyes and stared at his face. I didn't want ten children hanging on to my skirts. I didn't want to get pregnant and stay in my mother's house, growing my mother's family. I wanted my own dream.

"You'll never want to leave me," he repeated, not so softly this time — not laughing either, but returning my gaze and pushing against me. He was ready now.

I slapped him so hard across the face, he pulled back and rolled over on the ground next to me, holding his hand to his cheek, and then he looked at me, dumbfounded. I grabbed at the dirt and threw it into his eyes, blinding him, and I hit him with my fists and screamed at him:

"Stop it! Stop it! You're all the same. You all want to keep me here. You think you're good enough for me? You're not! Go to the lake and take a look at yourself. I hate you! I hate you! I hate my mother! I hate this place! I hate everything about this place." He looked at me, his eyes wounded and full of dirt, not understanding, and the more I saw his eyes, the more furious I grew. I was standing up above him by now, and I started kicking him very hard and screaming and crying with rage. I was mad with rage. "I never liked you! And I never want to see you again! Never! Never! I hate you."

I did not mean it, I did love him. I loved him. But I also hated myself.

Geko had rolled onto his side and was holding his arms around his head for protection. When I finally stopped kicking, he slowly uncoiled himself and kneeled before me. His face was bright red, already bruising. He looked stunned, bewildered, horrified. "You are crazy," he said at last, his voice hoarse with emotion, fighting the tears welling in his eyes.

"You think you can leave and make it big in the outside world? Well, go! Go and find out who cares about you!"

He put his pants back on and started down the hill. He never once looked back toward me.

I just watched him disappear, breathing easier, feeling calmed, hardened, saying to myself, "That's how it has to be." I pulled my clothes together and walked over to the pool to wash my face. To wash Geko's kisses off my skin. The sun was very low now, and the rain had begun. I loaded my basket on my shoulders and headed back to the school.

That evening the teachers had to wait for their meal, and by the time they sat down to eat, they were too hungry to notice that my silence was darker than usual. They ate and smoked and chatted away until they grew sleepy enough to retire to their rooms. I didn't care what they did. I had almost tasted Geko's body. I had almost lost myself forever. But I did not want to be in love. I wanted to belong to myself. I only wanted my dream.

I sat near the fireplace far too late into the night, drinking strong green tea. When I went to bed I could not sleep. I replayed the scene near the pond over and over. Geko laughing. Geko in pain and disgusted with me. Then I thought of my mother, and almost immediately I thought of Beijing. And the more I thought of Beijing, the further away from my heart I pushed my mother and my village. All I wanted was to go back to the city, to take a shower and wear red lipstick and walk in high-heel shoes. And I wanted to sing, my eyes blinded by the heat of the stage lights and my ears deafened by the applause of strangers.

Next day my body ached from Geko's embrace. He had been too rough with me, and I felt angry. Outside it was raining, and the dreariness of the rain matched the state of my heart. It rained for a week without stopping. On the seventh day I went home. The road was very muddy. I had no shoes and the thick, sticky red clay was caking my feet, and when I slipped and fell flat on my back, I was covered in it. My anger turned to rage again. I hated everything, the rain that would not stop, the mud that stuck to my feet and my clothes, my hair, my face, inside my ears. And again, I hated my mother. And I so wished I had a friend I could talk to. I so wished I did not have to feel so lonely.

When I walked through the gates, Zhema burst out laughing. "What did you do, Namu? Did you try sleeping in the mud?"

I did not answer. Ama took me into the house and brought hot water for me to wash and she asked my sister to fetch me some clean clothes. But I could not speak to my mother either.

"Have you lost your tongue?" Zhema teased again.

This time Ama cut her short. "Don't tease her, maybe she is going to have her period. Do you want some chicken soup, Namu?"

The chicken soup cheered me enough to talk. "I beat Geko," I said, looking into my bowl.

Ama did not reply immediately. "I heard about it," she said slowly. "His mother told me that he came home black and blue, wearing the imprint of your hand on his face." She gave a little laugh that gave me no reason to believe that she approved of what I had done.

"Anyway, you don't need to worry about Geko," Zhema joined in. "There are plenty of girls in the village who will take care of his wounds."

I glared at my big sister and snarled, "I'm not like you, Zhema. I don't think all there is to life is a man."

"Oh, what's wrong with you!" she snapped back. "Did you swallow gunpowder?"

"Come on, both of you!" Ama intervened again. "Be nice to her, Zhema. Namu's just arrived home."

So we were quiet for a while, and then Zhema left the room. "I think I'll go feed the pigs," she said.

When she was gone, I asked Ama, "Did I cause trouble between you and Geko's mother?"

My mother sighed and sat down next to me. There was a dark scowl on her face. "Since you came back from Beijing, you have been very strange. Geko's mother can see this. Everybody in the village can see this. You are worrying me. I have worked very hard to raise this family. I would like to see you become Dabu when I am too old. I want you to run the family after me. Your sister is a good girl but she is too timid, she can't stand up as tall as you can. You are special, and you have been special since you were a little baby. Everyone knows this. And everybody likes you, especially the old people. I know that the day you take charge of this family, I will not have to worry about anything."

This was an astonishing speech. I had never thought my Ama had such high expectations of me — Zhema was such a good girl — but I knew that if I let her continue, she would begin to cry, and I did not want to see my mother cry. "Ami, I have to go back to school. I have to feed the teachers."

Back at the school, I heated the water and prepared the tea, and I cooked the vegetables and the meat dishes. But I did not go up to each classroom to call in the teachers. Instead I stood on the doorstep and hollered in the rough Sichuan dialect, "Your dinner is ready! If you want to eat, come over and get it! If you're not hungry, I'll give it to the pig!"

Minutes later the teachers traipsed into the kitchen, looking sheepish. I greeted them with a dirty look and a gray face. "What's wrong with you?" one of them dared ask.

"Full bellies will explode," I answered him in Moso, and then switched to the Sichuan dialect: "Do you want more food or have you finished?"

EIGHT DAYS HAD PASSED since I had beaten Geko. It had stopped raining but now the fire had gone out overnight. At sunrise I had hiked into the mountain and brought back a basketful of wood, but it was too wet and the fire would not light. I would get an ember going, and thick gray smoke, and I blew and blew until I was dizzy but the fire just ate the kindling and died out.

Resigned to the fact that I had to build the fire all over again, I went out into the garden to cut a long piece of bamboo — I did not want to blow and get dizzy and get more soot on my face. Back at the stove, I reorganized the charred pieces, added kindling, and threw the match on the wood. I began blowing long slow breaths into the end of the bamboo. I blew until the kindling crackled and began to glow. I blew until a bright flame licked the bottom of the larger pot, and then I blew until another flared up under the middle pot. Then I took another breath and forgot to take my lips away from the bamboo stick, and the fire blew back into my lungs. The heat licked my throat and burned into my chest — that very place where I had been simmering with anger for so long now that it seemed I had wanted to scream since the day I was born. I fell back and rolled on the ground, and I screamed and screamed.

One of the teachers came running in, and when he saw the bamboo stick lying near the stove, he burst out laughing. "How can you be so silly! Here, put the fire out," he said, handing me an enamel cup filled with cold water. And he went back to his room, to his bed, still laughing, to wait for his breakfast.

I threw the cup against the wall and cursed the teacher. Eventually the pain receded and I stopped screaming, but it took a while before I could get off the floor, and when I did, my anger did not subside. I looked around the room. The breakfast wasn't made, the fire wasn't lit. Nothing was done.

I stood up, walked outside, and grabbed the ax. I came back into the kitchen, I lifted the ax as high as I could over my head, and then I brought it down, as hard as I could, crashing over the stove. In three furious blows I smashed the three earthenware cooking pots. Then I smashed my plank bed, and I smashed the low table and the stools and the rice bowls and the drinking bowls. When there was nothing left to break, I ran all the way back to my mother's house.

She was tidying up the pantry.

"What kind of wind blows you back here?" she asked. "Don't the teachers want their breakfast this morning?"

"They have diarrhea!" I answered, looking at the wall. "They don't want to eat."

"Oh!" She closed the pantry door and pointed to the enamel basin on the floor near the lower hearth. "Why don't you help me grind these soybeans?"

I followed her into the courtyard and helped her turn the millstone. Every time the dog barked, I imagined that the teachers were already at the gates, that they had arrived to complain about me. I had done a terrible thing. I had broken the whole kitchen. I had smashed the cooking pots that had come by horse caravan all the way from Lijiang. It must have taken at least seven days to bring them back to Zuosuo.

"Have you lost your soul?" my mother asked. "Why are you so quiet?"

And then I said, "I want to go to Beijing." Just like that. I just blurted it, without thinking, without pretending. I just said it, because that was what I wanted and because I wanted it so badly that there was nothing left for me to want, because

I wanted it so badly that I might as well die. And while I was at it, I might as well say it all. "I want to leave Zuosuo. I can't stand this place anymore. It's too quiet for me here. The village has become so boring to me. Everything bores me now." And I looked straight into her eyes, the rudest way to look at somebody.

My mother opened her mouth, but nothing came out of it. She just stood there, mouth opened, paralyzed, rooted to the ground — until, without any warning, she grabbed hold of the bowl where the soybeans were soaking and threw the lot at me. Then the words came. A lot of words. "Are you mad?" she screamed. "How dare you talk to me like this? Who do you think you are? You think your wings are strong enough that you can fly on your own? You think you don't need me anymore? You want to become friends with the Han? Is that it? Who will know you in the outside world? Do you think you are so extraordinary? Go! Go live with the Han! Go on! Leave! Go! The farther away from me the better!"

I began to sob. My mother's anger was terrifying me. If she screamed now, what would she do when she found out what I had done at the school? She surely would do more than shout angry words! She would lock me up. She would beat me. What else could she do? She would have to punish me somehow.

I ran upstairs to my flower room and quickly stuffed the beautiful white skirt and the pink vest I had worn at my ceremony into a canvas bag I had brought back from Beijing. Then I ran back downstairs and into the kitchen. I was hoping to take some cookies and some ham for the road but my mother was standing in my path. Her eyes were black and her mouth set so hard, it looked as though her face would break. But she was not angry anymore. She was afraid.

Because a long time ago, she had left her own mother's house, and when she had come home, it had been too late, forever.

"Don't go," my Ama said, her voice breaking. Jiama and Homi started screaming.

But I had to go. I had broken the school kitchen and the teachers would be here at any moment now. "I'm going," I said. "I am going." And I took off, through the gates and into the village streets, with my mother running after me, calling for me to stop, to come back.

I ran and ran, holding my little bag against my heart. Past the last house and onto the mountain trail. My mother's voice grew more distant, but just as I slowed my pace a little, out of nowhere something bit at my back.

I turned around. My Ama was still chasing after me, throwing stones at me. She could not run fast enough to catch me, so she was hunting me down. In her youth my mother had used the bow and arrow as well as any man, and she still knew how to throw. She never hit where she could really have caused damage. The next stone hit my elbow. Another hit me between the shoulder blades and then another hit at the same place. That one broke the skin. More stones. I ran faster and harder up the hill, toward the mountaintop.

At last I reached the edge of the forest. My Ama had given up a long time ago now. When I stopped and turned back, I saw her standing on the trail, very small, looking in my direction, silently pleading for me to come back. I knew that she was crying. I was crying too, without tears in my eyes, but I was crying. And I could not go back. I could never go back. Not after what I had done to the school kitchen. I looked toward the school. There was no smoke coming out of the roof and I wondered if the teachers were still lying in their beds, waiting for me to bring their hot water and to call them for breakfast. "Full bellies will explode!" I wanted to shout, but I was out of breath.

I turned around and ran.

I ran, and when I had no more breath I walked, and then I ran again — for the rest of the day, through the night, and the next day and the next night. I ate nothing and I did not sleep. I was neither hungry nor tired. I was scared. I was so scared that I could not even swallow my saliva. At some point I had thought of singing, but the sound of my own voice alone in the mountains had terrified me. On the third night it began pouring with rain, and I stopped running. The ground was too slippery and I could not see where I was going because it was too dark. I tied my little bag on my back and got down on my knees and began crawling along the path, feeling the slippery ground with my hands — until, after what seemed hours and hours, the mud receded and at long last I could stand up again. By this time, however, I was completely lost.

That night I sought refuge in a Yi village. I was a sorry sight — soaked and muddy and bleeding at the knees where my nylon trousers had torn. But my hosts were very kind. The woman of the house heated some water so I could wash my knees. She gave me some roasted potatoes, and when I had eaten, she spread a blanket on the floor, where I dropped and instantly fell asleep. The next morning I had breakfast and washed my knees again, and gave up on trying to dislodge the little stones encrusted in my flesh. I thanked the Yi family, and I took off.

My hosts had explained that to get back on the road to the cement factory, I needed to backtrack a couple of kilometers. Now, I hated the idea of crawling in the mud on my hands and knees again, but I had to get on the right trail. As instructed, I retraced my steps and then took a turn at the crossroad and walked ahead, until the track began running along the hillside, where it narrowed rather suddenly to only a foot or so in width. Since I had been walking for a long time and still had seen no sign of the muddy grounds, I began to worry that I had lost my way again. I stopped and looked back, and then I looked up the hill and down — and I saw the mud, quite a way below where I was standing on the trail. And I understood that I wasn't lost. The night before, in the darkness and the rain, I had somehow gone off the main path and ended much too low on the hillside, where there was no trail at all but slippery mud and then a vertical drop, and a long way down at the bottom, the river roaring and churning brown torrential water — and there I had crawled, for a good length of the gorge, on the very edge of the precipice.

Looking down the hill in broad daylight, I could not believe that I had gone for so long without slipping. And if I had slipped, no one would ever have found me or even known where I had disappeared. I began to shake uncontrollably.

I was shaking so hard that I feared falling over, and I had to sit down on my heels for some time before I could regain the courage to scramble on along the path, my knees still giving way underneath me, my heart pounding in my chest. And now I thought of my Yi sister, Añumo, who had run for two days and two nights on her own in the mountains, and how I had worried about her. But Añumo had run to earn the respect of her people. I was running because I had disgraced my family and I could never, ever return to my village. I was running because I had shamed myself beyond forgiveness. But also, I was running because I wanted my dream.

On the fifth day I reached the cement factory, where only a few months before I had stood with Latsoma and Zhatsonamu waiting to see the world. This time there would be no green Jeep. I walked on the asphalt road, resigned to the fact that I would have to make my way to the city on foot, but I had not gone very far before a log truck drove by and pulled up on the side of the road. When I came up to the cabin, the door opened, and I saw with some relief that the driver was Tibetan and no one we knew.

As I was covered in mud, he told me to sit on top of the logs. It was terrible, very painful and very cold, and I began to sing to cheer myself up. I was singing very loudly, as loudly as I possibly could—screaming really—but it paid off. The driver stopped the truck and told me to come down into the cabin and sing for him. It was a perfect arrangement. He loved the singing, and I loved the ride. This time I did not even throw up.

In the evening we stopped in Yanyuan at the Horsemen's Hotel. The truck driver bought me dinner and I ate like a hungry and terrified dog, constantly looking over my shoulder to make sure that no one in the room was likely to recognize me. After dinner the driver paid for my room, a two-person room where I was the only one sleeping. But now that I was contemplating which bed to lie in, I remembered Nankadroma's stories about Tibetan men, and I began to worry that the driver might be hoping to keep me company later in the night. Of course, the room did not lock—because in China in those days, the needs of hotel patrons always came second to the wishes of hotel personnel. Only service people could lock and unlock bedroom doors, and only from the outside. So I piled the two beds and every other piece of furniture against the door and crawled in between the sheets, muddy clothes and all. I was so tired I could not have cared less.

The service woman woke me early the next morning, beating on the door and yelling something about regulations and doing her job, and when she came into the room, she added something about dirty girls and something else about my mother that I was glad I could not understand. Leaving her to curse and tidy up, I picked up my bag and hurried out of the room, where I found the truck driver waiting for me in the corridor.

"You were scared I come in your room last night?" he asked, laughing, showing off the traditional gold tooth at the front of his mouth.

"Why?" I said, trying to fight back the heat rising in my cheeks.

He patted me on the back. "I saw all the furniture! Ah, you're good! You can take care of yourself." And he led me to the dining room, where he ordered steamed buns and tea for our breakfast.

A little while later, we were on our way to Xichang. Passing through a village, he took his hand off the wheel and put his fingers to his mouth. "You hungry? You want watermelon?"

"What's watermelon?"

We stopped and went for a walk through the market to buy a watermelon. When we got back to the truck, he chose a nice flat stone, where he carefully balanced the melon. Then he drew his knife from his belt and halved it in one clean blow. It was red and sweet and it tasted as good as pink ice cream. And the truck driver was so kind, and very handsome. For the first time in almost a week, I was no longer afraid. I felt very happy now; I felt as though I had gone traveling with my uncle.

We arrived in Xichang in the late afternoon, where the driver dropped me off on the main street. "Here," he said, handing me a couple of notes. "If you don't find your people, come look for me at the Number Two Hotel. I'll take you back to your mama. Number Two Hotel. You understand?"

But I had no trouble finding my people at the Cultural Bureau.

Xichang Again

Luo Juzhang was engrossed in a pile of paperwork. On hearing me enter his office, he lifted his head, and a look of utter surprise came over his face. "Oh, little Namu, what have you done? You're so dirty!" he exclaimed.

"I rode in a truck from Yanyuan this morning," I answered.

"Well, it's nice to see you," he continued slowly, at a loss to comprehend what I was doing there. "Did you come here by yourself?"

"Yes."

"Does your family know?"

"No."

Luo Juzhang gazed at me for a moment and the expression on his face changed from surprise to worry. He shifted in his seat and pursed his lips, and at last he said, "Wait for me outside. I'll be about half an hour, then I'll take you home for some dinner."

A weight had just lifted from my chest. If Mr. Luo was not turning me out, if he was taking me home to his family, then maybe he could give me a job. I went out to wait for him in the yard. The afternoon sun was still high in the sky and it was very hot. I found the faucet and turned on the water to wash my face, my hair, and my arms and watched with calm satisfaction as red mud poured down through my hands and into the drain. I felt much better, cleaner and in no hurry. I sat on a bench to dry myself in the sun.

We went to Mr. Luo's apartment in the chauffeur-driven car the Cultural Bureau assigned its most important cadres. Mr. Luo's apartment went with the car. It was a typical cadre residence, fit for a typical government official: a green-and-white-walled apartment with bare concrete floors, a small kitchen, a flushing, seatless toilet, and a living room and three bedrooms crammed with books, trophies, and photographs glued behind glass. The furniture was neatly arranged against the wall, including, in the living room, a TV and a green refrigerator. There was nothing extraordinary about Mr. Luo's apartment. In China all modern apartments looked like this, with minor variations in floor size and the number of rooms.

Likewise, there was nothing extraordinary about Mr. Luo. He was graying and balding. He had a paunch, acquired from too many banquets and too little exercise. He wore a gray Mao suit, and except in the hottest weather, he always carried a sweater on his shoulder in imitation of our great helmsman. He even paused for photographs holding his cigarette between two fingers at about shoulder level as Mao Zedong had done. Mr. Luo always called people comrade, teacher, or little So-and-So, and I felt very comfortable in his company. Luo Juzhang was the type of person who found it almost impossible to say no. And you could always tell when that was about to happen because his face went bright red before he even began to speak.

Luo's three daughters were practicing dance steps in the living room. In their black trousers and white shirts, they made a sharp contrast with their mother, who was dressed in the traditional Yi multicolored skirt. Mr. and Mrs. Luo were both of the Yi nationality, but Mrs. Luo had been born into the slave caste, and she spoke only Yi, while Mr. Luo always spoke Chinese with his daughters. I had a lot of respect for Mr. Luo. He was a dedicated Communist and an idealist, and he had managed to make a good life for himself and his family, working in the local Cultural Bureau. Mr. Luo asked his younger daughter, Xiao Mei, to lend me some clothes and to take me to the public showers to get washed. There was no bathroom in Mr. Luo's house, although he was a county official.

In the shower I closed my eyes; I did not want to see the look on the other women's faces when they saw how dirty the water was. After the shower I ate a bowl of noodles, and almost immediately I went to sleep in Xiao Mei's room. I woke up the next morning, with the other three girls, to a Chinese-style breakfast.

"Aunt Luo," I asked Mrs. Luo, pointing to the rice porridge, "you eat rice porridge?"

"*Aya!* Of course not! But the children love it."

And she explained that this was the modern way of things. The younger generation spoke Chinese, they wore Chinese clothes, and they ate Chinese breakfast.

I helped Aunt Luo wash the dishes. Then I swept and cleaned the floors, and I cut up vegetables for lunch — doing my very best to ingratiate myself, so that by the time Mr. Luo came home, Aunt Luo was ready to sing my praises.

Over lunch I told my story the best I could, in bits of three languages — how I had run away from home because I did not want to have a boyfriend and I only wanted to sing. Mr. Luo listened and ladled more rice into my bowl.

"How old are you, little Namu?"

"I'm not sure," I said, vaguely ashamed of my ignorance. Two New Year festivals had passed since my Skirt Ceremony. "Maybe fifteen. . . ."

Mr. Luo cleared his throat. "What's your zodiacal sign?"

"Horse."

Mr. Luo got up to fetch his almanac. "So, you were born in 1966. And since we are now in 1982, that makes you about sixteen. We'll have to age you two years if you want to get a job with us. You can't read Chinese, can you?"

"No." I could not read Chinese, and I could not read Moso either, since our language has no written form and I had never been to school. But there was a word for this in the city: I was illiterate, and Mr. Luo thought he could do something about it.

The next day I was admitted into the troupe as a singer. It had so happened that a singer had recently left, and since there was no representative of the Moso people, I was a perfect candidate. I was to receive thirty yuan a month and three meals a day, and sleep on a makeshift bed in the meeting room at the Cultural Bureau. Mr. Luo provided me an identity card and a work permit with an official circular red stamp, Aunt Luo gave me a blanket, and the director of the troupe offered some gym clothes. I was overjoyed. I ran directly to the Horsemen's Hotel to pass word that my mother should not worry, that I had a job in Xichang, and that it paid twice as much as the job at the school.

Life with the performing troupe was very exciting. We were forty performers from the different nationalities of Sichuan: Yi, Tibetans, Lisu, Miao, Hui, and a few Han who could impersonate various ethnic peoples. In actual fact, since we were not a very large troupe, we had to learn something of everything. We all trained in singing and dancing and playing musical instruments, and we all trained in the different nationality styles, and this time, unlike what had happened in Chengdu, and to Mr. Luo's surprise, I had no trouble learning new songs. All I had to do was listen a few times and I could do it.

My daily routine began a little before nine, when the songwriters came into the meeting room. I got up, rolled up my bedding, got dressed, and went down to the dining room to have breakfast—warm water with steamed buns, and every time I had breakfast, I missed my mother's butter tea. After breakfast, while the songwriters organized our repertoire in the meeting room, I joined the other artists for the daily practice, learning and rehearsing new songs and dances. Once a week we piled into a big bus and traveled to different towns and villages, where we sang and danced in front of factory workers or schoolchildren. Sometimes we also went on longer tours, staying out for a few days, visiting schools and work units farther afield. My first performance was at a meeting of cadres, and we had to sing "Mother's love and Father's love are not as good as Mao Zedong's love. Mao, Mao, we the poor common people love you." The music was really heartwarming. It made you feel so grateful and ready to lay down your life for your country, but the words puzzled me.

"How could Mao's love be stronger than a mother's love? We Moso believe that nothing is better than a mother's love."

"Mao Zedong is a god," the teacher answered sternly.

How could Mao Zedong be a god? I wondered. Mao Zedong was neither a mountain nor a lama. And I had seen him in Beijing, lying in his glass coffin. He had a mole on his chin just like my mother. . . . But my teacher was not in the mood to discuss either Mao's mole or his coffin. "Let's get on with the song." She cut my questioning in the same tone as my Ama had used on a couple of occasions when I had said something improper in front of my brothers.

Besides the music, what I liked best about Xichang was the moon. Another name for Xichang is Yuechang, which means Moon City. The moon in Xichang was more shiny, more silvery, and much bigger than it ever was in Zuosuo. At night I often rode my bicycle to the outskirts of the city and looked at the moon rising high into the sky.

When all was said, however, Xichang was a small place. A few months went by, then New Year, and I began to feel bored.

One spring day I was washing my clothes in the yard, dreaming of all the places I had visited in the world besides Xichang, only half listening to the conversations of the singers who were chewing on sunflower seeds on a nearby bench, when something caught my ear and made me look up from my laundry.

"Why are you showing me this? I don't want to go to Shanghai!" Xiaolan was laughing. "Do you want to go?"

"Are you dreaming? The conservatory?" Shaga replied, spitting out the shells of the sunflower seeds on the ground.

"But why not? They have a special class for minority students. You won't have to sit the academic examinations."

My heart suddenly began to beat wildly. I knew only two things about Shanghai: what Dashe the horseman had once showed us on the label on his sweater — "Made in Shanghai" — and that it was a long way from Xichang and a lot bigger. I dropped my clothes back into the soapy water.

"Xiaolan! Are you going to Shanghai?" I asked.

"Of course not! What would I do there? Imagine if I went all the way there and they didn't take me! What shame. I could never show my face again."

"Do you mind showing me the pamphlet?"

Xiaolan paused and looked at me for a moment, and she laughed again. "Here, you can have it!"

I wiped my hands dry and took the pamphlet and asked Xiaolan to show me the characters that said Shanghai Conservatory — I already knew the character for *music*. Then I carefully folded the piece of paper and put it inside my pocket.

"What do you mean, you want to go to Shanghai?" the director of the performing troupe asked, looking at the pamphlet. "Your ass hasn't warmed up the bench you're sitting on, and already you have ambitions to outdo all of us. Shanghai Conservatory is the best music school in the country!" But later that week, after he had spoken with Mr. Luo, he came to find me. "If you want to go to Shanghai, you can go. But we won't pay for it."

But how could I pay for a train ticket across China? With only thirty yuan a month, I had no savings. And I owned nothing of value. I owned nothing but my identity card, the clothes on my back, the costume I had worn on my ceremony, and another the Cultural Bureau had made for me — and the jade bracelet my mother had given me. The bracelet was very old, it had belonged to my mother's grandmother. It had to be worth something.

I sold my mother's bracelet for 140 yuan.

At the end of June, the director of the troupe handed me a letter of recommendation with a red stamp on it, and another piece of paper I was to give to Djihu, a Yi student at the conservatory. "Mr. Luo will be sending a telegram to Shanghai to let them know you're coming. There's just enough time for you to make it to the auditions," he said. And he added with a strange sort of smile: "And you better get in, because we don't want you back here."

I thanked him and packed my costumes. The next day I said good-bye to Mr. Luo and my friends and walked to the station, where I took the train to Chengdu. I rode third-class, standing for twelve hours between squawking chickens and peeing babies. This was a very different train trip from the one I had made to Beijing almost a year before.

In Chengdu I had to wait another twelve hours before boarding the train for Shanghai. After purchasing my third-class ticket, I had seventy yuan left. Feeling flush, I went to buy some food for the trip—a whole smoked duck, some oranges, duck tongues, and bread—and came back to the noisy, crowded, outdoor third-class waiting hall to sit and wait out the hours. I soon became very anxious, and I started to pick at the duck, a little bit, then another bit, and before I knew it, I had eaten the whole duck, the oranges, the duck tongues, and the bread. Still, I had sixty yuan left, plenty enough to buy more food from the vendors on the train.

Riding third-class all the way to Chengdu was bad, but three days to Shanghai was much worse. After a few hours, the train attendants had given up on trying to sweep the overcrowded, foul-smelling carriage, and soon enough I was above my ankles in trash, choking on air thick with tobacco smoke. Next the ninety-degree inclination of the seat got the better of my back, and then my bladder filled. But I did not dare go to the bathroom for fear of losing my seat. I didn't want to stand up for the next two days. When I couldn't hold on anymore, I plucked up the courage to ask the woman sitting next to me to keep my seat. It felt good to stand up and stretch, even in such cramped quarters, but when I got to the toilet, it was in such a state that I almost threw up. It was blocked, yet people had continued to use it, and urine was running down the alleyway. Meanwhile, they stood in the overflowing piss, seemingly unaware. "What kind of people stand in their own piss?" I asked myself as I pushed and shoved my way to the equally fouled-up toilet in the next carriage. "And what kind of world is this?" On the second night, an exhausted man shoved the garbage to one side and curled under my feet while people threw wrapping paper and orange and apple peelings and spat out the shells of sunflower seeds over him, so that by the time he woke in the morning, he was almost completely covered in garbage. But he just shook himself and sat up, resting his back against my right leg, until it cramped and I had to tell him to move.

At the end of three long days and two yet longer nights, the train pulled into Shanghai railway station. I was so tired and dazed it took me some time to realize that at last it was over. I looked out the window. The station seemed so gray and rundown compared with Beijing. I couldn't believe this was Shanghai. I sat on my seat, not daring to move, until the train attendant came to sweep the garbage. She swept high and low, and as I was in her way, I was soon covered in it.

"Hey!" she cried out, looking up at my dirty trousers. "What are you doing sitting here? Everybody's got off the train."

"I'm going to Shanghai," I said stupidly in the Sichuan dialect.

The Audition

The taxi fare to the Music Conservatory was fifteen yuan, and I had to pay the driver before he would let me in the cab. I didn't blame him. I could only imagine what I looked like—but as we drove along the wide, shaded, tree-lined streets, I wondered if I had been robbed or if Shanghai was really that expensive. I had only thirty yuan left—one month's salary—and no job . . . but this was a very beautiful city—and nothing at all like Beijing. It was very hot. I wound down the car window and let the city air flood the taxi. It took my breath away, and for a moment I forgot about the money and the stickiness of my nylon trousers and that I had not washed or slept for three days. I was in Shanghai.

More streets and brick buildings with slanted roofs and shuttered windows, houses unlike anything I had seen in the other places, and then we stopped. "Here's the conservatory," the driver said. I looked around, puzzled—I expected a large, tall, square building with lots of glass windows, but we had stopped in front of a double gate in a wall, and there was nothing to distinguish those gates from the others in the street. "See? Music Conservatory! It's written above the gates," the taxi driver said, pointing across the street at the Chinese characters.

I did not dare go up to the gates just yet, and so I stood on the pavement and watched the students riding their bicycles, going in and out of the conservatory, waving at the old man who was guarding the gates and who was glaring at me from the opposite side of the street. They looked so elegant, so pretty with their long hair tied in ponytails, their white blouses and black trousers, their hips swaying as their feet pushed on the pedals. One carried a violin case under her arm. "One day I will be just like that. I too will ride through the gates of the music school on my bicycle with my hair in the wind, wearing a beautiful white blouse and clean black trousers." And I crossed the street.

But the old man would not let me in. I tried showing him the documents Mr. Luo had signed for me, but he would not even look at them and shooed me away like a dirty beggar. "Go! Go!" he shouted in a thick Shanghai accent, his mouth snarling over black teeth. So I moved out of barking range, and he sat back on his stool, sipping green tea from a big glass jar and puffing on one wet cigarette after another, occasionally darting a black look in my direction. And I waited anxiously, trying to think of what to do next, fearing the worst — could I have come all this way only to be turned away at the gates? And with only thirty yuan left in my pocket, not speaking beyond a spatter of standard Chinese, and barely able to read beyond a few basic characters . . . what was I going to do here in Shanghai? At the first opportunity, when the old man had run out of tea and gone into his little room to fill up his glass jar from his thermos flask, I sneaked past his back, through the gates, and kept running.

Inside the conservatory, it was a brand-new world. The buildings, I would learn later, were in colonial style, with white walls and red tiles. Instead of a concrete yard, there was a green lawn shaded by tall leafy trees. I walked around the campus excited, dazzled, and then gradually I began to feel self-conscious, ashamed of myself, of my dirty cheap clothes and my dirty face, feeling so like a dirty country girl. No one had paid any attention to me, but I suddenly felt an irresistible urge to wash and do my hair, and I rushed into the first bathroom I found.

When I had done my best to look like the students strolling on the campus lawn, I approached a couple of girls and showed them the piece of paper the director had written for Djihu, the Yi boy who was to help me. They shook their heads and said something I could not understand and called out to someone who then pointed me toward a building.

"How brave! You made it here all by yourself," Djihu said.

"You look surprised!" I replied, fishing for a compliment. I was rather proud of the fact that I had made it all the way to Shanghai and to the conservatory all on my own, and that I had even managed to find him.

But there was a simple explanation for Djihu's surprise. "I was expecting to be called to the gate to meet you. Also, I thought you would be here a bit earlier. Did you know that the deadline to register for the auditions is tomorrow?"

Djihu took me to the student guest house, but all the beds were already taken. Thus I spent my first night at the conservatory on a cotton quilt on the floor in one of the dormitories. And since I was so tired and I knew no one aside from Djihu, I went to bed a long time before the other girls got back to the dorm around midnight, laughing and shouting and eating late snacks as is the custom in Shanghai. As they passed by my bed on the floor, one dropped water over me and another a piece of greasy paper, but I was too tired to fight back.

The next morning I woke up to the inquiring looks of my roommates. Not knowing how to respond, I rolled up my bedding, picked up my bag, and went into the bathroom, where I changed into my white skirt and pink shirt and wrapped a wide black turban over my head. And I went out to meet Djihu, in traditional Moso costume, holding my head high and keeping my eyes on the space ahead, doing my best to ignore the curious faces turning toward me.

Djihu was waiting on the football field. We had to go to the registration office so that I could enroll for the auditions. There was a long line and it was perhaps two hours before we finally stood in front of the clerk's desk.

"Do you have an ID photo?" the clerk asked.

I gave her my papers and realized with a panic that I could not find my Xichang identity card. I had only two photographs of myself: one was on that card and the other in the newspaper cutting glued on the pantry door in our house. But the clerk was a stickler for the rules, and she would not hear of my enrolling for the audition before she had a photograph. We had no choice but to leave the campus and go to the photographer's. When we got back to the registrar's office, the clerk closed the door after us. I was the last student to register.

"Name?" the clerk asked.

"Yang Erche Namu."

"Strange name," the clerk said. "What nationality are you?"

"Moso."

"I've never heard of a Moso nationality." And she began enumerating the names of the fifty-five official Chinese minority nationalities.

"She means Naxi," Djihu interrupted her.

"Naxi?" the clerk continued, with a frown on her face. "Your costume doesn't look Naxi. Where do you come from?"

"I am from Sichuan, and I am not Naxi." I glared at Djihu.

Djihu smiled. "Actually, you're right." He turned to the clerk. "In Zuosuo the Moso are classed as Mongols."

The clerk looked at both of us in turn. "Can you make up your mind? What nationality are you?"

"Moso," I said firmly.

"Okay, Moso nationality." The clerk laughed. "Are all Moso girls as pretty as you are? Anyhow, what's your date of birth?"

"I'm not sure. . . ."

The clerk tilted her head sideways. "You don't know your date of birth?"

"What about the girl who enrolled before me?" I said, thinking that the girl looked about my age. "What's her date of birth?"

The clerk looked through her papers. "August 25, 1966."

"Mine, too. August 25, 1966." And it was about right, since Mr. Luo had said that I was born in 1966, the year of the horse. I handed her my brand-new identity photograph.

Half an hour later I had a new temporary identity card bearing the number 223. And I now had a day on which to celebrate my birthday.

The week of the auditions, a few hundred students, many of them accompanied by their mothers and fathers, sat on both sides of the wide corridors outside the audition halls. Above each door hung the most wonderful signs, announcers of dreams—opera, piano, orchestral instruments, composition, musicology, ethnic music, ethnic singing. The students held their music sheets and the parents carried bottles of water. Every now and then the mothers wiped a trace of smeared makeup off a tearful cheek, and the fathers whispered encouragement. The air was crammed with jittery expectation and the cacophony of stray notes escaping from the audition rooms. Shanghai Music Conservatory was the best music school in China. There could be no greater honor for the winners and no greater disappointment for the losers.

On my appointed day, I took a seat in the corridor. I was alone, without mother or father to encourage me, but I was almost a professional now, having spent so many months with the troupe in Xichang, and I remembered how we had won the competition in Yanyuan, and then in Xichang and Beijing. I could win in Shanghai too. Besides, I had to win. I had nowhere else to go.

As their numbers were called, students stood up and disappeared into the different halls — some almost running, others so slow that the parents had to push them. When they came out again, their eyes were bright and shining, searching eagerly for their parents' faces, or else downcast, as though they were looking for their parents' feet.

There were about forty students to audition for the minority music department. Because I had enrolled so late, my number was last. It seemed that I would never be called, and as time passed, the tension permeating the air began to get to me. I shuffled in my seat and rubbed my hands together. I felt very hungry as well. I stood up and began pacing up and down the corridor. For a moment I even thought of pushing in ahead of the others. Instead I peeked through the door into one of the audition halls, where a girl was singing in a weak trembling voice, until her mother tapped me on the shoulder and I went back to my chair.

More students disappearing and then reappearing, eyes bright with hope or shiny with tears. Suddenly a girl — not the girl with the weak voice but another — ran past me. She was covering her face with her hands and sobbing her heart out. And chasing after her was her mother. I couldn't help thinking of my Ama chasing after me on the mountain path.

What would she do if she were here, sitting next to me? And what if I were to fail, like this girl, what would my Ama say then? And what if I couldn't control the fear that was now coming over me? What if I were so scared that I could not sing?

I can hardly remember how or when my number was called. What I do know is that I walked straight up on the little stage, bypassing the pianist (I had no sheet music to give him), and I began singing immediately, without introducing myself or the song, barely greeting the examiners sitting at the table below me, cups of tea and notebooks in front of them. I also remember that I felt very annoyed at the examiner who had fallen asleep on the table, his white head on his folded arms. My first song was the song of our mountain goddess Gamu, and I wanted to wake that examiner. So my voice rose very high, high as the mountain peaks I had run away from, and loud enough to rattle the windows and for the old man to finally lift his head from his arms and reach out for his cup of tea.

After the song to Gamu, I sang the "Ahabala," the joyful song of the herdsmen, and then I began to sing "Madami," the love song, but the chief examiner said: "All right, all right! That's enough." And I knew they were pleased with me.

Life at the Conservatory

During the five years I spent at Shanghai Music Conservatory, I learned a great deal. I learned to sing and to read music and play the piano. I learned to speak Chinese correctly, and to read and write. Not a day went by when I did not feel grateful for what the conservatory was making of me. Whenever I went out of the school gates, I never failed to wear my student badge right in the middle of my chest for everyone to see that I was a student at the most prestigious music school in China. And every time someone looked at my badge, I felt my mother's pride, and I knew that at last I was making up for breaking up the school kitchen and running away from home. Every day I thought of my Ama, of my empty room at home, of my little brothers and my little sister, of Zhema. Sometimes I also thought of the teachers. And I thought of writing home. But I never did.

After the audition results had been posted, all the students had gone home, but I had nowhere to go and no money to go anywhere. The administrators thus considered my case and allowed me to stay in the guest house for the rest of the summer, even providing me with a small stipend. Minority students, I soon discovered, were especially well treated by the school administration. We had our own dining room that catered to dietary restrictions, and we were allowed to take days off on our traditional holidays—which would not be very useful to me because we Moso eat just about everything (though, unlike the Han, we do not eat dogs), and we only have two fixed holidays, New Year and our goddess festival, both of which take place during school vacations. Meanwhile, however, I spent the rest of that first summer staring out my bedroom window, strolling on the green lawn, or talking with the janitor, who had become my only friend and even lent me a small radio to practice Chinese. I did not dare go outside the conservatory, for fear that the old man guarding the gates would not let me come back in, and also for fear of ridicule—because I had only my gym clothes and Moso skirts to wear.

When school began in September, I requested to share a dormitory with Han Chinese students rather than with other minority students. I wanted to keep learning Chinese and speak it as well as I could, and I wanted to learn the ways of the modern world. And now I was walking up the corridor toward my room, my heart beating fast, my hands nervous, acutely aware that I was not only beginning a new life but that here my dream began.

We were five students per room, and in each room were two long tables, five chairs, and three beds, all double bunks. Since there were neither closets nor wardrobes, the bottom bunk nearest the door was used to store suitcases and personal effects. When I arrived, my roommates had not stored or organized anything and the room was in chaos. Each girl had brought at least two suitcases and there was stuff spread all over—clothes, special foods, extra blankets, books, soft toys. I had never seen so many personal effects. Even the gifts I had received for my Skirt Ceremony did not amount to anything when compared with what these girls had brought with them. And as I stood there, on the doorstep of the dormitory room, looking at all these things, a new emotion came over me, a sort of sadness wounded by humiliation, something I had never felt before, not even when I was hugging the yaks to keep warm or when I was too ashamed of my clothes to leave the conservatory. For the first time in my life, I felt poor.

I hugged my canvas bag and stepped through the doorway. My roommates stopped unpacking. They stared at me and then at each other. "Why did they put a minority girl in here?" one of them asked.

Although I was not as yet very familiar with the Shanghai accent, I understood the remark perfectly clearly. I also understood the long looks they were giving each other. The only thing I did not immediately grasp was that, being the last one to arrive, I had been left with the last of the bottom bunks, directly under the girl who had made the comment. Her name was Hong Ling and I was going to sleep under her bunk for the next five years.

Thankfully, during my first two years at school, I did not have much to do with my roommates or, for that matter, other students. I was enrolled in a two-year preparatory program for minority students designed to improve our Chinese language and to bring us up to standard academic level. When it became obvious that I was illiterate, however, my teachers organized to supplement my education with individual tutorials. I gradually moved back into the mainstream minority classes during my second year, although reading and writing remained a huge hurdle for me, and I often got into trouble for copying other students' work or cheating on my tests. Unfortunately, my teachers' sympathy did not extend to the effort that even plagiarism demanded of me.

But I truly was hardworking, and I loved student life — the laughter, the chatter and the tears, the mess in the rooms, the communal showers and the noise of the instruments, and of course the classes. My favorite were the ethnic music classes, where we learned songs from all the different nationalities of China. And singing practice was the class I enjoyed least, just as had happened in Chengdu, when I had rehearsed for the singing contest with Nankadroma. Voice training went so much against my own nature, and I proved so resistant and argumentative, that, in my first year, two teachers gave up on me—which says quite a lot because our teachers were almost always kind and very understanding, even if they never failed to voice genuine surprise when any of us performed as well as or better than the Han students.

FROM THE VERY START of my residence at the conservatory, I sought the friendship of foreign students and other minority students. Foreign students and ethnic minorities had one thing in common—we were not Han. "We Shanghainese don't do that," Hong Ling would say whenever she saw or heard of anything beyond her range of experience or when she was really in a bad mood: "Namu, something stinks in here! Did you eat mutton in the minority kitchen again?" Whereas my roommates saw themselves as models for ethnic minorities to follow, the foreign students were curious about our languages, our religions, our foods. They wanted to sing our songs, even try out our clothes and wear our jewelry. Conversely, all of us, including the Han students—even Hong Ling—wanted to know everything about the foreigners. China had been closed to the world for too long and everyone was hungry for everything foreign. But perhaps my own interest in foreigners was just a natural outcome. Now that I was living outside our mountains, wasn't it my destiny that I should befriend the blue-eyed, blond-haired people of my childhood fancies?

The whole world seemed to live at the conservatory—students from all over China but also from America, Europe, Africa, and Japan. The foreign students' dormitory was adjacent to our building. Like my four roommates, I envied the foreigners' living conditions. Whereas we fitted six beds in our dorm, they had one room each, or at worst shared a room between two. Where we had bare floors, they had a carpet—although it was thin and somewhat wrinkly—and their rooms were heated in winter, and they had access to hot showers whenever they wished. But from the very first day, I was also fascinated by the white, pink, and black skins, the strange-colored hair and eyes, the facial features so different from our own, and the loud alien sounds coming out of the rooms, the music and the laughter. Right in front of our window, there lived a Congolese student who spent all his spare time blowing discordant rhythms out of his saxophone instead of practicing the marching tunes his teacher had instructed him in. Next to the Congolese was a Dutch student. She was in China for only a semester, to work on Chinese language and opera singing. She practiced for hours and hours and she sang so badly. Once, when she was doing scales outside in the yard, I could not bear it anymore and leaned out the window to sing back to her. She stopped and looked up at me and applauded.

"You sing so beautifully! What's your name?"

"Namu."

"Come down! Come to my room and have some coffee."

I liked the coffee, it was unctuous and simultaneously bitter and sweet, and it had milk in it and looked like butter tea.

"Do you like jazz?" she asked, tapping on her cassette player.

Jazz sounded like the Congolese student's music, and I was not sure what to make of it, and we could not talk a great deal on account of her limited Chinese, but we became friends immediately. I liked everything about her, the way her green eyes narrowed when she laughed, the way she moved her hands when she spoke, and how she sat cross-legged on her bed. She was very tall, and she had very white skin. One hot sunny afternoon, she lay on the lawn for a couple of hours to try to get a tan, but instead she turned bright red.

"Now look what you've done!" I said, laughing at her. "Your face looks like a monkey's butt!"

She found that funny as well, and from that time on, whenever she wanted to have coffee with me, she shouted under my window, "Namu, come and have coffee with Monkey's Butt!"

I went to the foreign dormitory as often as I could, in spite of all the obstacles the school administrators put in our way—the registration process, the guard at the bottom of the stairs, and the service people who would glare and follow with their eyes burning into your back as you walked down the corridors. If you visited too often, the administration would ask you to explain why you spent so much time with the foreigners. And there were other risks. That same year, a Chinese student became too friendly with one of the Africans. She loved the way he walked and how he always wore freshly ironed clothes. One night she slipped back into the dormitory and recounted for her girlfriends how it felt to make love with the black man. Within a few days, everybody in the school was talking about it as well, and they were looking at her as though she were dirt. The next week she was expelled.

One Saturday night the Uygur minority students from Xinjiang province had a party and I was introduced to two new foreigners, exchange students at Fudan University in Shanghai. One was Turkish and to my amazement looked just like the Xinjiang students. He spoke Chinese with an accent, of course, but then so did the Uygurs—and he did not shake my hand but instead kissed my cheek. And I found myself recoiling from his thick mustache.

"A kiss without a mustache is like bread without butter!" he said, laughing out loud. Then he turned to the other foreigner and introduced Umbalo.

Umbalo was from Mexico. She was wearing huge glasses and her black hair was cut short, and very messy. The way she was drinking warm beer straight from the bottle truly impressed me. At this time I drank only tea and coffee and right away I thought of Nankadroma and her broken heart, and how close we had been. I felt immediately attracted and the feeling was mutual; we spent the rest of the evening together. After the party, Umbalo came again to visit me at the conservatory, and before long we were going out riding on our bicycles almost every day. Unlike my Dutch friend's, Umbalo's Chinese was perfect. Indeed, in those early days she spoke much better Chinese than I did. When we became closer, I found out that her parents were also living in China. Her father was Mexico's ambassador to Beijing, on his second appointment to the People's Republic, where he had first worked when Umbalo was a little girl. Umbalo had lived in many countries and she spoke eight languages, although she insisted that she did not speak all of them as well as she spoke Chinese.

Umbalo was the first true friend I ever had. She introduced me to all the people she knew, artists, scholars, musicians, small-business people, money changers, and still more foreigners. Every time we stopped to greet a foreigner, she spoke in another language. Every now and then we also came across somebody she would later describe as "my original boyfriend." And I would tease her, saying that she sounded like a woman from Lake Lugu. Yet we certainly had very different views of life. Umbalo had been raised with all the comforts in the world and cared for none of them. She wore baggy torn-up jeans and never put on makeup or did her hair, and she liked to talk about politics and the environment. For my part, I could not get enough of the material world and its superficialities. In fact, I had one burning wish at this time — to go into the special Friendship Stores and the hotels where only "foreign friends" were allowed to shop. I wanted to buy nice clothes, a silk dressing gown and silk underwear, and a suitcase and coffee and the other things the foreigners had access to. But then again, my friend Umbalo was a sophisticated world traveler and I was prepared to learn whatever I could from her. So I began to take an interest in the finer things of life and accompanied her to the theater and the museums. And the following November, I met her mother.

My teachers had decided to send me to Beijing to record some music for a documentary about the Moso people. I was very excited, as I had not gone to the capital since the contest with Nankadroma, nearly three years before. But Umbalo was almost happier than I was. She wanted me to visit her parents.

When I told my roommates that I was planning to stay with Umbalo's family at the Mexican embassy, they were horrified. "You're crazy! The embassies are full of cameras. All the foreign diplomats are spies. You're going to get into big trouble." What they said worried me so much that when I got to the beautiful streets of San Litun, where the embassies were, and I saw the soldiers posted at every gate, I almost turned back. But Umbalo was my friend, and I had spoken to her mother on the telephone only half an hour or so before; I could not let them down now. I took a few deep breaths, tried my hardest to stop my knees from shaking, and moved on. As things turned out, I did not have to test my resolve for too long before I heard someone calling out to me from across the street: "Namu!"

It was Umbalo's mother. She had been waiting outside the embassy gates, looking out for me, and had no trouble recognizing me from the description I had given her over the phone.

From the moment I set my eyes on her, I forgot my fears. I was spellbound. I had never seen Umbalo dressed in anything but jeans and old sweaters, but Mrs. Ambassador was pure elegance. And Mrs. Ambassador dressed not only better than her daughter, but better than anyone I had ever seen.

She greeted me warmly in very good Chinese and brought me past the guard into the compound, where we walked arm in arm.

Inside the embassy house, everything was comfortable, luxurious, and tasteful in a way that I had never experienced. There was central heating, and colorful rugs were on the floor. The rooms were furnished in Mexican style and the bed where I was to sleep (Umbalo's bed) had large, square, fluffy pillows and crisply ironed sheets. At dinner I was mesmerized by the chandeliers, the tall wine glasses, the silver cutlery, the way Mrs. Ambassador spoke to her maid, with consideration and respect—and how she ate quietly with her mouth closed, and how she addressed Mr. Ambassador. Mrs. Ambassador was very refined and cultured—there seemed to be books about every subject and in every language in every room. I loved Umbalo dearly, but meeting her mother had the same power of revelation I had experienced when I had stepped out of the Jeep and into the grimy shower room in Yanyuan. Before I met Mrs. Ambassador, I thought that China was the whole world, but now I knew that outside our middle country there was yet another world perhaps as large and as beautiful as China. And I wanted to see that world, to travel. I wanted to be just like Mrs. Ambassador.

I stayed in Beijing only two days, just long enough to complete the recording for the documentary—which incidentally was to win a major prize at an international festival a year or two later, only to be censored by the Chinese authorities and never shown to the Chinese public. I was very sad to say good-bye to Mrs. Ambassador, but at the same time, I could not wait to get back to the dormitory and see Hong Ling's face when I opened my little suitcase filled with all the wonderful things Mrs. Ambassador had put in there—clothes, books, and music cassettes and exotic Mexican foods.

Almost all students at the conservatory received parcels of food and clothes as well as spending money from their parents. The better off had perhaps one hundred yuan a month. I had only the thirty-yuan stipend that the school provided me, which left me feeling not only inferior but hungry. It was such a small amount that I had usually spent everything on buying meal tickets by the third week of the month. To earn extra meal tickets, I ran errands for my roommates, fetching their mail from the post office and their thermos of hot water for making tea and washing their faces. Still, I never seemed to have enough to eat. I was always hungry, and in the winter, sitting in the unheated dorm, I was always cold. Some mornings, I was so cold that I could not bring myself to get out of bed. I would lie there under my quilt until the last minute before class time, thinking of the fireplace at home, of hot butter tea and roasted potatoes. And then I would think of my Ama's face in the glow of the fireplace. Was she thinking of me? Did she miss me? Would I ever see her again? But of course, I would see my Ama again. When I was famous. When I could make up for the terrible thing I had done and she could be proud of me again. And that was why I was here, at the best music school in the whole of China. Because I wanted to show my mother that I could have my dream.

On the weekends my roommate Hong Ling went home to her parents' house, and on Sunday nights she always brought dumplings back to our room. The next morning she would eat a couple and then look at me, sigh, and hand me the rest. "Here, you can have them. I eat this sort of thing all the time!" There was no mistaking her condescension, but I did not know the meaning of the word *full,* and my stomach always won over my pride, if not my resentment.

Sometimes Teacher Cui, our ethnic music teacher, also took care of my stomach, inviting me to his house for all sorts of delicious spicy food. Once he put on a record for me and played it at low volume.

"Hey! What is this?" I shouted with enthusiasm. "It's so beautiful. Why don't you turn it up?"

"Shhh, listen," Teacher Cui hushed me. "It's from Taiwan. We're not supposed to be listening to this here. It's decadent music."

I liked decadent music. It was so unlike the Communist repertoire we learned, which always had something martial about it, something to raise the collective spirit and send you marching off for the glory of country and revolution. The Taiwanese music was soft and romantic and moved only your heart.

EARLY IN THE SPRING I was sitting in the dining hall, eating a bowl of noodles and listening to a conversation between two boys at a nearby table. One of them had caught my eye because of the showy way he dressed and a very short haircut that made him look like a foreigner. He was not a student at the conservatory. He was a guitar player, with his own band, making twenty-four yuan an hour playing gigs in restaurants and nightclubs, and he was looking for a singer.

"Hey! I can sing in your band!" I called out to him. "I'm a singer!"

His name was Zhu He, and we became friends immediately. In less than two hours, I was at the restaurant, rehearsing with the rest of the band, singing decadent, fluffy, beautiful Taiwanese pop songs. Most were by Deng Lijun, whose music was officially forbidden but, thanks to the black market economy and the national disregard for copyright, was at the time so popular that cassette tapes were available at every street corner. That year you could hear Deng Lijun's songs in every Shanghai street, coming out of restaurants, apartment buildings, or small stores, whistled on all the building sites, hummed on everyone's lips.

From the first day of rehearsal, Zhu He was very pleased with me, and so was the owner of the Four Seasons restaurant, who quickly reckoned that since I was a student, there was no reason to pay me a professional fee. Thus, instead of the twenty-four yuan the other members of the band earned, I got seven, and a small picnic bag with a cup of orange juice, a piece of cake, and an apple. But I was more than satisfied. In the mid-1980s, orange juice and cake were luxury foods in China, and seven yuan for one hour of singing three times a week made twenty-one yuan a week, which was no small supplement to my thirty-yuan monthly stipend. Besides, Zhu He soon had more work to give me. Within a few weeks I was singing in three venues at least three nights a week — starting at 7:00 P.M. at the Four Seasons and ending after eleven at the Cherry Blossom nightclub, just in time for me to cycle back to the conservatory before the old man closed the gates. Meanwhile, Zhu renamed me Yang-yang, which was cute and much easier for customers to remember than Yang

Erche Namu, and he taught me to introduce myself by speaking in a sugary Hong Kong accent: "Hello, everyone, my name is Yang-yang! Welcome to you all." The effect was pure kitsch — so kitsch that I could not bring myself to invite Umbalo (who hated anything cheap and fake) to come and watch me perform. Well, it was fake and it was tacky, but I loved being onstage, and it paid well.

In fact, I was not only eating very well now, I also had a disposable income, and I was not averse to showing off. I asked Umbalo to take me to the Friendship Store and help me buy a new suitcase, lipstick, coffee. I borrowed fashion magazines from the foreign students and had new clothes made, including a bright yellow jumpsuit and a pink miniskirt. One day when I was wearing the miniskirt, an American boy called out to me, "Namu, you have beautiful legs!" I looked at him and I looked down at my legs, not understanding, and he said, in English this time, "Sexy!" Now, *sexy* was one of those English words we all understood, but I felt intrigued. It had never occurred to me that legs could be beautiful or provocative; I had never thought of legs as anything but a means of getting places. I just showed mine to look like the foreign models in the magazines. For us Moso, sexy and beautiful were the same thing, and beauty was a woman's face, a man's long graceful hands, a tall gait (for both men and women). "Yes, really sexy!" the American repeated, laughing at the puzzled expression on my face. I too laughed, at the compliment, but then I thought of Geko, who would never have thought to tell me that I had sexy legs.

In the village that was the Music Conservatory, conspicuous consumption and outlandish dress could not fail to set tongues wagging, and since I had kept my work a secret, all sorts of rumors and speculation were circulating about me. It did not take long for the noise to reach my teachers' ears.

When they found out about my work, they were not impressed.

"No student from the conservatory has ever sung in a nightclub," they said.

But I objected that my stipend was so small, that I had no family support, and that I really needed to earn money — and if they did not want me to earn money, they would have to feed me. The battle went on for a few days but the teachers grew tired before I did. After all, these were the mid-1980s, a time of liberalization, economic and social reforms. Shanghai was fast renewing with its cosmopolitan past, and the young had freedoms their parents had never dreamed of. Eventually I heard no more about it and I assumed I had won the argument.

Next I became an entrepreneur. At this time in China, everybody was crazy for everything made in Taiwan — not only pop music but also books and movies. Things made in Taiwan or even Hong Kong had all the appeal of things made in the capitalist foreign world but with the advantage of Chinese language and culture. At the conservatory, students craved Taiwanese romance novels filled with heart-wrenching individualistic bourgeois sentimentality, and the books were so hard to find that some students had taken it upon themselves to sell handwritten copies, while others were causing huge backlogs at the school's photocopier. On a tip I had been given at the nightclub, I decided to go to Beijing to buy a supply of books by the two writers most in demand, San Mao and Chong Yao. I had made enough money that I could purchase a plane ticket, so I flew to Beijing one morning (my very first plane trip) and returned that same evening with two huge boxes filled with books, including several dozen copies of *Outside the Window* by Chong Yao. I soon became the most popular girl on campus, renting the books out for five yuan each, and in a short time I had made back my plane fare.

Chong Yao's novel, however, almost cost me my place at the conservatory.

According to school rules, all lights had to be turned off in the dormitory by 11:00 P.M., so that after eleven, we read by flashlight. One evening Hong Ling, who was reading *Outside the Window*, called out from the bunk above me:

"Hey, Namu, pass me your light for a moment! I'm out of batteries."

I handed her the light and took the opportunity of the break to put my own book down and go to the bathroom. But when I came back, Hong Ling wanted to keep the light a little longer, just to finish a sentence, then just to finish another paragraph, and another, and then a page. . . .

After fifteen minutes or so, I grew impatient. "Hong Ling! Give me back my light, now."

But she had no intention of giving me the flashlight. She made more excuses and ignored me, until I pressed her more and she snapped, "Hey, muddy butt, what's your hurry?" and she turned over on the bed, showing me her back. This was no longer about Chong Yao's novel. Hong Ling had decided to teach me a lesson, to remind me that I used to fetch her thermos flask and feel grateful for eating her dumplings and that however I dressed and whatever money I made on renting books and singing at nightclubs, I was and would always be a peasant girl who had dirtied her butt in the mud of the fields.

"It's my torch and I want it now!" I raised my voice. "Get up and get your own batteries!"

"Oh, fuck your mother!"

That was it. I'd heard enough. I'd heard enough the very first day I had walked into the dormitory, three years ago. I grabbed at her blankets, and then at her pajama shirt. The flashlight flew across the room, and at last I got hold of her hair and pulled her off the bed, screaming and crying in terror, and I thrashed her. When I finally let go of her and went to turn on the light, she was whimpering on the floor, her face all red, her hair a mess, her pajamas torn off her back. The other three girls were sitting on their beds looking on, terrified. Still furious, I grabbed everything I could find that belonged to Hong Ling, including her suitcases, and I threw the whole lot out the window. The light had now gone on in the corridor and other girls were at our door. "What happened?" "Hong Ling, are you all right?" And seeing the fear in their faces, I stormed past them, out of the room and into the corridor, where I went banging and shouting at the doors that had not opened yet. "If you want to know what this minority hillbilly, muddy butt, country bumpkin did to Hong Ling, come out of your beds and see for yourselves!"

That night, when everyone had gone back to their beds, I slept very well. Next afternoon, however, I was called to the director's office, where Hong Ling, her mother, father, and brother and three administrators were waiting for me. I was soundly chastised, reproached, and required to apologize. But I could not apologize. Hong Ling had insulted my mother. What she had done was worse than anything. She could not have hurt me more if she had stabbed me in the heart. I turned to Hong Ling's mother. "I know I should not have hit her. You're her mother and she's your own flesh, but I am also my mother's flesh. Hong Ling should respect my mother. She should not insult my mother. And she should not insult me because I am a minority and I am from the countryside. Even a rabbit will bite if you taunt it long enough."

In the end I had to write a self-criticism, and my name and the story of Hong Ling's beating were put on the disciplinary notice board for everyone to see, and for weeks afterward, I would hear students whisper as I walked past, "This

minority girl can really fight." But it was better than being expelled. And no doubt I would have been expelled if I had
been a Han student, because I had committed a very serious
offence by thrashing my roommate, and Hong Ling was the
daughter of an influential family—but no administrator at
the conservatory wanted to risk my lodging a complaint at
the Nationalities Institute in Beijing.

Still, the thought that I had almost lost my place at the
conservatory sent shivers down my spine. Where else could
I go? What would I do if I lost my dream? And how would I
ever face my mother again? Because one day, yes, one day, I
would go home to my Ama. I would become a famous singer
and bring glory to my people, and I would go home to my
Ama with my head high, and she would forgive everything.
She would have to forgive me.

The experience with Hong Ling left me very nervous and
more conscious of the boundaries I should not attempt to
cross. Two things had always struck me as especially worth
avoiding: politics and sex, my own knowledge of which was
extremely rudimentary and almost entirely derived from
the compulsory classes everyone was officially subjected to,
everywhere in China.

In actual fact, in the mid-1980s no one in China cared
about politics, or more exactly, no one cared for politics
classes, but in the five years I spent at the conservatory, I
never dared miss—because I never felt entirely secure of my
own position, at first because of my poor level in Chinese
class, and later on, on account of my work at the nightclubs
and then the incident with Hong Ling; or perhaps I did not
dare miss classes simply because the conservatory was my
dream and I would not have risked my place for anything,
least of all by breaking a rule no one really cared for. As
things were, however, politics classes were mandatory but I
was often the only student in the classroom. No one else

bothered to come and the few who did usually got so bored that they fell asleep on their desks before time was up. At times I even wondered if they did not just come to class for a nap, for the opportunity to recover from the previous night's party.

Sometimes even the teachers fell asleep. But occasionally they talked from their hearts, mostly of their experiences in the Cultural Revolution. Of course, I too remembered the Red Guards putting up their posters on our village walls, and I had not forgotten the worse details of the stories the horsemen told around the campfire, but I had somehow assumed that this cruelty was something the Han—that imaginary bogeyman our mothers threatened us with when we were naughty—had done to get *us*. Until I heard my teachers speaking in the politics class, I had no idea that the Cultural Revolution had happened all over China—neighbors spying on neighbors, friends betraying friends, children spitting on their own parents, students beating their teachers. And as I watched my teachers speaking with trembling hands of the ten years of bitterness, all I could think was, these people are mad. These people are mad and dangerous. But as to who "these people" were exactly, I had no idea.

Sex for its part was entirely devoid of poetry—taught not in songs and clever improvisation but as part of the general curriculum in physical hygiene during which we learned about the various body parts that distinguished men and women and thus enabled the mechanics of procreation. As for sex without procreation, our teacher told us it was a healthy hobby in which married couples could safely engage up to twice weekly. I thought of Moso women singing around the bonfires, making love under the stars, lighting the fires in their flower rooms, not too bright, not too hot, but just right so that their bodies could relax. Perhaps Moso bodies were different from Han ones. When I had first walked into the communal showers at the conservatory, I had found the Han girls so white and their bodies so flat, their breasts so small. No wonder Han people did not need to make love, I now thought, listening to the teacher. For the Han girls had looked at me as well. They had stopped talking and fixed their curious eyes on my dark skin. Then one of them had said, "Why does she have such big breasts?"

"All minority women are like her. They're like foreigners. It's because they eat dairy products," another diagnosed.

But a year or so into my schooling, I discovered that it was not Han and Moso bodies that were different but our minds. Students at the conservatory were just as interested in lovemaking as Moso peasants, and eager to take advantage of any dark recess that could offer privacy. And others also took advantage of the dark recesses — the security personnel who seemed to enjoy peering at the couples even more than they did catching them out. Nonetheless, if and when students were caught, there was only one punishment, and it was swift and disgraceful — expulsion from the school, as had happened to the Chinese girl who had fallen in love with the African.

And now there was another girl everyone talked about, a beautiful Han girl who had fallen in love with one of her classmates. She had taken the train to a country town to have an illegal abortion, and she had come back in such a terrible state that the teachers soon discovered what had happened. When she came out of the hospital, the girl was called by the school's administration to be criticized and was told to write a confession, to name the father of her baby, and to give all the details of their encounters. But she was not so easily subdued. Instead of writing her boyfriend's name, she gave the names of eleven teachers — so that when the administrators and the teachers read her statement, they decided to forget about the confession altogether, and she was not expelled.

But the school had to make an example of her, and the story of her abortion appeared on the disciplinary notice board for everyone to sneer at. This terrified me.

When male students looked at me, I looked away, no matter how brightly their eyes shone. I laughed and joked and went to parties, where we danced cheek to cheek to slow, decadent music, but I never danced with the same boy too many times, and I never let anyone walk me back to the dorm late in the night. Yet, before I went to sleep, I often thought of Geko, and as my body grew older, I thought of him more and more often. What was he doing now? Who was loving him? What would he think of me riding a bicycle in the streets of Shanghai? In these sweet waking dreams, I imagined myself alone in my flower room and Geko tapping on my window. I always got up and opened my door now. But this was only in my village, in my imagination. Here in Shanghai, love was the most dangerous thing of all, and I stayed well clear of it.

One day a classmate told me that there was a letter for me at the office.

"Are you sure?" I asked incredulously.

I had never yet received a letter. I had thought of writing to my mother many times — surely she must be anxious to know what was happening to me. But every time I thought of writing, I decided against it. My Ama could not read. If I wrote, she would have to find someone to read the letter for her, and that would probably cost her at least a chicken. There was no point in making life harder than it needed to be.

But who could have written to me? Could the letter be from Zuosuo? Could something have happened to my Ama? I ran to the school post office. My classmate was right. My name was on the notice board.

The envelope was thick. It was not from Zuosuo, but not so far from home either; the sender's address was in Lijiang. I turned the letter over. The handwriting was very beautiful, so beautiful that I hesitated before tearing open the envelope. Inside there were eight pages, and at the top of each page, a beautiful letterhead saying *Camellia* magazine. I started to read.

Dear little sister Namu,

My name is Lamu Gatusa. Please forgive me for writing to you without a formal introduction. I am from the Moso village of Labei, in the mountains. Last year I graduated from Normal University in Kunming, and I am now working in Lijiang as a writer for the Camellia *magazine. Two months ago I went home to my family, and I stopped in Ninglang on the way, to visit our Living Buddha, who has just been reinstated by the government. He told me your story and asked me to write to you because we are two young Moso who are making a name for ourselves and our people in the outside world. Our guru says that we have been isolated by the mountains for so long, our people need scholars and gifted artists. He thinks you are the pride of our people.*

Dear little Namu, I wish I had met you before you left. Everyone speaks so well of you, and I am still a single man. . . .

But how are you? Did your lips who loved drinking butter tea get used to eating rice porridge? Did the bare feet that climbed the side of the mountains get used to walking in high heels on the streets of Shanghai? Did your ears used to the sighing of the mountain pines get used to the din of city traffic? . . .

I READ THE LETTER OVER AND OVER. Suddenly my village seemed so close. Suddenly, it was as though my Ama was standing next to me, smiling, her beautiful face glowing with pride, just as it had when I had come back from Beijing with two hundred yuan rolled in pretty red paper. And Gatusa, who had written, "I am still a single man...." I laughed out loud. A Moso man just could not waste an opportunity! And the Living Buddha, who had been recalled from farmwork and who was saying such good things about me. And all the people were proud of me. "They've forgiven me," I thought. My Ama has forgiven me! I can go home now! I can go home anytime I want. I'm going to see my mother again, and Zhema and my brothers and little Jiama, who must be so grown up.

I ran back to the dormitory, took out a letter pad, and sat down to write my very first letter. I sat, and I thought about what to say, acutely aware that whatever I wrote, I could not write only for Gatusa but also for my Ama and my little brothers and my sisters and all our neighbors—for the Living Buddha even. All of which, in the final count, proved a rather tall order. I did not know what to say or where to start. When at last I had put a few lines on the paper, my handwriting looked so clumsy, my sentences seemed so banal by comparison to Gatusa's beautiful prose, I could not bear it. I tried for a whole week; I wrote a few pages, and then I tore the letter and threw it in the wastebasket.

At the end of the week, I thought, "Lijiang is in the middle of nowhere, surely you can't buy *Outside the Window* over there." And I took the book off the shelf. Chong Yao was such an eloquent writer, I was sure I could find something in her novel that could express my emotions — something beautiful, something worthy of Gatusa's letter. I began carefully selecting passages, copying, editing names and places. At last my own eight-page letter was ready. I sent it off, and the following week I had a reply from Gatusa. He thought I wrote beautifully.

For the rest of the school year, I received a letter from

Gatusa every week, and I never failed to reply to him, always matching the exact number of pages. Over the months, he wrote ever more poetically and I plagiarized ever more efficiently. I now spent all my spare time in the library and the bookstores, reading, researching, looking for a poem, for a dedication, a prologue, a story that could express what my heart felt and my talents failed me to write. And if nothing else should come of it, I thought, my reading skills were improving dramatically.

In the meantime, I kept all of Gatusa's letters inside my pillowcase and I read them again and again. I thought of him constantly. I was in love. I imagined, quite naturally, that he looked something like Geko — tall with dark skin, beautiful long and strong fingers, and I pictured him sitting at his office desk at the *Camellia* magazine, writing, smoking a cheap cigarette, blowing smoke rings into the air, searching for inspiration. I saw myself serving him butter tea, standing by his side, my hand resting on his shoulder, my fingernails painted pink. I slowly massaged his tired shoulders and then I bent my head to his and whispered softly in his ear, leaving a trace of pink lipstick on his delicate earlobe. I imagined we were just like the lovers in *Outside the Window*.

I was never so happy. My heart was filled with Gatusa's poetry. Even the voice lessons became easier. I listened to my teacher, and I smiled at her. That year I also made my first professional recording. It was called *A Moso Girl Sings of Love,* and I sang every song for Gatusa. The world seemed such a joyful place and the future was so bright. Time flew. In the summer I spent part of the long vacation in Beijing with Umbalo and her family, and when school began again in September, I was already looking forward to the New Year and the winter holidays. I had decided to go home — to see my mother and to meet Gatusa. Or perhaps it was the other way around.

Coming Home

In China the idea of spending New Year apart from one's family is almost unbearable, and I had spent too many New Year holidays on my own in the miserably cold dormitory, dreaming of going home. Early in the fall of 1986, I wrote to Gatusa that I had made up my mind to come home for New Year. It had been such a long time since I had seen my family. And such a long time since I had broken up the school kitchen, surely I no longer had anything to fear. I was now the pride of my people — I had recorded my first professional cassette, and I was two years from graduating from the best music school in the country.

This time I would not travel to Chengdu but to Kunming, in Yunnan province. Gatusa had arranged to meet me in Ninglang, where we were to visit the Living Buddha, and from Ninglang I could go all the way to the eastern shore of Lake Lugu by Jeep.

I carried two suitcases filled with gifts — clothes, coffee, tea, candy, tiger balm ointment. I also had a gold ring for my mother, a long wool coat for my father, and two boxes of American cigarettes for Gatusa. The gifts had stretched my resources somewhat and I had to travel third-class on the train, but the thought of Gatusa waiting for me at the end of the journey made everything so much easier to bear. In addition, I was with five classmates from the conservatory—Han, Bai, and Yi students who were going home to Yunnan province. We had four seats among us, which made things more comfortable. At night we took turns resting on the benches or sleeping against each other's shoulders, and during the day we played cards and sang and told jokes and made the best of it. In Kunming I said good-bye to my friends and took the twenty-four-hour bus to Lijiang, and after a night's sleep in Lijiang, the twelve-hour bus to Ninglang, via Huapin and Yongshen. On that last leg, everybody seemed to be throwing up, and all I could do not to lose patience was to remind myself of the first time I had traveled by car on the mountain road. And then, as we neared Ninglang, the sight of the open blue sky and the red mountains, and thoughts of Gatusa, almost made me forget my grief.

The bus drove into the station and stopped, and the passengers rushed out of their seats, lighting cigarettes, pushing each other, tripping over bags and feet; they could not wait to get off. I took the time to pour a little water from my drinking bottle onto a cloth and to wipe my face clean. I put on my pink lipstick and brushed my shortish hair. I really wanted to look my best.

Careful not to tread in anything disgusting in my slick city boots, I got off the bus and stumbled past the others on the uneven concrete pavement toward the back of the bus, where I picked up my two cases. Then I went to stand on the porch, from where I gazed anxiously about the yard, looking among peasants in blue cotton garb and Yi women in colorful dusty skirts for a tall, dark, handsome Moso writer wearing a gray wool sweater, a white-collar shirt, and a long black coat.

There was no one fitting this description.

But I noticed, a few feet away from me, a short man in

white sports shoes and a ridiculous white jacket who was staring at me. Meeting his eyes, I felt uncomfortable and turned away. And when the short man walked over toward me, I suddenly became desperate for Gatusa to arrive.

"The bus came in early," he said in Moso.

"Where is Gatusa?" I answered him, barely looking at him, worried that something wrong had happened. Maybe there had been an accident.

"But I am Gatusa!"

I looked at him, incredulous. This was Gatusa! No, that just could not be!

A mischievous twinkle flashed in his black eyes. "Maybe I'm not as you imagined . . . ," he said, his smile broadening.

I glared at him.

"I really am Gatusa," he said again.

Oh, he was so right. He was nothing like I had imagined! Nothing like Geko! And that awful smile of his! How dared he?

"You're Gatusa?" And I threw my shoulder bag at him and shouted in Chinese, "How dare you be so ugly?"

And then we just stood there, silently staring at each other in common disbelief.

Gatusa did not stoop to a reply. He only bent forward to pick up my bag from the ground and hand it back to me. Then he picked up my suitcases and said in a calm voice, "Come on, let's go. You must be hungry."

Oh, how could I not have thought of asking him for a photograph? But I had never even sent him a photograph of myself! Why should I have asked one of him? We were Moso people, we did not exchange photographs! Oh, but I felt so cheated, betrayed. How could *he* write such beautiful things? How was such a thing possible? I did not want to walk next to him. I fell back three feet behind him.

Gatusa had made arrangements for us to stay with his

friend Qin Zhengxing and his family. Qin's wife had prepared a feast in my honor and by the time we came in, everything was ready to be served. Touched by all this kindness and cheered by the excellent food, I somehow managed to put a smile on my face and even to feel a little ashamed of myself. But when, after dinner, Qin called the children away and they all retired to another room to let us have some privacy, I was furious all over again. I sat in my chair looking vacantly ahead of me, as though Gatusa had become invisible, refusing to talk.

Meanwhile, he drank his tea, ignored my mood, and began to tell me about his work, his dreams, how he was planning to collect and translate Moso oral literature for *Camellia* magazine, and his ambition to record every Daba ceremony and every song and story. "It will take years, but I am young. . . . You'll see, things have changed a lot since you left. Almost all the children go to school now. They learn Han values and the ways of the modern world, and if we do not record our culture, in another generation everything may be forgotten. We Moso must not stay out of the world." He gazed at me thoughtfully, his eyes shining with intelligence and perhaps a little scorn. "The problem is, how do we become part of the world without losing ourselves in it?" But I had no answer to that question, and he went on talking about other things concerning our people, about our past and our future — things I had no idea about. He was often very funny, and he spoke more beautifully and he was more intelligent than anyone I had ever met. I felt myself charmed again, as I had been by his letters, until later in the evening, when it was time to sleep, and I asked Qin's wife to show me to her youngest daughter's room.

Next morning at breakfast, I was in a bad mood again and there was an awkward tension all around, relieved only by the chatter of the children. The Qins must have felt grateful when Gatusa looked at his watch and announced that we had to leave because the Living Buddha was waiting for us.

We hurried to the ugly modern building where our guru resided under the official title of Chairman of the Chinese People's Political Consultative Conference, the CPPCC. Gatusa pushed the door open, and a sweet scent of incense enveloped us. I followed him inside and then up a dark staircase and into a large hall cheered by the warm glow of butter lamps. As my eyes adjusted to the half-light, I made out the couches and the low tables, the mural paintings, the butter sculptures, incense burners, a photograph of our Living Buddha in his yellow robes, and next to it, a larger portrait of Mao Zedong. The hall was something halfway between a Communist Party meeting room and a Tibetan temple, but everything here was clean, pure, calm. I gazed at the mole on Mao's chin . . . just like my Ama's — and I realized that this was the first time since the bus had pulled into the station at Ninglang that I thought of my Ama. I realized that all this time, I had been so preoccupied with being angry with Gatusa that I had completely forgotten about my Ama. And yet it was not only for Gatusa that I had come home after all these years. The truth was, I was afraid. I was terribly afraid of going home. What if my Ama had not really forgiven me? What was the point then? What worth were all the dreams in the world, if I did not deserve my mother's love?

Guru came in from a side door, wearing a gray Mao jacket and a People's Liberation Army winter hat, with the fur ears tied in a bow at the top of his head. He looked just like a party cadre but for the rosary around his neck, his face filled with kindness, his thick eyebrows and large forehead radiating intelligence. He was a living god and even under his PLA headgear he had what we call a Buddha face. On seeing him, on feeling his presence, I felt unworthy of the honor.

We kowtowed with our heads to the floor. Guru touched

my head and then Gatusa's, and he invited us to sit next to him on a couch while a servant brought us butter tea. I took a sip and looked at Guru's portrait. He was so much more handsome in his tall yellow hat than in his PLA headgear.

"How is your life at the conservatory?" Guru asked.

I described my life the best I could. I told him about Shanghai, about my friends, my voice teachers, but I did not talk about my gigs at the nightclubs.

Guru listened carefully, smiling and nodding, and when I had finished talking, he crossed his hands in his lap and said, "You must study hard. You must become a great singer. And you, Gatusa, you must continue to write about our people's customs and our history. You two will let the world know about the Moso. You two will tell the world about our culture. Don't forget your roots." He paused for a moment and took a sip of tea, and then continued in the same tone, "You two must continue to love your people. You two are an example for the younger generation. I am old. You two must work together."

Gatusa glanced at me and I shot him a dirty look in return. Although Guru's attention filled me with pride, I was beginning to get irritated with all the advice and especially with the way he kept saying "you two" — as though Gatusa and I were already a couple. I was beginning to feel as I had when my mother had left me alone in the house with Geko. It seemed that someone was always wanting to arrange my life. Why should I love a Moso man? Why did they all want to keep me in the mountains?

Guru spoke with us for more than an hour. Before we took our leave, he handed me a hundred yuan, to help with my schooling. I was touched and very embarrassed. One hundred yuan was no longer such a lot of money for me, now that I worked at the nightclubs, but it was certainly over a month's salary for our guru. I refused to take it, but he insisted, and Gatusa also insisted. So I thanked him for his kindness and kowtowed one last time. On the way out, Gatusa tried to hold my hand to help me down the stairs. He meant well — there was no electric light and the stairs were pitch black — but I pushed him away. We returned to Qin Zhengxing's house without talking. Qin's wife brought us a cup of tea and Gatusa lit a cigarette, and seeing I was not in the mood for a conversation, he told me Guru's story.

Our Living Buddha, Losan, was born on Nyoropu Island on Lake Lugu. His mother was the wife of the old Yongning feudal lord. When she was pregnant, she had a recurrent dream that she was standing in the library of a monastery, surrounded by holy books. There was no way out of the room, there were no doors, only shelves filled with books. In a later dream, a voice called out to her, "Dear precious lady, don't worry. You will give birth to a little Buddha." The day our guru was born, half of heaven turned bright red and a dragon flew from Mother Lake toward the sky, churning torrents of water in its wake, and it hovered above the mountain goddess Gamu until our lady gave birth. When little Losan was three years old, Tibetan lamas came from Lhasa looking for the reincarnation of a former saint from Delimin monastery in Sichuan, and they took him back with them. He did not return to our Moso country until 1954, when he took charge of the monastery and the temples in Yongning, but the following year the People's Liberation Army came to liberate us from our feudal oppressors and our guru was sent to live in Ninglang town. Then, during the Cultural Revolution, after Mao Zedong declared religion a poison, the Red Guards destroyed the Dgebo lamasery and our guru was sent to work on a collective farm, where he lived like a simple peasant, growing vegetables and herding goats in the mountains. Everything he had learned had become useless, but he never gave up hope. He always believed in our people. After the Cultural Revolution, our guru was moved back to Ninglang, where he was given the title of Chairman of the CPPCC. And the previous year he had presided over the festival of Goddess Gamu, for the first time in more than two decades.

Gatusa paused. "Did you know that the county government insisted we build a wall to separate women and men at the hot springs?" He laughed. "It's only shoulder high, so it's completely useless!"

But I wanted to talk about something else. Better even, I did not want to talk at all. I barely excused myself and went out for a walk. I could not bear to hear any more about our country and our people. I could not bear to think about home, until I had seen my mother.

THE NEXT MORNING I WOKE VERY EARLY. Gatusa was already up, waiting for me in the Qins' living room. He suggested, perhaps only out of politeness, that I stay in Ninglang for a few days, but I declined. "I miss my mother too much. I want to go home." Besides, I had arranged with the Living Buddha's driver to take the Jeep to Luo Shui, and no doubt he was already waiting for me. I gave Gatusa the American cigarettes I had brought for him, and some tea and candy for his mother.

Outside, a fine cold rain was falling. I had gone only a little way down the street when I heard footsteps and turned to see Gatusa running after me, carrying an umbrella. "What now?" I thought. But he wanted only to give me the umbrella.

"I don't need it!" I snapped.

"Ooooh, but where did you get such a bad temper?" he answered, partly talking to himself. He took his umbrella back, turned around, and walked away without turning again.

I sat next to the driver and we began the thirty-mile, five-hour drive to Luo Shui. It was still dark. I looked at the cold rain beating on the black window, and Gatusa's words rang in my ears — Where did you get such a bad temper? Yes, I thought, where did I get such a bad temper? I thought of Geko and how much I had hurt him, and Hong Ling. Ah, but Hong Ling had asked for it! And what about Gatusa, what had he asked for? For months I had lived by the thought of him, my heart filled with joy and light, my thoughts striving for beauty. It had been the happiest year of my life, and I had achieved so much: I was thoroughly literate now — reading all those books, looking for that perfect sentence, the exact word to echo the love singing in my heart — and I had recorded my first cassette, and I was no longer alone, I had a soul mate, I was in love. . . . And in a single moment, in the little time it takes to place a name on an unfamiliar face, I had thrown everything away! How could that be?

It never occurred to me that I was shallow, superficial. I just felt sorry for myself and angry at myself too, but even angrier at Gatusa. But just below the surface, right under my skin where the anger burned, there was yearning and wanting, but I did not know what for. And that hunger is still with me, but I can see it now, just as I can still see myself clinging to the muddy edge of the precipice on the way to Yanyuan, crawling doggedly toward my dream, oblivious of the torrential water churning below, deep in the valley, where, should I fall, I would be lost forever. No, I was not shallow. But I was seething, and there was no end to it.

I stayed in this black mood for the rest of the trip, not talking to the driver, hardly noticing the sunrise or that it had stopped raining or the white peaks of the mountains — until we reached the last pass and Lake Lugu appeared before our eyes in its eternal magnificence.

Mother Lake, eternally blue, and our mountain goddess

crowned by feathery clouds. There was no purer beauty than my country.

The dark cloud lifted from my heart. I could already see my mother in her festival dress, her long blue skirt, her red jacket, and our garden and my big sister smiling and little Homi and Jiama, and Howei and Ache. . . . I could already taste the butter tea and feel the heat of the fireplace.

The Jeep reached Luo Shui, where I went to pay my respects to my old relatives while my cousins prepared the boat. Everyone was so pleased to see me, and so astonished at my clothes, my short haircut, my boots. . . . We had to row across to the other side of the lake—an hour and a half, and then walk again for two hours. At last the children appeared to greet us, but I didn't know who they were, and when I did, I did not recognize them. And they stood before me smiling, fascinated, confused, knowing I was one of them and yet unable to deny the absence of sameness their eyes could not fail to see.

My Ama was alone in the yard, chopping wood, her back to me. I did not dare approach her. I did not want to give her a shock. Besides, I was terrified. My knees were shaking, and my heart was beating wildly. What would she say? What was she going to do? What was I going to do? I asked the children to go and tell her I was there. She put down the ax and turned to see me, but she did not move. She stood and smiled and wiped her hands on her cotton trousers.

"Ami, I'm hungry!" I said, my voice breaking.

My Ama wiped her eyes. "Come inside, come inside!" And she called out, "Howei, come out! Quick, go and kill a chicken, Namu's hungry! She's come from such a long way!"

We brought my suitcases inside the house and I took out my gifts. Before I had opened the third bag of candy, our house was filled with little children, and I gave everything away. Then I gave my watch to Homi, and at last we sat down, all of us, near the fireplace. For a moment, everything seemed so simple. We were together, sitting at the hearth as though nothing had ever happened, and the thought crossed my mind that nothing ever did happen in our village.

It had been almost five years since I had run away on the mountain path. And now everything felt so familiar and yet so strange, time-warped, dislocated. Could they even begin to imagine how much of the world I had seen? Or ever understand how much I had changed? Homi and Jiama could not take their eyes off me, but then, they had grown so much, I could not stop looking at them either. They were going to school, and Jiama could already read and write, my Ama assured me. And my little brother Howei had become such a handsome young man! He must have dozens of girlfriends, I thought to myself, because this is the sort of thing you cannot talk about with your own family. My Ama had changed as well, but she was so happy it hardly showed.

Zhema brought me some tea. She too looked different—not just older but just like a Han woman. She had left home a year after me and gone to live and work in Yanyuan. And she had come home again, just as I had, to visit for New Year.

"A lot has changed in the past few years," Howei said, echoing my thoughts. "There's even a cinema now. They show movies from Hong Kong and America. Everybody knows what trains and airplanes and telephones look like."

And Ache, where was Ache?

There was an awkward pause, and then Ama said, "Ache is living in the village . . . like a married couple. Do you want more tea?"

I looked at my mother and felt my heart break. What had become of her dream?

After lunch Ama took out the Sulima wine and all the people in the village, including my brother Ache, came to our house to visit—everybody except Geko.

I had brought three photo albums with pictures from Shanghai and Beijing, the conservatory, the Mexican embassy, Umbalo and me at the Peace Hotel, my Dutch friend and me drinking coffee, me singing at the nightclub, me in the pink miniskirt—at which Dujema burst out laughing. "Is there a shortage of cloth in Shanghai?" And once again I was the center of attention, and once again I was my mother's pride, and she poured the wine and joked and smiled and showed off the beautiful gold ring I had given her.

When the guests went home late in the evening, I was exhausted from the traveling and the emotion, but before taking my suitcases up to my room, I remembered to take out the can of coffee and place it on the shelf in the pantry, ready for the next day's breakfast. I did feel a little conceited but I had lived in the world now, and I had changed so much. I would rather have coffee than butter tea for breakfast.

The next morning the winter sun was streaming softly through the window and I noticed that everything in my room was new. The bed, the little side table, my comforter. At first I felt moved at the thought that my Ama had gone to all the trouble and expense of providing a brand-new room for me. Then it struck me as a strange thing to do, since I was no longer living at home, and I suddenly missed my old comforter.

Downstairs, Zhema was drinking butter tea with Ache. I walked over to the pantry to prepare the coffee and found the can filled with water and a beautiful red camellia flower. "Hey? What happened to my coffee?"

"Ask Ama," Ache said.

My mother was in the pig yard. "Ami, what happened to my coffee?"

"What coffee?"

"You know, the black stuff inside the can!"

"Oh, that stuff! I gave it to the pig. It tasted horrible!"

I looked at the pig. She was scratching and scratching at the ground with her front feet. She had dug a big hole. Then I looked at my mother. She was holding her cigarette in her left hand, and with her right she was twiddling a long bamboo stick into the pig shit.

"What are you doing, Ami?"

"Last night, when I was feeding her, she grabbed at my finger and I think she swallowed my ring."

I glanced at the pig shit. "Do you think you'll find it?"

"I hope so. Gold must be very bad for a pig. I am worried she'll get sick. See, she's acting very strange."

"I don't think it's the gold," I said.

The poor pig acted strange all day, twitching, jumping about, scratching at the ground. Thankfully, she survived the caffeine, and my sister found the gold ring under the pig trough.

I was at home for ten days only, and everyone treated me like an honored guest. Every day I was invited out for lunch, and every evening Ama cooked my favorite foods, always serving me first and more than anyone else. And yet I did not dare to look into her eyes, and she avoided mine. We never spoke about what had happened, why I had left, or that we were sorry, or that we had missed each other so much. There were no embraces and no kisses. There were no explanations, no excuses, no making up, no regrets, no affirmations, no pledges for the future. Nothing. Not because we didn't feel anything but because talking about it was not the way we did things. We said nothing because we wanted to believe that nothing had ever gone wrong, because this is the only way we could truly forgive. We buried the past. We banished it from our talk and from our memory. We remembered only what should have happened. And so for ten days, we would live side by side as though nothing had ever gone wrong, as though I had never left the roof my mother had built for her family, where I had come screaming into the world near the woodstove, where I had burned my little red shoes, and where she had given me her jade bracelet.

"Hey, what happened to your bracelet?" Ama asked the first time she caught sight of my bare arm.

I hesitated. . . . "I sold it to go to Shanghai."

Ama was quiet for a while. "Do you think we could buy it back?"

"I don't think so, Ami."

My mother nodded her head, and she said no more about it. The bracelet had now vanished to the void of memory, together with the smashed-up kitchen stove and the other unspeakable things. The past was done and there was nothing she could do to change this, nothing but to begin forgetting, one wordless moment at a time. One evening I went to sit in Zhema's room to talk, and to try to make things the way they had always been. I so desperately wanted things to be as they had been. But when was this "always"? When I was living with Uncle and came home from the mountain? When I had come home for my Skirt Ceremony? When I had beaten Geko? And then something occurred to me. "Zhema, why is everything new in my room?"

Zhema winced.

"What is it?" I insisted.

"After you left," she finally said slowly, looking away from me, "the teachers came and told her what you had done . . . so she knew that you wouldn't be coming back. One day she took the ax and went into your room. She broke everything up, your bed, the chest of drawers. She threw everything downstairs and made a fire in the yard. She burned all your things, even your clothes." Zhema paused and looked at me, her eyes filled with tears. She had told me a terrible thing. The precipice on the way to Yanyuan suddenly opened up again in my imagination. I had come so close . . . And my Ama had meant to destroy all traces of me. "Now, do you understand?" Zhema sobbed. "She thought she had lost you forever."

I stared at my big sister. I felt sick inside. I pictured my mother burning my things, smashing my bed as I had smashed the kitchen stove at the school. . . . But what was I thinking? That I could run away from home and bring disgrace to my family, and my Ama would just get on with life as though nothing had ever happened? Of course my Ama had to do something!

"Yes, I understand," I said to Zhema.

The next day, when my mother served me the best pieces of meat, I did not protest, and when Zhema gave me a whole portion of blood sausage, we all burst out laughing. And when my father came to visit and handed me two small leather purses filled with deer musk, which he had been saving for a year, I took those gratefully too, my eyes brimming and my heart full of love. "In Shanghai," my father said, "they'll fetch a good price. That will help you with your school." I still felt strange and uncomfortable, and I knew they all felt the same way, but somehow we would have to live with it. Besides, I was home only for a few days. Could we not simply be happy that it was all over, that we were together again, that we would always come together like this, around the fireplace, drinking butter tea, laughing, and forgetting what we did not want to remember?

When it was time for me to leave, all the villagers came to our house to wish me a safe trip. Everyone except Geko. They came with bamboo boxes filled with the same foodstuff: boiled eggs, salted pork, ham, chicken breast. "Take this to eat on your journey." There were so many boxes I began to worry. According to our custom, each box would have to be returned, filled with other food, and since I could not possibly carry or eat all this, I had to leave everything for my mother to take care of. As for my Ama, she gave me a pot of fresh butter and a leg of ham wrapped in red silk to take to the Living Buddha, for a temple offering. It was not important that the Living Buddha was, like all Buddhist saints, vegetarian.

Ama walked with me all the way to the lake, chanting mantras, counting her prayer beads with her right hand, and holding a cigarette in her left. Every so often she stopped to admonish me to be careful, to take care of myself, to try to get the jade bracelet back, and to write, because Jiama could read the letters, and to come home again soon. You can take the plane, it's faster. Come home in the summer . . . or else next winter. . . .

My cousins were waiting for us at the boat. They loaded my suitcases, and I stepped into the canoe and took my seat. Then Ache pushed the boat off into the water, and I turned around to say one last good-bye. Zhema waved back. Ama was crying. "Come back soon," she called. I nodded. We both knew now that I would always come back. I waved again and turned, and I stared through blurry eyes straight ahead of me, toward the other side of the lake, toward Luo Shui and the road back to the city, where the whole world was waiting.

Afterword

I first heard of the Moso in 1988 when Lü Binghong, my Chinese language teacher, suggested I research a lost matriarchal tribe of the remote mountains of the Tibet-China borderland. He had himself discovered the Moso a couple of years previously when he had written English subtitles for a documentary film entitled *The Country of Daughters.* The Moso, Teacher Lü explained, practiced "walking marriage," whereby men visited their wives at night, and husbands and wives did not live together; here also women ruled society and people favored daughters over sons.

I was intrigued but also skeptical. Like all other anthropology students, I had learned that contrary to popular conviction, there exists no such thing as a matriarchal society, that what goes by matriarchy is in fact matriliny—a system of inheritance determined by maternal lines. Matriarchy, indeed, implies the opposite of patriarchy, a social and political system where women have privileges and power at the expense of men, and this is not something that maternal inheritance automatically guarantees. As a dear old professor had put it, "The difference between a matrilineal society and a patrilineal one is that in a matrilineal society, women are bossed by their uncles and their brothers rather than their fathers and husbands." Among the relatively few matrilineal societies of the world, some could perhaps claim to be gender egalitarian but none had as yet satisfied Western anthropologists' criteria for women's rule. Listening to Teacher Lü, and peering over the newspaper clippings he had brought out for my perusal, I was not convinced that Moso society was the exception. But just the same, I was interested.

Library research, however, soon turned curiosity into confusion. To begin with, there was not a great deal of information on the Moso, and what there was did not fit with Teacher Lü's description. Firsthand reports fell almost entirely to three prerevolution writers, renowned East Asian scholars Jacques Bacot and Edouard Chavannes, and an American botanist explorer by the name of Joseph Rock. Jacques Bacot, the first to publish anything of true scholarly interest on the Moso, had passed through Lijiang in 1912, where he had obtained a copy of the genealogical chronicle of the long-deposed Moso kings, which he had then given to Chavannes to translate into French. Chavannes quite rightly described this document as a precious resource for historians, but such as it was, the Moso chronicle showed that the Lijiang kings were actually hereditary feudal lords, vassals of the Chinese emperor who had inherited their position *patrilineally* for centuries. And neither Bacot nor Chavannes made any mention of matriarchal or matrilineal customs.

Joseph Rock, for his part, had done a lot more than pass through Lijiang; he had spent almost thirty years in northern Yunnan, until his expulsion in 1949 following the Communist revolution. He had also published extensively. From Rock I now learned that the people Teacher Lü called Moso were in fact the neighbors of the Moso described by Bacot and Chavannes, and that the "real Moso," so to speak, lived in Yongning and not Lijiang—where people called themselves Na-khi. By a mystery that puzzled Rock for years, it so happened that for centuries the Chinese had referred to both the Na-khi of Lijiang and the Moso of Yongning by the name Moso.

Yes, of course, Teacher Lü further enlightened me, because the Moso and the Na-khi had once formed a single tribe called Moso. Even today the Naxi (current spelling) and the Moso were still classed under one name, for the Moso were not considered a national group in their own right but a branch of the Naxi nationality, one of fifty-six official ethnic categories that make up the Chinese socialist state. In other words, in the People's Republic of China, the Moso and the Naxi were once again regarded as a single tribe but now under the name Naxi!

Although I was still confused as to who the Moso and the Naxi were exactly, and as to why they should have had two or one name, thanks to Rock I could at least situate the Moso in Yongning and the Naxi in Lijiang, and I also had access to a wealth of mostly arcane historical and geographical data that he had compiled into a monumental opus entitled *The Ancient Na-khi Kingdom of Southwest China*. And from those I learned that in more recent history, northern Yunnan had been home to a powerful kingdom centered on Lijiang. Beginning with the Mongol conquest in 1253 and ending in 1723 with the annexation of their territory by the Manchu emperor, the Lijiang kings had ruled over a vast territory that, for a period of a hundred years at its foundation, had even included Yongning. So perhaps the confusion between the Moso and the Naxi had begun with Kublai Khan.

By Rock's time, however, all that was left of the ancient Naxi kingdom were a few crumbling feudal enclaves plagued by local tyranny, opium addiction, and banditry, among which Yongning was the only vital exception. In Lijiang the Naxi had been subjected to Confucian administration for two hundred years, and they had adopted so many Chinese customs that even Jacques Bacot had thought them just like the Chinese. But Rock quite rightly saw that the Naxi had also retained extraordinary traditions, in particular an ancient religion called Dongba, whose ceremonies were written in an exotic pictographic script unknown anywhere else in China. Rock, who believed the Dongba had originated in the pre-Buddhist Bon religion of Tibet, devoted the rest of his life to the translation of Naxi ceremonial texts. Now, the Moso also had a folk religion, called Daba, but they did not have manuscripts or pictographs. The Daba religion was purely oral, and Rock assumed that it was nothing more than an impoverished version of the Naxi Dongba.

It is truly a great loss to anthropology that Rock's intellectual passion lay with the religion of the Naxi and did not include Moso culture. For whereas his translations of Naxi ceremonies are unsurpassed for the attention he paid to detail, when it came to the Moso, he was anything but precise. Although Rock had been a close and loyal friend of the Yongning feudal lord with whom he had spent "many happy and peaceful hours," what he had to say of Moso society could be summed up in a few acerbic generalities to the effect that women owned houses and took lovers for as long as they wished, and that the Moso had such an "inordinate number of bastard children" that the word *father* was altogether missing from their vocabulary—a phenomenon that he further attributed to the many Buddhist monks who lived in Yongning and whose vows of celibacy "did not refrain them from sexual activities."

As I was to discover some years later, the Moso themselves have kept very fond memories of Dr. Rock, whom they credit with legendary deeds of kindness, including his fathering of many blue-eyed, blond-haired children. These stories, however, are probably just stories. Rock was a formidable figure, a bad-tempered and opinionated man who never went anywhere without his portable bathtub and an armed garrison but who nurtured a timidity toward women that bordered on the pathological. If we believe his biographer, the late Sylvia Sutton, he was the least likely man to have fathered anyone.

In the fall of 1990, I enrolled as a scholar at the Academy of Social Sciences in Yunnan to research a Ph.D. topic I was still at great pains to define beyond the stubborn notion that I wanted to learn about the Moso. By then I had read all of Rock's books and I still knew little more about the Moso than what I had found out from Teacher Lü's newspaper articles. Worst of all, I had visited Lijiang the previous year and discovered that it was impossible to travel farther. The Country of Daughters was closed to foreigners. The region was too backward, Comrade X of the Public Security Bureau had explained, there were no roads and no way to guarantee the safety of foreign friends. And now my professors at the academy confirmed what I already knew: that non-Chinese scholars were not allowed to do fieldwork in Yongning. But they proposed a solution. The academy had just hired a brilliant young man, Lamu Gatusa, the first and only Moso academician. I could get all my information from him, and I could also study Naxi culture with the Naxi scholars — since, after all, the Naxi and the Moso were the same people.

"Really? They are the same people?" I asked, hopeful.

"Maybe not," said Lamu Gatusa, who informed me that the Moso had petitioned the central government to be identified as a "Moso nationality" entirely separate from the Naxi.

From our first meeting, Gatusa and I became friends, and like all good friends, we talked a lot — about the Moso, their family life, their extraordinary sexual customs, their moral values and religious beliefs, and the differences between them and the Naxi. Within a few weeks, and by complicated means, we had obtained permission to travel together to the valley of the Yangtze River that divides Naxi and Moso territories and where the Moso are neither matriarchal nor matrilineal but patrilineal and therefore believed to be a "link population" between Naxi and Moso. This, my first introduction to Moso culture, to the beauty and majesty of Moso country, and to the kindness and generosity of Gatusa's family, made an indelible impression on both my heart and my memory.

Back in Kunming, we began working on the translation of ceremonies from the old Daba religion that we had recorded in Labei, as well as others Gatusa had collected over several years. And, of course, we kept talking. One evening Gatusa told me about a beautiful Moso singer called Erche Namu who now lived in Beijing. He had visited her some months before. "We were pen friends when she was at the Music Conservatory in Shanghai." He laughed, his dark eyes shining. "She married an American. He speaks Chinese just like a native. . . . True, his Chinese is perfect! Oh, yes, that American husband, he's really something!"

I wondered if I would ever meet Namu, and if my Chinese would ever be perfect. Then, as the months passed, I wondered if Gatusa would ever realize his dream of recording the entire Daba ceremonial corpus and how much of it I would ever get to translate. By then I was devoted to our religious studies.

Examining Daba liturgy and ritual, I had been struck by fundamental differences between Naxi and Moso religions that fueled other questions I had begun formulating ever since our visit to Labei. In particular, I was not convinced by the description of Labei Moso as a "link population" whose customs were derived from both Naxi and Moso cultures. As far as I could tell, the people of Labei were very different from their Naxi neighbors, even those who lived closest to them on the opposite side of the Yangtze River. It seemed to me that the Labei people were Moso in every way but one: they were not matrilineal.

Gatusa's work on the Daba was entirely original. No one else knew anything about the old Moso religion. Joseph Rock had simply *assumed* that the Daba was a poor relation of the Naxi religion. And a few decades later, Chinese scholars (and others) had done the same thing in order to provide evidence of the common origin of the Moso and the Naxi, a proposition sorely lacking in historical documentation that appeared to me in an ever more interesting light. For Naxi and Moso history, I had found out, was far from a proven fact. It was a matter of theory, of ethnohistorical reconstruction, of detective work based on a patchy historical record and correlative evidence: linguistics, customs, genealogies, religion, and thus it was open to discussion, to further enquiry and research. In other words, it was a Ph.D. topic. But it was also a significant political issue that my teachers at the academy were now advising me not to bother exploring. Because the idea that the Naxi and the Moso were once the same people was the very thing that legitimized the Moso's official classification into the Naxi nationality—and the very thing the Moso were now contesting.

But my teachers were too late. Curiosity had already grown into a fixation that was to drive me for the next six years to do nothing else but attempt to unravel the mysteries of Moso and Naxi history. During these six years many things happened, but of special interest: in 1992 I obtained a restricted permit to visit Yongning for the first time; and some months later, northern Yunnan was unconditionally opened to foreign visitors; then in 1993 the Chinese government rejected Moso demands for national identification; and I met Erche Namu in San Francisco.

Seven years later Namu sat at my desk, next to me, and she began to tell me stories about her childhood, what it was like to be a girl growing up in Moso country. And so she talked, and we cried and we laughed, and then we cried again, and in this way we drafted the stories from which I wrote *Leaving Mother Lake*. But this story, the story of Namu's girlhood among her people, is in every way an extraordinary one, telling of a unique experience, a unique destiny, and an inimitable personality. It is not the story of all Moso.

What I present here is not the story of all Moso either, but rather a little of what I have learned about their society and what I have hypothesized of their history. And I can only hope that it speaks on their behalf as helpfully as Namu credits me for speaking on hers. Because ever since the Communist revolution intruded into their world in 1956, the Moso have been under great pressure to explain themselves, and few of China's ethnic people have been so consistently misrepresented and misunderstood and at times, indeed, mistreated.

The Naxi nationality, to which the Moso belong, number about 309,500 people and dwells in northwest Yunnan province on both sides of the Gold Sands River, as the Yangtze is known in these parts. On the western shore, Lijiang Autonomous County is home to people who are identified specifically as Naxi (pronounced Na-shi). The Moso (also Mosuo) live on the eastern shore in Yongning and nearby territories, and number about 30,000. The Yangtze has divided the Naxi and the Moso for centuries, at the very least since 1381, when the Ming court established Lijiang and Yongning as separate feudal districts. And with this ancient administrative boundary came important developments. In Lijiang, Confucianism and Chinese culture increasingly influenced the Naxi, and especially after they came under direct Chinese rule in 1723, they took part in all the major political upheavals that befell the Chinese nation. In 1949 the Naxi were at the vanguard of the Communist revolution. By contrast, the Moso were oriented toward Tibet and Tibetan Buddhism, and today they are still devout followers of the Gelugpa, the Yellow Church of the Dalai Lama. And although Yongning was a feudal district administered by Chinese decree, the Moso lived almost entirely isolated from the rest of China — until 1956, when the People's Liberation Army turned their world over.

Nestled in the spectacular mountains of the southern China-Tibet borderland, Moso country begins east of the Yangtze and extends from the mountains and terraced fields of Labei across the Yongning plain and beyond Lake Lugu into the territories of Qiansuo and Zuosuo in Sichuan province. The lake, which the Moso call Xienami, or Mother Lake, lies at about ten thousand feet of altitude. It is immense. Towering above it is the squat figure of the sacred mountain Gamu, the mother goddess who watches over the Moso people, and perhaps also the tourists and other alien visitors who have come to experience "matriarchal life" in the Country of Daughters.

As could be expected, Moso country is more complex than tourist guides and the mass media may ever care to explain. To begin, the Moso are not the sole inhabitants of the Country of Daughters so much as they are the dominant ethnic group. Other groups include Pumi, Lisu, Yi, Tibetans, Naxi, Han Chinese farmers, and also traders who settled in town centers. As to the Moso themselves, they do not form a strictly homogeneous cultural group but rather several local groups. Thus, in the mountains of Labei where Gatusa comes from, the Moso trace their genealogies from fathers to sons and they also contract marriages in a way fitted to a larger cultural complex spanning the Himalayas from western China to Ladakh. Until 1956 there were three Moso districts, the largest of which was the feudal principality of Yongning in Yunnan, while the smaller districts in Sichuan —

Qiansuo and Zuosuo, where Namu comes from—had seceded from Yongning in the early eighteenth century. Today the Moso are still divided on either side of the administrative line between Yunnan and Sichuan provinces, with the Sichuan Moso being officially classed as Mongols and the people of Yunnan as Naxi.

Yet, in spite of territorial and administrative differences, all Moso identify themselves as Moso as well as share essential cultural traits that not only make sense of their common identity but also readily distinguish them from both the Mongols and the Naxi. All Moso speak and understand the same language, worship common gods, eat the same foods, sing the same songs, and wear similar traditional dress, and all Moso, even the patrilineal people of Labei, share the belief that the true Moso family, that essential, founding unit of society, is the extended maternal household.

And certainly, from the perspective of those on the other side of the mountains, this matrilineal Moso family cannot help but fascinate—for the Moso are reputed to be the only people in the world who consider marriage an attack on the family. In fact, marriage was never entirely absent from Moso society, and Moso families have grown ever more diversified since the revolution, but formal marriages and nuclear families are still relatively few. Outside patrilineal Labei, the ideal family is a large group of people, all related through the women of the house—grandmothers, maternal great-uncles, mothers, sisters, maternal uncles, daughters, sons, grandchildren, nephews, and nieces. At the core of this family, there may be no husband, no wife, and no father, but, instead, brothers, sisters, mothers, and maternal uncles. Ideally, Moso families should never divide, wealth should be held communally and shared equally for the benefit of all family members, and there should be no need for inheritance rules because property may simply pass on, down the generations, as children succeed their mothers and uncles in the ancestral home.

While the Moso uphold this ideal of an indivisible family, however, they also keep sexual relations strictly out of the family—a rule of conduct that finds its most concrete expression in the fact that in a Moso house, only women have their own bedrooms, evocatively called *babahuago*, or "flower rooms." Old people and children under thirteen sleep in the main room, near the fireplace or in wooden alcove beds alongside the walls. Adult men are expected to sleep at their lovers', or if they don't have lovers, in one of the outhouses or guest rooms if the family has those. And Moso custom not only forbids adult men from sleeping under the same roof as their sisters, it also prohibits any type of sexual talk, allusion, joking, or even the singing or humming of love songs in the family home. Although women and men are free to choose their lovers and to maintain sexual relations for as long or short a time as they desire, what a woman and her "friend" *(azhu)* do in the privacy of her bedroom is left to individual discretion. If a couple decide to make their relationship public, they can spend time together with each other's relatives, but their romantic involvement should not be discussed in front of family members of the opposite sex, including their own children. These rules of sexual propriety are so strict that ideally, and this was the case until the Communist intervention, they would qualify the public disclosure of children's fathers. In the past, people often learned about their fathers indirectly, or they might not have known at all. And although there are two words in the Moso language for father, *abo* and *ada*, fathers were commonly addressed as Awu, which simply means uncle.

Because the Moso arrange sexual relations as men's visits to their lovers' houses, the custom is sometimes called visiting marriage, or also walking marriage. The latter, which is the term preferred by Chinese anthropologists, is derived from the Moso's own terminology, who refer to sexual relationships as *sese,* meaning "walking." By any stretch of the imagination, however, *sese* are not marriages. *Sese* are of two types — they are entirely private and usually short-lived, or they are more stable and publicly acknowledged, but all *sese* are of the visiting kind, and none involves the exchange of vows, property, the care of children, or expectations of fidelity. Now of course, even among the Moso, people are not entirely immune from jealousy or heartbreak, but Moso moral codes strongly discourage public displays of jealousy or amorous despair, or for that matter any display of negative emotion. Jilted lovers may receive sympathy from neighbors and friends up to a point, but they will lose face and ensure that sympathy shifts to the faithless party if they cannot keep their feelings under control. Ideally, there should be nothing, aside from desire and mutual affection, to decide on the freedom and frequency of sexual relations. Indeed, when Chinese officials first encountered the Moso in the 1950s, they were flabbergasted by their relationships, both because of the sheer number of partners women and men claimed to have had and because of the complete lack of self-consciousness people exhibited.

Seen from the Moso perspective, however, free visiting relationships strengthen and support the stability of the family. Because sexual relationships are assumed to be limited in time, because they take place outside working hours, and because they do not engage partners economically, love affairs don't intrude on the family's economic life or compete with the brother-sister and mother-children bonds that are at the affective core of the family.

The economic organization of Moso society, for its part, reflects these same sexual patterns. In the simplest terms, women's work centers on the house, while men's takes place outside. Thus, women grow, cook, and distribute the food, while their male relatives engage in all other outside activities, such as house building, herding animals, trade, and so forth, and bring home whatever cash they make in the outside world. In the same vein, women and men are responsible for different religious spheres, with women taking care of daily libations to the house gods and ancestors, while men are engaged in organized religion — Tibetan Buddhism, or where it still exists, the Daba tradition. Having said as much, I must also point out that while these divisions of labor are prevalent, gender boundaries are easily crossed when circumstances require it, and as schooling and the cash economy make headway into Moso society, women's roles are also changing. Today both women and men are involved in work activities connected with the local tourist industry, and although it may not be a first choice, daughters as well as sons will travel to the cities to earn badly needed cash.

The relative positions of men and women in Moso society are not easily gauged. Moso social etiquette clearly stresses the importance of age over gender and thus demands universal deference toward older persons irrespective of sex. But even a senior woman who is Dabu (household head) does not have undue authority over her relatives. In ideal terms, Moso families are democratic units where all relatives expect to be included in decision making. From another angle, Moso divisions of labor and religion conform to the general rule of segregation between women and their brothers and may be perceived to create complementary rather than hierarchical roles. Males and females have separate spheres of responsibility and they also have limited authority over each other. Thus, maternal uncles are supposed to be knowledgeable and wise in the affairs of the outside world, and mothers and sisters are supposed to know best how to run the household.

And these roles are not better or worse, they just are. From an outside perspective, however, it is difficult not to notice that male occupations are highly valued, that women shoulder a far greater burden of physical labor than men, and that men command respect and authority and more, because of the aura of knowledge they carry with them from their activities in the outside world.

What is beyond argument, in any case, is that Moso society is not ruled by women as is invariably publicized by the mass media. Before the Communist revolution, the Moso were governed by male chiefs who inherited their position from their fathers and passed it to their sons, while aristocratic women could and did hold high offices but not because they were women so much as because they were aristocrats. Today, although there are no rules barring women from office, the administration is dominated almost exclusively by male cadres. Unlike women, who are constantly preoccupied with housework and farmwork, men are available to pursue positions in the outside world, to become village chiefs, administrators, cadres, technicians, teachers, traders, and so forth, and in all evidence, they have a fair share of authority in public and family life. Of course, in the Moso family, the maternal bond determines blood ties, but this makes Moso society matrilineal, not matriarchal.

But if Moso society is not matriarchal, it is nonetheless remarkable. In many societies, even patriarchal ones, women are often more powerful than social convention would have anyone believe. As these expressions go, women may get to rule the roost or to be the power behind the throne; in other words, they may usurp the authority that is ideally vested in men. But Moso women do no such thing. They are *legitimate* figures of family authority, managers of family wealth, coowners of family property, caretakers of ancestors, and owners of their own bloodlines. Not least, they have personal rights and freedoms in the domain of sexual relations that are unthinkable in much of the rest of the world. Indeed, above and beyond gender relations, Moso society is extraordinary for its institution of visiting relationships, which may well claim to have solved a universal conundrum of human existence, predicated by the desire for sex and love, and the requirements of family continuity and economics.

As French anthropologist Claude Lévi-Strauss and others have shown, marriage is a form of exchange through which bloodlines, family names, wealth, and other forms of privilege and social status are actuated and legitimized. Marriage, in other words, is the glue that holds societies together.

But in most societies, for marriage to work, something usually has to give. In patrilineal male-dominated societies, that something is very often romantic love, and almost always (female) sexual freedom and pleasure. In more extreme cases, male lineages may well depend on the exclusive sexual cooperation of wives and daughters, a thing that women are not naturally inclined to provide. Such societies have to work hard to keep women's sexuality in check, and they often take drastic measures to achieve this goal, among the most infamous, female circumcision, bound feet, widow burning, burkas, and all forms of social seclusion.

On the other hand, where marriage is based on ideals of romantic love, sexual compatibility, and the equality of two individuals rather than concerns for family lines and property, it is the economic stability and the very unity of the family that risk coming unraveled. As our current divorce rates testify, love and sex provide a lofty ideal and a tenuous basis on which to build enduring marriages.

The Moso have made an extraordinary cultural choice — they have sacrificed neither sexual freedom nor romantic love nor economic security nor the continuity of their bloodlines. Instead, they have discarded marriage. What they have gained is a society where all the essentials of existence (food, affection, property, and family lines) are birthrights established by the most evident fact that is the maternal tie. And interestingly, from the perspective of family continuity, not only women but men find fulfillment in this way of life, which frees them from the anxiety of ensuring descendants — with multiple sisters, Moso families are almost guaranteed a next generation.

The Moso advocate this idealized maternal way of life as the best possible, and the most likely to foster happiness and harmony. Visiting relationships, they say, keep relations between men and women pure and joyful, and people who live in large maternal houses do not fight like married people do. We can trust that they are speaking from experience, because many Moso have tried marriage, under pressure from the Communist authorities, and most gave up. Unfortunately, the Moso can articulate the positive attributes of their family system with so much conviction because they have had a few decades to reflect on its benefits. For whatever advantage may be perceived in their tradition, the Communists failed to see. Instead, they judged Moso custom feudal and incompatible with socialist ideals.

There is no doubt that the Moso feudal rulers encouraged both the matrilineal family system and the custom of visiting relationships. For a start, the large maternal households were found in the feudal center rather than in the peripheral mountains of Labei, and indeed, closer to the feudal center, not only the Moso but also the Pumi were matrilineal. Here, all classes of Moso engaged in visiting relationships, and apart from the ruling family itself, almost all Moso, including aristocrats, traced descent matrilineally. But the feudal lords nurtured local custom in numerous other ways — through proverbs and songs extolling the virtues of the indivisible matrilineal family; through the sponsorship of communal cults dedicated to the mountain goddess and other mother figures; through the taxation and corvée system, which levied households rather than individuals and thus encouraged families to stay together.

On the other hand, the fact that men engaged in long-distance trade, and therefore could be away from home for months at a time, no doubt encouraged sexual infidelity and made sense of leaving the running of farm- and housework to women. And finally, if Buddhism did not contribute to the system, it was certainly well adapted to it. In the old feudal world, every Moso family, whatever class it belonged to (aristocrat, commoner, or serf), was required to give up one son to study the Buddhist scriptures. It is estimated that in 1956, at the time of the Communist takeover, one-fifth of Moso males were monks vowed to celibacy but, as Joseph Rock had observed, not chastity. Evidently, visiting relationships were well suited to Buddhist Yongning.

But to claim that the feudal system nurtured Moso culture does not in any way explain the origins of Moso customs or why the Moso should be alone among all their neighbors to have institutionalized the matrilineal family and the absence of marriage. In other words, it does not answer to the questions of where the Moso come from and how old their matrilineal system might be.

Although the name Moso appears in ancient Chinese records as early as the seventh century A.D., the Moso's ancestral origins, their extraordinary family system, and not least, their historical relationship with neighboring Naxi remain steeped in mystery. In truth, the historical record is very incomplete and at times filled with so many obscure or contradictory details that it seems indecipherable. But perhaps even more problematic is the fact that neither the Moso nor the Naxi appear to have traditional claims to this ancient name Moso. Today the Naxi take offense at it, and the Moso request it as their own in order to distinguish themselves from the Naxi. *Moso* is never mentioned in the old Naxi pictographic manuscripts, or in any of the Moso legends and ceremonial texts. The Naxi and Moso respectively call themselves Naxi and Nari in a similar vein to their Yi neighbors, whose own name is Nosu — *na* and *no* both meaning "black," while *xi, ri,* and *su* mean "people." As to the name black, it is almost certainly derived from an ancient tribal system that for centuries divided the various peoples of southwest China as Black and White tribes.

Putting aside the old name Moso, however, the historical record, oral tradition, and linguistic analysis all suggest that the Naxi and the Moso trace their origins neither to a single "Moso" tribe nor to two distinct tribes but to several people who arrived in Yunnan under different circumstances and at different times — Qiang, Tibetans, and Mongols, as well as ancient indigenous tribes. For, quite aside from being subjected to invasions by outsiders, the native people of Yunnan were at war for centuries, engaged in conquest, feuding, raiding, dispersal, intermarriage, and regrouping under the banner of various federations, kingdoms, and empires. Not surprisingly, the historical record mentions dozens of tribes whose names have now entirely disappeared. When groups were conquered, they were either enslaved to provide labor and/or military service or assimilated into the system of tribute payment to local feudal lords. In fact, even as late as the sixteenth century, Chinese and local historians report that northern Yunnan was inhabited by congeries of rebellious tribes whom the local feudal lords were still trying to pacify under their respective tax and corvée systems.

By 1956, whatever their more distant past, the Moso and the Naxi were entirely different people who shared neither territory, language, religion, nor custom — even though

Chinese historians had confused their identities for centuries and the Communists were about to class them as a single nationality group. And undoubtedly, whether in Yongning or Lijiang, people owed much of their cultural particularities to local elites who had exerted themselves to impose laws and customs upon previous generations.

Now, on both sides of the Yangtze, the feudal lords believed themselves to be descended from an army officer left by Kublai Khan during his conquest of China. But whatever this common claim to a distant Mongol ancestry, the family histories of the Moso and Naxi rulers are entirely distinct. Not least, the genealogy of the Lijiang chiefs shows consistent father-son successions from the Mongol conquest, while that of the Yongning chiefs makes no mention of any Mongol ancestor and shows a messy line of inheritance passing as often as not from fathers to sons, brothers to brothers, and uncles to nephews. It is only after primogeniture and patrilineal succession were mandated by Imperial edict in the eighteenth century that the names of official wives even appear in this record. In fact, the old Moso elite may look not only to the Mongols to seek their own splendid origins.

Yongning lies south of an ancient Qiang state described in the imperial histories of the Sui (A.D. 581–618) and Tang dynasties (A.D. 618–907) as a Country of Women (*Nü Guo*), which certainly appears to have been not only matrilineal but also matriarchal. These documents are remarkably detailed, for they provide a precise geographical position, naming rivers, towns, and territorial boundaries, as well as information on economic, social, and political organization. The Country of Women was ruled by queens and a council of state made exclusively of female ministers. Men, the imperial scribes tell us, were not held in high esteem; they took the names of their mothers, tilled the soil, and went to war. The record also provides the names of several queens who paid

tribute to the Chinese court, among whom figures a Ngue —
which is the clan name of the old aristocracy of Yongning and
which is not found among any of the Naxi in Lijiang.

As I had discussed with Teacher Lü so many years ago
now, Western anthropological theory does not believe in matriarchal states; it believes only in myths about matriarchy —
but knowledge of the Country of Women has not come to us
via mythology. It has come to us in written, official documents. The Country of Women disappeared from the imperial record during the ninth century, after the Sino-Tibetan
wars, but if it ceased to exist as a state, is it not possible that
some of its clans, among them the Ngue, made their way to
Yongning? And if this is a possibility, the Country of Women
may not only throw light on the validity of current ethnic
boundaries between Moso and Naxi but also reopen the case
of the matriarchy in Western anthropological theory.

Until the late 1980s, the Moso were virtually unknown outside western China. There were several reasons for this, such
as extreme geographical isolation, and not least the fact that
for several decades after the revolution, they did not have a
name of their own but were simply called Naxi. Isolation is
still the most prominent feature of Moso country and one
need not go far off the beaten path to discover picturesque
villages without running water or electricity, and a virtually
cashless economy where trade and barter are still done by
horse caravan. Amid these tall mountains where modern
commodities and infrastructure are practically invisible, the
illusion of going back in time is almost perfect. Here one gets
the feeling that history has stood still. But appearances are
deceiving. For the Moso have never truly been sheltered
from the great historical movements that have shaken the
Tibet-China frontier. And the more recent watersheds of eco-

nomic liberalization and globalization have not passed them
by.

So much has changed in the past fifty years. So much has
changed for China and for the Moso. As China has become
more urban, wealthier, and open to the world, news of Moso
culture has spread beyond Yunnan to the rest of the country
and, in the past few years, to the world. Today foreign journalists and filmmakers can travel freely through Moso country, and even Western anthropologists can take up residence
for as many months as their research visas allow. To date,
German scholar Susanne Knödel and Americans Shih
Chuan-kang and Eileen Walsh have contributed doctoral dis-
sertations and publications in Moso studies. But the great
majority of visitors to Moso country are not scholars or journalists but the thousands of Chinese and increasingly also
foreign tourists who come to Yongning in ever greater numbers every year. Most stay only a few days, just long enough
to look, to do a little horse riding, to paddle across the lake
and visit the temples, to sing and dance around the bonfires
and speculate on what it is like to live in a society with no fathers or husbands, where free love and women rule — the ex-
oticism of it all, the innocence or the wantonness, depending
on where you happen to stand on sex and morality.

In the space of a decade, Yunnan province has become
one of the most favored tourist destinations in China, and
tourism has wrought stupendous changes there, creating
great wealth matched by an enormous gap between those
who are involved in the new industry and those who are not.
In Yongning, in spite of local efforts to spread both the industry and the wealth it generates beyond the lucky few, tourism
is still very much concentrated in the village of Luo Shui near
the lake, where hardworking, entrepreneurial families have
turned their log homes into spacious guest houses. In only six

or so years, standards of living in Luo Shui have increased dramatically, with many families having a television set, running water, a telephone, and plenty of cash in the bank — a material comfort that is in stark contrast to much of Moso country.

Meanwhile, as the outside world increasingly intrudes into their own, many Moso are voicing concerns that their traditional way of life may be enduring on borrowed time — and, ironically enough, when there is no longer a need to fear government interference. Today almost all Moso children go to school, where they learn the Chinese curriculum, and with it, to define themselves beyond Moso language and culture, beyond subsistence farming, and perhaps also beyond the extended maternal family. In the more remote villages, economic urgency is pushing young people to leave and seek work in the cities, where some will inevitably end up settling for good. And in the wealthier communities where tourist dollars make television sets affordable, the young now have access to a world their elders never dreamed could exist.

Few in Moso country would disagree that tourism holds the surest promise of economic well-being. But can tourism alone sustain economic development and stem the migration of young people to the cities? And if not, what then? And if yes, at what cost? The "matriarchy industry," indeed, creates a strange paradox, for it makes the promise of modernity dependent on the preservation of tradition. But then again, since the Communist revolution, visiting relationships and the maternal family have acquired much more than market value, they have come to symbolize the best in Moso tradition and to embody Moso identity itself. And surely, this is more than an incentive for cultural preservation.

The Moso say that the future lies behind us while the past is before us. By this they mean that the past is what we know, because it is what is in front of our eyes, while the future, since it is behind our back, cannot be seen. I am now thinking of those sacred images of snakes that swallow their tails, bringing end and beginning together in a gesture of eternal regeneration. I am also thinking of the resilience of a family system that has survived the tribulations of centuries of history, and not least, of the unique genius of a people who made freedom to love the keeper of their collective happiness, and who are still doing so even as they dance around the bonfires, hand-in-hand with curious visitors.

Christine Mathieu
San Francisco
November 2001

THE LAST WORD

I have long understood that my life is different. As I grew up in my village, and then traveled to Shanghai, Beijing, and later to America and Europe, I was always conscious of being different—different from my family, my own people, and others. But I also knew I was carrying a treasure—the treasure of my birth in the Country of Daughters. Although I have chosen to make my life mostly in the Western world, it is only this country that gives me an inner peace that I know I cannot find anywhere else no matter how long and how far I travel. I think I always knew this, but I could never find the words to truly explain myself to others until I began working on writing my story with Christine Mathieu. After many years of friendship, I discovered I could connect with Christine in a way I have never done with anyone. She knew where I came from; she had walked our mountain paths and drunk our salted butter tea, and even sat with my mother in our house in Zuosuo. More than that, she could make sense of my confused, emotional recollections. I had never before reflected so deeply and I had never trusted anyone with so many secrets. Although I had written about my life and told my story many times in interviews with the Chinese media, I had only ever skimmed the surface.

I spent three months in San Francisco with Christine, telling her my story. In those three months, we talked over every minor and major event and explored every visual and sensual recollection I could bring to mind, so that I found myself not only talking about my life but reliving it and recovering feelings and incidents I had buried very deeply long ago, deep enough so that I might forget them. Our talks were often painful but also very funny at times, and almost always surprising. This experience of deeper reflection and memory was completely new to me; it was as though I were seeing my village, my mother, myself even, in an entirely new light, as though I were making new acquaintances, discovering new depths of understanding.

More than a year has passed, and I have now read the final manuscript. I was not prepared for this story of my youth, to see so much of myself in those English words, filtered through another's imagination. Yet this is me, who I was and who I am, and it is a beautiful, sad, and hopeful story. It is very hard for me to take in so much emotion. I couldn't leave the manuscript in Geneva, where I first received it; I took it with me to Italy and then to Beijing, and now I am here in Lake Lugu, where I have come to visit my mother, to spend three weeks in my village. This is my longest visit since I ran away in anger so many years ago. I am sitting by the fireplace on the mud floor of the kitchen, looking over the manuscript again. The wood is too wet from last night's rain and smoke is filling the room, giving me a perfect excuse to let the tears flood my burning eyes and roll down my face. I have always found it so hard, almost impossible, to cry, but now it seems that I cannot stop!

Through the window I can see my mother feeding the pig, caressing her gently. The old lady's face is sweet and tender. There is an aura of warmth around my mother. She is finally in harmony, I tell myself, and as if she could hear my thoughts, she turns and looks over her shoulder. Her eyes meet mine and she smiles. It is as if I were hit by a ball of fire. I smile back, and the tears fall on yet another page of my life.

It has long been clear to me that my past is what makes my present. Always an outsider, always different, I hope my story can contribute something of importance to anyone who has felt different, and that I may be an ambassador for my people and give them the pride and confidence they deserve.

Namu
Lake Lugu
November 2001

AUTHORS' ACKNOWLEDGMENTS

We wish to extend our warmest thanks to our agent, Richard Balkin, and our editor at Little, Brown, Deborah Baker, for the enthusiasm, hard work, and encouragement that made this adventure possible. We also give very special thanks to Eileen Walsh for her support, and to Thoralf Stenvold for all his patient support and dedication. And we thank Peter Shotwell, Sandra Steele, Cassis Lumb, Harley Blakeman, and Lisa Cody for their comments on the work in progress; and Paola Zuin and Matt Forney for relaying messages between San Francisco, Geneva, and Beijing.

Yang Erche Namu was born in the year of the horse (1966) in Zuosuo village by Lake Lugu. At the age of eight, she was sent to live with her maternal uncle and herd yaks in the mountains. She did not return to live in the village again until she was about thirteen years old, entirely illiterate, yet ready to undergo initiation as an adult woman. In 1981 she left her mountain home for the first time to partake in a series of singing contests sponsored by the provincial Cultural Bureau, which led all the way to Beijing and the discovery of her talent. A few months after returning home, she ran away from her village and joined the Liangshan Minority Singing and Dancing Troupe in Xichang, Sichuan province. The following year she was accepted in a special minority program at the Shanghai Music Conservatory, where she not only studied singing but also learned to read and write. After graduation she joined the China Minority Singing and Dancing Ensemble in Beijing. In 1990 she left to reside in San Francisco for several years. When she returned to China in the mid-1990s, Namu had lost all her hearing in one ear and was forced to abandon singing professionally. She then pursued a career in modeling, which took her to Italy, Japan, Hong Kong, and the United States. In 1999, she won

Cosmopolitan magazine's first annual fashion award in Beijing. Over the past ten years, Namu has published several books in China about her life and career, including a book co-authored with Moso scholar Lamu Gatusa. Today, Namu divides her time among Beijing, Lake Lugu, and San Francisco.

Christine Mathieu was born in Paris, France, in 1954 (another horse year). When she was sixteen, she went to live in England and from there emigrated to Australia, where she studied anthropology. After graduating, she pursued various interests and a career in teaching. In 1989, she began doctoral research in the comparative histories, customs, and cultures of the Moso and Naxi peoples of Yunnan province. There she met Moso academician Lamu Gatusa and through him Namu. Christine divides her time between San Francisco and Australia. She teaches part-time at Saint Mary's College of California.

Leaving Mother Lake

A GIRLHOOD AT THE EDGE OF THE WORLD

by Yang Erche Namu and Christine Mathieu

A Reading Group Guide

A Conversation with Yang Erche Namu
and Christine Mathieu

Leaving Mother Lake is a memoir by two authors. Can you say a little about your collaboration?

Namu: Christine and I worked together several days a week over a period of three months. After a couple of weeks, we had decided on chapters and where the book would end, and we had the opening paragraph. As we talked, Christine would write straight into the computer. Then she would re-shape the text before the next session and read it to me. We never taped anything. We just talked, and Christine wrote. When we had put the first draft together, I went back to Geneva and then to China, and Christine continued writing. We kept in close touch, speaking on the phone and via email, but I did not see the book again until she was finished rewriting a year later.

Christine: We had decided from the beginning that the book would be a memoir, not a biographical or ethnographic piece. This was Namu's story, it was not a story *about* her, or about the Moso. As far as crafting the book, I needed to provide Namu with a voice in English. She needed to speak as a storyteller but also to have an internal voice, the voice of a child, and that of an adult reflecting on her memories. Evidently, the process is very similar to constructing a character for a novel, except that since this is real life, you really have to "get" that person — and what a person Namu is! But we were very close, and we became closer, and we went through each experience in the minutest detail. I was able to inhabit her interior world. Another challenge was to make Moso culture accessible to Western readers, to tell just enough to help suspend disbelief. Mostly, I needed to draw the reader into a world that Namu, as an insider to the culture, necessarily took for granted. Of course, Namu provided the songs and much of the dialog, and I retained some of her own expressions when those translated perfectly into English.

Why did Namu wait for a year to see the final version of the manuscript?

Christine: We had agreed that Namu would be in a much better position to judge the book if she did not read the manuscript through several drafts. This required a great deal of trust on her part, but she never hurried me. As could be expected, the final manuscript had an emotional and aesthetic dimension that we had not developed in the original draft. But I had painted as faithful a portrait as I could and trusted that if Namu felt misrepresented or misunderstood, she would let me know. It was very rewarding for me that she truly recognized herself and did not want to change a word of the story.

How did you feel, Namu, when you received the manuscript?

Namu: This book is very beautiful and very special. It is also very hard for me. I am naked in this. Reading in English is difficult for me, and so to begin with, Thoralf [Namu's boyfriend at the time] read for me. But as he read, I found myself so moved, I could not stop crying. This was me, my life. I had to take the manuscript and go and sit in a room by myself and try to read for myself, difficult as it was, one word at a time.

But this book is also about the relationship between Christine and me. For two people who come from such different cultures to get as close as we did was an amazing experience. We were speaking in English and in Chinese, and sometimes we couldn't understand each other and we had to draw on a piece of paper. I had never been so intimate with anyone before, and I had never spent so much time reflecting on my life and my relationships with my family. It was often hard, really hard. But often it was also very funny. And what was incredible is that we had known each other for years, but we had never really talked about our past. We discovered that we'd had so many similar experiences. We both had very strong, rebellious mothers, and we both had difficult relationships with our mothers. Both of us left our homes when we were sixteen and lived our adult lives outside our own cultures, speaking in second and third languages. And then, of course, Christine knew my country and my people, and China. Our collaboration was perfect, and I don't think anyone else could have written this book.

When I went back to Geneva, I wrote a book on my experiences in the U.S. and Europe, which I published in Beijing some months later. I had included a chapter about working with Christine on *Leaving Mother Lake*. It was called "Can you hug me?" I wanted to tell Chinese people that in our country we take for granted that children should just love their parents. This is what we call filial piety. But it is not enough to expect children to love their parents. Parents have to do something to earn their children's love as well. They have to spend time with them and hug them and talk to them, and make them feel like they are important persons, even if they are only small children. I received dozens of letters after this, from women all over China who told me very sad stories about their childhoods. One woman wrote that she had sent the book to her mother and that after her mother had read this chapter, they had finally made up. They had not spoken for years.

After *Leaving Mother Lake,* something really changed inside me. This book washed my heart. Because this story was not just about getting my dream, but about my relationship with my mother. That's why so many readers like it. Because everyone has a mother. And so many people love their mothers and they are lonely.

How is your relationship with your mother today?

Namu: We forgave each other but we find it very difficult to talk intimately. It's hard for us to get close. I know she loves me, and she knows I love her, but we cannot be affectionate with each other. My mother is my greatest fan. She has pictures of me all over the house, but she can't hold me in her arms and hug me. And I don't think I could hug her either. We have never done this. Moso are very reluctant to show physical affection towards their relatives.

How often do you go home to Lake Lugu?

I visit often, and these days I stay a lot longer—this year I spent over two months at home. Things are very different in my village now. There are so many visitors, and the standard of living is better. In some parts of Moso country, we have telephones and televisions and modern conveniences like washing machines and refrigerators. We are joining the modern world and life is not so hard for many people. Lake Lugu attracts a lot of attention. There have been several international women's conferences held there in the past few years.

And what about your career?

Namu: I have just moved into a new apartment in Beijing. I am doing so many things, writing, fashion and media and television work. I am also promoting tourism in Lake Lugu and doing fundraising to build schools in Moso country.

Do you worry that tourism will have a negative impact on Moso culture?

Namu: Tourism brings wealth to my people. The problem for Moso is that we have no industry. Before communism, we had long-distance trade as well as agricultural production. After Liberation, during the Mao years (1956–1976), the long-distance trade stopped. Mostly, we relied on agriculture and rations from the government. Under Deng, we were allowed to sell farm surplus at local markets, but we live in a high mountain region and we had no roads and no motorized vehicles. Even today, the Moso transport goods on their backs, or on the back of horses and sometimes by bus, and in this modern world, they can't compete with producers closer to the town centers in the plain regions. So people grow what they eat and do a bit of bartering in nearby towns, and young people go to the cities to find work and earn cash. Most of them work for a while and then they come home. But some stay. And unless we have means of earning money in the villages, more and more young people will leave and not bother coming back because life is too hard at home.

Given the realities, tourism is a lifesaver because it provides young Moso with good, well-paid jobs. Also, because visitors come to Lake Lugu to see Moso culture, tourism gives us more incentive to preserve our culture. International tourism can be good for our self-esteem. After decades of government pressure to change our culture, we can tell the younger generation that our way of life is important and good and so interesting that it attracts the attention of people from all over the world.

But there are problems as well. We have to take care of the natural environment, the forests and the lake, and make sure that people don't dump garbage. Some of the Chinese tourists also come to Lake Lugu for the wrong reasons, and they lack respect for the people. They have heard so many stories about us, they imagine that Moso women are indiscriminate and are there for their convenience. And tourism has also created economic inequalities among the Moso. Wealth has made some people conceited, and some of the less fortunate have become resentful. One very important thing is for us to retain control of the tourist industry, and not to allow big hotel chains and outsiders to take over. This may prove difficult in the future.

Now that you live mostly in Beijing and the West, what family do you want for yourself?

Namu: That is a very difficult question for me. Like everyone, I would like to have my own family, and, unless I settle back at Lake Lugu, this probably means marriage. I have tried marriage and it did not work out very well. I think because I never had a model, I never saw couples doing things together, working out conflicts and managing the house. I found it very difficult to cope with married life, and my husband, Adrian, found it very difficult to cope with me. But I haven't given up!

Christine, you said earlier that Leaving Mother Lake *was a childhood memoir, rather than a story about Moso culture. Yet the book has received a great deal of attention from the media and from readers because of its cultural content. Surely there is something of interest here for anthropology?*

Christine: Yes, *Leaving Mother Lake* is literary anthropology. Namu's story allows readers to experience Moso culture from within and to reflect on the wonders and the limitations of traditional and modern life, love, and family, our common and diverse human nature, and the relative nature of time and place. And this is what anthropology is all about.

The book is what it is because I spent years immersed in the mysteries of northwest Yunnan and, not least, months with Gatusa translating Moso poetry and folklore. Anthropology combined with our personal experiences made it possible for Namu and me to connect at a deeply empathetic level. But the funny thing is that it was not until we began writing this book that I realized just how Moso Namu had remained, even after all the years she had spent traveling the world in haute couture outfits.

Is Moso culture unique?

Christine: The Nayar of South India have a similar system to the Moso. They too are matrilineal, reside in maternal houses, and engage in "free" visiting relationships. But the Nayar also have marriage ceremonies, even though marriage is largely symbolic since married couples do not reside together. Nevertheless, the Moso are unique because they have instituted visiting relationships with no symbolic marriage at all.

In the book's afterword, you mention that marriage was never entirely absent from Moso society and that Moso families have become more diversified since the revolution. Can you say more about this?

Christine: The Moso have several relatively marginal forms of marriage. Families can split if there are too many people or, as in Latso's case, if there is conflict. And when a family splits, the new branch is just as likely to be founded by a cou-

ple as by a sister and brother. Families also contract perma-
nent or temporary marriages/cohabitation to balance gender
ratios. For example, if in one generation a family is missing a
son or, more problematically, a daughter, and there is no opportunity to adopt or exchange children, then a husband or
wife will be taken in. But as the anthropologist Shih Chuan-
kang explains, such arrangements are more akin to adoption
than to marriage.

Finally, the Communists introduced new forms of marriage, or rather extended an old principle. In the past, Moso
feudal lords took wives to satisfy the Chinese emperors.
Today Communist authorities require all Moso government
cadres to marry. The Communists also forced marriage on
the Moso during several political campaigns. Among the couples who married under government pressure, most went
back to their extended families, but some lived happily and
stayed together. And today it is not so uncommon for young
people to opt out of the extended family and start their own
families, as Namu's brother Ache has done.

Namu: Some young people who have been educated and
lived in the outside world also question traditional Moso culture and do not approve of visiting relationships. Also, there
is government pressure for couples who have children to
make their relationship public and to remain monogamous,
to act like married people even if they don't actually live together.

*Chinese anthropologists have claimed that Moso society is proof of an
ancient matriarchal past. Do you agree with this proposition?*

Christine: There are several reasons for objecting to this view
of Moso society. The theory of an ancient, primitive matriarchal stage was a creation of nineteenth-century thinkers such
as Bachofen and, more significantly, Marx and Engels. In the

twentieth century, this theory had the status of scientific truth in Communist regimes, but it is a utopian view of human history for which there is no hard evidence. Now, eminent archaeologists and mythologists such as, for example, Marija Gimbutas have argued convincingly that ancient societies gave central place to the sacred feminine. But scholars fail to convince when they try to explain (after Engels) that Stone Age people were mother-centered because they did not understand the part played by men in procreation. Indeed, anthropology cannot support this idea.

In very ancient cultures — for example, Australian aboriginal cultures which have roots going back forty thousand years — people are perfectly clear that sexual intercourse between male and female is a necessary condition for the production of offspring (human, animal, and vegetal). Even as they explain the mysteries of procreation through religion and mythology, basic physiology is obvious to people whose lives are entirely dependent on nature's regenerative powers.

There is no universal psycho-cultural explanation as to why some cultures stress the feminine rather than the masculine, or vice versa, or, indeed, give equal importance to both sides. This is not to say that these ideologies are not without significant consequences. Evidently, cultural systems that stress the masculine at the expense of the feminine tend to give rise to societies where anxious men spend much of their time controlling women. But, whatever the more distant origins of their customs, the Moso feel deeply insulted by Stone Age references. After the revolution, the primitive matriarchy theory provided Chinese authorities with a rationale to force monogamous marriage upon them. It also fed wildly exaggerated or misconstrued claims about their sexual customs that the Moso found invasive and distasteful.

But if marriage is universal, how do we explain the Moso exception?

Christine: We can be relatively sure of one thing: visiting relationships helped the Moso feudal lords to pacify the various tribes under their rule. The ancient people of southwest China were tribal. In tribal societies, marriage fulfills an important political function because it is through marriage that family groups organize into clans and tribes. The rules of marriage govern many other forms of exchange — goods, land, and labor — and marriage also institutes obligations of reciprocity for mutual help, common worship, and the defense of persons and territory. But wherever there is obligation, there is also potential for conflict. Ironically, marriage not only cements families into tribes and nations, it also creates the conditions for conflict within the tribe — when someone betrays an obligation, as, for example, when a man "steals" a bride, or when dowry is not paid, and so forth. And because of the rules of obligation between relatives and in-laws, a skirmish — whether between two tribes or within the tribe — always has the potential to involve ever larger numbers of people and escalate into full-scale warfare.

The historical record shows that tribal warfare prevailed in southwest China well into the middle feudal period (seventeenth century). But the Chinese emperors invested local feudal lords to collect taxes and to keep peace among the various tribes, and it follows that in Yongning and in Lijiang local rulers reformed tribal marriages in order to weaken tribal politics. In Lijiang the Naxi feudal lords did this by instituting a politically restrictive form of cousin marriage and the mandatory suicide of illicit lovers, and by shifting society towards stricter patriarchy. In Yongning the feudal lords consolidated the matrilineal family system by encouraging visiting relationships: People who don't marry don't have allies to organize for warfare.

But as I mentioned in the afterword, if feudalism provides an explanation for the success of visiting relationships into the modern period, it does not necessarily explain the origins of Moso custom. For Moso matrilineality may have ties to a far more ancient world. Chinese chronicles describe the ancient Qiang, who are among the Naxi and Moso's more distant ancestors, as people who "knew their mothers but not their fathers." Other records give the details of a Qiang matriarchal state called Dong Nü Guo—the Eastern Country of Women. And Chinese legends have long spoken of the high mountains of the Tibetan borderland as the mythical paradise of the Queen Mother of the West.

Reading Group Questions
and Topics for Discussion

1. Namu says that her mother rejected her because she was a third daughter and her mother needed to have a boy. Are you convinced by this? How do you explain that people can love their children and yet exchange them? Why do you think Namu stopped crying after Ache came to live with them? And what do you make of Dujema's explanation, that Namu had cried a lifetime of tears in her first three years?

2. Of all the relationships Namu had with her family members, which do you find the most intriguing? The most complex? Which is the least complicated? Which relationships do you think most influenced Namu's own emotional development? Might Namu have become a different person if her mother had not left the maternal home in Qiansuo? What moved you most in her story?

3. Alice Walker has said that Namu's childhood experiences reminded her of growing up in the South. Did you ever feel that Namu's story was in some ways typical of stories about growing up in a small town?

4. Why was life in the mountain never boring for Namu? Do you think she ever missed home? Why was she in such a hurry to go back to the village for her skirt ceremony?

5. What did you think of Namu's skirt ceremony? Why did her mother entrust her ceremony to a friend? What did you think of Namu selling her jade bracelet to go to Shanghai, and of her mother's reaction to the news at the end of the book?

6. Imagine yourself in Namu's shoes on the occasion when she visited the city for the first time and sang in the competition. Imagine what life would be like if all the people you knew were relatives or friends, if no one you encountered was a stranger. Why did Namu suddenly yearn for the admiration of strangers after she sang on stage for the first time? Why was her reaction to the city so different from that of her girlfriends?

7. How do you explain Namu's adoration of Nankadroma?

8. Discuss life at the Music Conservatory. How did Namu's experiences at school reflect daily life under communism? Were you surprised at the degree of prejudice she encountered? How did Namu play the "ethnic minority card"?

9. Were you surprised that Namu's mother sent a gift of ham to the Living Buddha? How could Latso, as a Buddhist, not be aware that the Living Buddha is vegetarian? Can you identify additional instances in the book when the values of Buddhism are balanced against other traditional and apparently contradictory views?

10. How do you view the relationships between Moso men and women as they are portrayed in *Leaving Mother Lake*?

Suggestions for Further Reading

There are virtually no books on Moso or Naxi culture written for the general public, and unfortunately, almost all that is available in the mass media and on various web sites presents a highly distorted picture. To interested readers, we recommend the following scholarly works: the anthology *Naxi and Moso Ethnography*, edited by Michael Oppitz and Elizabeth Hsu; *A Society without Fathers or Husbands: The Na of China* by Cai Hua; and *A History and Anthropological Study of the Ancient Kingdoms of the Sino-Tibetan Borderland* by Christine Mathieu. Readers may also consult the web and relevant databases for articles, theses, and forthcoming books by the above authors, as well as by Eileen Walsh, Yan Ruxian, Shih Chuan-kang, Weng Naiqun, Guo Xiaolin, and Susanne Knödel. Regrettably, Lamu Gatusa's work is not available in English.

For the general reader, we recommend *In the Remote Country of Women*, a brilliant satirical novel by the Chinese writer Bai Hua, set in the worst years of the Cultural Revolution. Here, Bai Hua presents Moso country as an island of innocence in the midst of a Chinese sea of lunacy, meanness, and hypocrisy. On Dr. Joseph F. Rock's life there is the wonderful book by S. B. Sutton, *In China's Border Provinces: The Turbulent Career of Joseph Rock, Botanist-Explorer*. For the truly dedicated, or those interested in photographs of Moso country before the Communist revolution, we recommend Joseph F. Rock's monumental opus, *The Ancient Na-khi Kingdom of Southwest China*.

The Unwanted
A Memoir of Childhood
by Kien Nguyen

"Nguyen writes with a voice of innocence that takes us into the heart and spirit of one person's underserved and tragic childhood."
— Carol Memmott, *USA Today*

"A remarkable tale of survival at all costs."
— Julie K. L. Dam, *People*

"Vivid and compelling. . . . A gripping, emotionally raw story. . . . It deserves a place with the best memoirs of immigration and exile." — Richard C. Kagan, *Minneapolis Star Tribune*

Candy
A novel by Mian Mian
Translated by Andrea Lingenfelter

"Perhaps China's most promising young writer. . . . Mian Mian's novel deals with issues — sexuality, drug abuse, China opening to the world — that touch the core of her generation's experience."
— Jonathan Napack, *International Herald Tribune*

"A fascinating mixture of tone, observation, and material. . . . In this well-written, beautifully translated novel, the only weapon of mass destruction is Western popular culture. American CDs, DVDs, dancing, drinking, and controlled substances entice an entire generation to throw away their lives."
— Carolyn See, *Washington Post*